Contingency Blues

The Wisconsin Project on American Writers

Frank Lentricchia, General Editor

Contingency Blues

The Search for Foundations in American Criticism

PAUL JAY

The University of Wisconsin Press

The University of Wisconsin Press
114 North Murray Street
Madison, Wisconsin 53715

3 Henrietta Street
London WC2E 8LU, England

Library of Congress Cataloging-in-Publication Data
Jay, Paul, 1946–
    Contingency blues: the search for foundations in
    American criticism / Paul Jay.
        234 pp.   cm. — (The Wisconsin project on American writers)
        Includes bibliographical references (p. 210) and index.
        ISBN 0-299-15410-6 (cloth: alk. paper).
        ISBN 0-299-15414-9 (paper: alk. paper)
        1. American literature—History and criticism—Theory, etc.
    2. Modernism (Literature)—United States. 3. Criticism—United
    States—History. 4. Pragmatism. I. Title. II. Series.
    PS25.J395   1997
    810.9—dc20   96-42533

For Darren, Lydia, and Isaac

Contents

Acknowledgments

This book would probably not exist if I hadn't met Kenneth Burke. There are no words to express my gratitude to him for his friendship, and for the intellectual stimulation he provided me in the last years of his life. I also owe a debt of gratitude to the late Malcolm Cowley, from whom I learned an enormous amount, and whose friendship I will always value. Getting to know these two critics was a privilege, not to mention a remarkable stroke of good luck. I can only hope that this book (with which they would have many arguments) can begin to repay my debt to them.

My work has also benefited from an enormous amount of helpful input from friends and colleagues over the years. Bill Rueckert and Frank Lentricchia were particularly helpful in getting me to understand and appreciate Burke. Early versions of part of this book were read at Seton Hall University, the University of Wisconsin–Milwaukee, and Pennsylvania State University. I thank those in attendance whose helpful suggestions stimulated me to rethink what I was doing. Portions of chapter 5 appeared in *American Literary History, Cultural Critique,* and *Genre.* I am grateful for permission to reprint that material in the present volume. My chairs at Loyola, James E. Rocks and Suzanne Gossett, were wonderfully supportive during the years I worked on this book, and I thank them for helping me to complete it. My work has also benefited from innumerable discussions with my wonderful colleagues in Loyola's English Department, and from the stimulating feedback I received from our graduate students over the years this material surfaced in my courses. John McGowan, Steve Mailloux, Vincent Leitch, Gerald Graff, Gordon Hutner, and Greg Jay read part or all of the manuscript in various incarnations, and my debt to them is huge. My editor, Allen Fitchen, has been a model of support and encouragement, and I thank him for the enthusiasm that brought this book to the light of day. Thanks, too, go to Ross Miller, Deborah Holdstein, Roger Gilman, and Criss Jay for all-around support when I most needed it, in the form of friendship, encouragement, and criticism. To my wife, Lynn Woodbury (professor, writer, and friend), and my dear son Darren, the joy of my life, I owe everything, for they have loved and supported me over the years I worked on this book in ways I can only begin to justify.

Contingency Blues

Introduction

Contingency Blues had a long and somewhat complicated genesis, and like many books it is not the one I set out to write. When I completed editing *The Selected Correspondence of Kenneth Burke and Malcolm Cowley* (published by Viking Press in 1988) I set to work on a study of Burke's literary and cultural criticism. By then, Frank Lentricchia had published his excellent book on Burke, *Criticism and Social Change*, a study that galvanized interest in the relationship between Burke's critical theories and poststructuralism while emphasizing the political and cultural orientation of his writing. I particularly wanted to follow Lentricchia's lead in looking at Burke as a cultural critic engaged with both the literary and the social ramifications of modernism. One of the ways I wanted to extend Lentricchia's focus on Burke's cultural criticism was to consider Burke as an *American* critic, to explore how his work was related to an American critical tradition stretching from Emerson and Whitman to Dewey. Setting out to write an introduction exploring this relationship, I was struck by the ambivalent response to modernity I found in both Emerson and Dewey. Modernity and modernism, of course, are not the same things (as I will explain later, I deal with modernity as the historical period ushered in by the Enlightenment, and with modernism as a set of complex philosophical and aesthetic reactions to forms of epistemological, technological, and social innovations ushered in by modernization). The more I began to consider Emerson's early work as a response to philosophical problems grounded in the Enlightenment, and the more I observed in Dewey's *Art as Experience* a surprisingly strong ambivalence toward modernization and forms of modern experience, the clearer it seemed to me that American cultural criticism in general constituted a long and complex reaction to modernity that was worth exploring at more length than could possibly be done in a book on Burke. Burke's modernism (his critique of modernization, his rhetorical turn, and his attempt to create a self-consciously modernist style of critical thinking and writing) marked

3

an important point of departure for American criticism, but it was only part of a longer story I wanted to tell, one that would work its way not only back to the cultural criticism of Emerson, Whitman, and Dewey, but forward from Burke to deal with contemporary rhetorical and neopragmatist criticism.

That longer story became *Contingency Blues*. It has three principal aims: to examine an influential set of American writers and critics as they collectively reflect an engagement with philosophical, cultural, and social problems related to the emergence of post-Enlightenment modernity, to trace within that tradition the persistent tension between a transcendentalist and a pragmatist impulse, and, finally, to relate contemporary critics working in a pragmatist or rhetorical mode to this tradition. All of these aims work together to ground the larger argument I make in my Conclusion: that American neopragmatist criticism has come to an impasse in its attempts to solve epistemological and cultural problems related to the legitimation crisis ushered in by modernity, and that we ought therefore to move beyond both the theoretical preoccupation with this crisis we find in poststructuralist pragmatists like Stanley Fish, Richard Rorty, and Barbara Herrnstein Smith, and the desire among ostensibly more traditional "literary" pragmatists like Giles Gunn, Richard Poirier, and Peter Carafiol to organize American literary and cultural studies around a return to some version of an Emersonian pragmatism.[1] I argue that we need to move beyond the *ethnocentricity* of this discourse (the term, of course, is Rorty's) and turn our attention instead to the *ethnocritical* discourse (this term is Arnold Krupat's) characteristic of border and postcolonial studies, a discourse that comes at the problem of modernity from a very different angle, and which takes up with greater force contemporary social and historical issues I find to be more urgent than the mainly theoretical and methodological ones treated by neopragmatic Americanists.

Modernity—or, more specifically, what critics like Habermas and Pippin have called the "philosophical discourse" or "philosophical problem" of modernity—is the point of departure for both my analysis of the tradition from Emerson to Dewey, and my diagnosis of what is wrong with contemporary neopragmatist American criticism. I follow Horkheimer, Adorno, Habermas, Foucault, Pippin, and a host of other critics in dating "modernity" from the Enlightenment, and in distinguishing it from "modernism," which can be defined either as a self-conscious association with beliefs, practices, and technologies related to modernity, or as a self-conscious critique of modernity.[2] My chapters on Emerson, Whitman, Santayana, and Brooks focus much more on their engagement with various forms of the legitimation crisis associated with modernity than on their relationship to "modernism," which begins to emerge as a specific challenge for Dewey and Burke in the first decades of the twentieth century. In linking the cultural, literary, and philosophical work of these critics to the discourse or problem of modernity, I begin with the historical fact that Emerson was writing in response to a range of problems connected to the philosophical and social discourses of the Enlightenment. As Pippin writes, "the original modern notion of Enlightenment was closely linked to a new view of nature, originally mechanistic, later more broadly materialist," and connected to "a tremendous confidence in a new, mathematically inspired method" grounded in reason (148). His comprehensive description of the "enterprise" called modernity is worth quoting in full:

> It is pretty clear that the enterprise included such things as: the emergence of the 'nation state,' a political unit constituted by a common language and tradition, with an authority transcending local feudal fealty and based on some explicit common representative . . . more and more ambitious claims for the supreme authority of 'reason' in human affairs, contra the claims of tradition, the ancestors, and, especially, the Church . . . claims for the authority of natural science (modeled basically on mathematical physics) in the investigation of nature (including human nature); the corresponding 'demystification' of life, especially natural phenomena; an insistence on the natural rights of all individuals, above all else the right to freedom, the maximum expression of an individual's self-determination; the domination of social life by a free market economy, with its attendant phenomena of wage labor, urbanization, and the 'private ownership of the means of production'; a belief in, if not the perfectibility, then at least the improvability of mankind . . . Above all else, modernity is characterized by the view that human life after the political and intellectual revolutions of the seventeenth and eighteenth centuries is fundamentally better than before, and most likely will, thanks to such revolutions, be better still. (4)

I do not deal with Emerson, Whitman, Santayana, Brooks, Dewey, and Burke because they endorsed all of these changes (or the progressivist narrative these changes often implied), but because their work deals in very specific ways with a range of problems related to them. American criticism—defined as a self-conscious attempt to theorize the lineaments of a national culture—began with Emerson and Whitman in the historical context Pippin associates with modernity.[3] Both write with the kind of self-consciousness Foucault associates with modernity, that is, with a strong insistence that the present historical moment repre-

sents a clear break with the past, and that the role of the critic is to reflect on the "contemporary status of his own enterprise" (38). In the cases
of Emerson and Whitman, that enterprise involved articulating a self-
consciously new and modern national culture grounded in a sharp
break from European cultural traditions. Their work in this regard developed out of the need to come to terms in an American context with what
Habermas, following Weber, has called *modernization:* "a concept . . .
that refers to a bundle of processes that are cumulative and mutually reinforcing; to the formation of capital and the mobilization of resources;
to the development of the forces of production and the increase in the
productivity of labor; to the establishment of centralized political
power and the formation of national identities; to the proliferation of
rights of political participation, of urban forms of life, and of formal
schooling; [and] to the secularization of values and norms . . ." (*Philosophical Discourse* 2).

Since I am particularly interested in how the critics I discuss found
themselves continually having to sort out and justify their theoretical
and methodological assumptions, I have focused less on their responses
to the material and social conditions outlined by Pippin and Habermas
and more on how that sorting out reflects their engagement with philosophical and literary-critical problems related to the discourse of modernity (for example, Emerson and Whitman were particularly concerned
with what Habermas characterizes as the "formation of national identities" and "the secularization of values and norms").[4] The major historians of modernity I have cited date its emergence, of course, from the
Enlightenment's steady replacement of metaphysics with reason and
scientific rationality. The main result of this replacement, as far as the
philosophical character of modern thought goes, was not the simple
displacement of faith by reason, but the undoing of any firm foundational basis for either. If, as Pippin puts it, modernity is characterized
by the "ever more plausible possibility that what had been taken to be
absolute and transcendent was contingent and finite, since always 'self-
determined,' a contingent product of human positing" (165), then how
are we to erect normative standards (either for inquiry into knowledge
or for ethical norms of behavior)? This dilemma inaugurates the philosophical crisis of modernity, for "once we give up the idea of a radical,
ahistorical self-grounding, either in a scientific or 'phenomenological'
method, or in a pure transcendentalism, the philosophical problem of
modernity in the European tradition cannot be resolved or avoided by
those convinced that . . . everything is 'interpretation all the way
down'" (Pippin 166–67). This fundamental problem, perhaps the cen-

tral one in philosophical discussions of modernity, dogs American cultural thought from Emerson to new pragmatists like Rorty. I think it is wrong to construe this problem as a "postmodern" condition, since it is an example of the "problem of self-grounding" Habermas identifies in *The Philosophical Discourse of Modernity* as the central dilemma of *modernity*, an era in which the "eternal" becomes the ground of illusion, and the "actual" seems riven with contingency.[5]

One of the reasons I set out in this study to discuss American criticism in the context of modernity's legitimation crisis is that the modernist tension Pippin points to here—between transcendental idealism and the belief that everything is a "contingent product of human positing"—runs like a fault line through American criticism. It marks *the* contradictory impulse in Emerson (was he a mystic, as Harold Bloom argues, or the father of pragmatism?), and continues over one hundred years after his death to be a central concern of neopragmatists like Rorty, Fish, and Herrnstein Smith. I want to argue that to continue to articulate this conundrum and finesse a resolution for it is a guaranteed dead end that too often transforms criticism into a metadiscourse about the contingent ground of knowledge, that is, into a bleak rehearsal of how modernity leaves us stuck with contingency "all the way down." American criticism in this neopragmatist vein seems condemned to what Rorty calls the perpetual redescription of previous vocabularies, but with the recognition that there is no way back to a vocabulary that will connect us with the actual nature of things. The deep irony here is that "contingency," originally developed as a critique of philosophical absolutism, has become an absolute truth about all critical discourses.

The neopragmatism of critics like Gunn, Poirier, and Carafiol attempts to deal with the legitimation crisis left over from modernity in a different way from that of the poststructuralist pragmatists, one that is consciously formulated to overcome the debilitating theoretical preoccupation with contingency I have been discussing. However, I will be arguing that their return to "experience" and the "actual" as characterized by Emerson, James, and Dewey attempts to purchase legitimation at too high a price, since it is grounded in a transcendentalist kind of essentializing that fails to come to terms with the powerful poststructuralist critique of foundationalism. Critics like Rorty, Fish, and Herrnstein Smith have what I call "the contingency blues" in the sense that their positions cannot get beyond rehearsing how we have gotten to an epistemological and ethical impasse stemming from our realization that all knowledge is contingent. Critics like Gunn, Poirier, and Carafiol are preoccupied with contingency in a different kind of way. They reject the

reluctant and ironic embrace of contingency we find in the poststructuralist neopragmatists. They want to return instead to a more innocent
kind of pragmatism rooted in what they believe is a focus in Emerson,
James, and Dewey on actual experience, experience that is ostensibly
freed from the bothersome complications of poststructuralism. The first
set of critics do not get us very far beyond the original legitimation crisis
of modernity, since they give us only ever more nuanced and sophisticated redescriptions of theoretical problems inherited from philosophers like Kant and Nietzsche. The second set of critics also fail to resolve this crisis because they fall back on an anachronistic version of
transcendentalized pragmatism, one that remains wedded to a completely discredited kind of foundationalism.

There are two basic problems with the neopragmatist positions I treat
in this book: They either perpetuate or deal in a theoretically unsatis-
factory way with the historical tension between metaphysical idealism
and pragmatism so characteristic of American criticism, and they work
within a traditionally narrow and in some senses arbitrary set of authors and texts that ignores the actual range and complexity of American literary and cultural discourse. For this reason, I argue that we
ought to abandon the revisionism of both camps and turn instead to the
work of another set of critics who have been associated with the field of
"border studies."[6] These critics (Saldivar, Anzaldúa, Owens, Krupat,
Jay, Porter, Hicks, among others) argue, somewhat paradoxically, that
what has been wrong with American criticism has been less its inability to resolve the historical tension between idealism and pragmatism
than its preoccupation with "America." In their view, American criticism has been too closely allied with inventing and sustaining an ideal
and essentialized national identity, a project that has produced a myth
of national origins (and a national culture) that has for too long circumscribed and distorted American literary studies. These critics have
turned their attention to the study of American literature as the product of specific locations that cut across national and cultural borders, locations (geographic, bodily, gendered, racial, and cultural) that betray
the illusory coherence of "American literature" as it ostensibly origi-
nated within the neat borders of an Anglocentric New England and
fanned south and west to organize less metropolitan regions.

A "border studies" approach to "American" literature reorganizes
and makes more concrete our interest in contingency by taking a more
historical, cultural, and sometimes anthropological approach to the invention of subjects, communities, and cultures. Focusing on the politics
of location, and the hybrid nature of cultural identity and forms of

cultural expression, such criticism has begun to develop a rhetorically persuasive approach to writing in the United States that explores the contingency of "American" values while challenging the kind of ethnocentrism openly embraced by neopragmatists like Rorty. This approach to the criticism of American literature, which I examine at some length in the conclusion of this book, is not without its problems, but I argue that it offers the best revisionist alternative we have to the contingency blues of neopragmatism.

Chapter 1 begins at the moment of Emerson's complex American reaction to the Enlightenment's privileging of reason and the instrumental use of nature over forms of metaphysical belief. Emerson inherits from the Enlightenment the challenge of working out in an American context a response both to the flight from metaphysical idealism and the emergence of a newly autonomous, secular subject.[7] To the extent that Emerson tried to recuperate metaphysics in his appropriation of European transcendentalism, I argue, he inaugurated a rearguard action against an unchecked instrumentalism and the valuation of scientific principles over spirit. Emerson reacted to the Enlightenment by reaching back beyond its valorization of reason and empirical measurement to a premodern conception of divine or universal spirit, where the validity of "self-grounded" knowledge was insured by individual access to an absolute spiritual truth.

What is important about the relationship between Emerson's cultural criticism and the philosophical problem of modernity, however, is not that he represents in America the first romantic rebellion against the Enlightenment, let alone its outright rejection. It is, rather, his *ambivalence* about modernity. This is particularly clear in his writings about nature, where I show how his commitment to a "rational," instrumentalist domination of material reality is regularly countered by his belief in a higher, transcendental reality, a belief that tends to complicate and limit his commitment to Enlightenment forms of modernization. This ambivalence also surfaces in some of his key essays on art, which I explore in a second chapter dealing with Emerson's approach to aesthetic creativity and its relationship to the development of a specifically "American" form of cultural practices. Here I show how Emerson's insistence that American art be rooted in the actual and the local is complicated by his further insistence that what is vital there has *its* roots in a higher, transcendental reality. The primacy of the specific and the local in Emerson is continually superseded by the primacy of Spirit, so that whatever begins as particularly "American" in his essays ends up getting validated by its participation in a larger, transcendent, timeless, and ahistorical reality.

Emerson's writings on art and aesthetics are connected, as I have indicated, to his larger interest in fostering the development of a specifically "American" set of aesthetic and cultural practices. Seen in this context, Emerson's engagement with a set of problems specific to the emergence of modernity gets channeled into the specific problem of defining a *national* culture. I explore this engagement in the second half of this chapter by turning my attention to a key text in nineteenth-century American cultural criticism, Walt Whitman's *Democratic Vistas*. Whitman takes up and extends Emerson's interest in American culture, insisting that while the United States has made great strides in the spheres of industry and national economy, it has failed to create a vital culture in the spheres of religion, morality, literature, and art. Whitman adds to Emerson's nationalist rhetoric a stress on the challenge of being "modern" (the cultural program he lays out is aimed at an "original" expression of "democracy and the modern") (456). I draw on the work of Lawrence Levine in *Highbrow/Lowbrow* to show how Whitman's engagement with the problem of culture in the 1870s was part of a larger discussion about how to define "culture," for this was the moment in America when the distinction between "high" culture and "popular" culture began to emerge and gather force. I argue that while Whitman took the side of a more populist conception of culture (as against a highbrow conception of culture then being popularized by enthusiasts of Matthew Arnold), the *metaphysical* rhetoric he used to articulate it in *Democratic Vistas* tended, like Emerson's, to undercut the specificity of its *local* grounding. That is, we find in Whitman the same tendency we found in Emerson to privilege the material and the practical over the ideal, while at the same time locating the very value of the material and the practical in their embodiment of universal or transcendental principles or forces—what Whitman frankly calls a "new world metaphysics."

Emerson's attraction both to metaphysical idealism, on the one hand, and to the virtues of practical reason and the instrumental uses of nature, on the other, is reflected in the way cultural historians tend to see Emerson as the father of both transcendentalism and pragmatism. Enlightenment thought attempted to replace a premodern transcendental ground for truth and knowledge with self-grounding, and transcendentalism and pragmatism in America responded to this change in very different ways. Transcendentalism attempted to recuperate a conception of divine or universal spirit that might function in a secularized religious and cultural context as a universal ground for individual and social behavior defined by the Enlightenment value of autonomy.[8] Pragmatism, on the other hand, responded by abandoning the concept of metaphysical idealism altogether in order to work out an instrumental and utilitarian philosophy in which the validity of "self-grounding" could be measured in terms of the practical efficacy of an idea or "truth." This does not mean that in a writer like Emerson a transcendentalist and a pragmatic impulse could not coexist (on the contrary, he insists in "Circles" that his "moods do not believe in each other"). Cultural historians have tended to foreground either one or the other of these moods, leaving us to choose between Emerson the pragmatist and Emerson the transcendentalist. On the one hand, claims for Emerson's pragmatism are accurate in a very general kind of way. The problem is that they are regularly overstated, and very rarely do the pragmatist Emersonians make an attempt to reconcile the so-called pragmatist side of Emerson with his mystical, transcendentalist side. On the other hand, critics like Harold Bloom, who insist on the fundamentally mystical side of Emerson (even while linking him to James and Dewey), routinely ignore the materialist, historical, and political orientation of much of his writing. I spend some time in my chapters on Emerson reviewing the shortcomings of this criticism, particularly the recent attempts by Giles Gunn and Richard Poirier to assert Emerson's "pragmatism" as a counter to what they perceive to be the debilitating effects of French poststructuralist theory on American literary and cultural criticism.

The chapters following the two on Emerson and Whitman chart the solidifying and formalizing of transcendentalism into what George Santayana dubbed "the Genteel Tradition." Examining the early twentieth century's critique of Emersonian transcendentalism mounted by critics like Santayana and his student, Van Wyck Brooks, I examine how the legacy of Emerson's response to modernity left American philosophy poorly equipped to deal with its challenges as they had evolved by the beginning of the twentieth century. Writing in 1911, Santayana found America divided into two mentalities, the one heavily invested in transcendentalism's radically subjective approach to knowledge (what he called metaphysical fables), the other oriented in a wholly pragmatic way toward harnessing instrumental reason to increase material production. Santayana deemed transcendentalism too preoccupied with the inner play of the mind, too disengaged from the world of practical affairs to assist the nation in its full emergence as a modern state.

Santayana wanted to distinguish between the systematic and the methodical sides of transcendentalism. While it was the systematic (metaphysical) side of transcendentalism that developed into the genteel tradition, Santayana argues that its methodical side developed into the pragmatism of James and Dewey. He finds James in particular moving American philosophical thought away from transcendentalism's paralyzing idealism, for James insists on using reason and knowledge instrumentally and on valuing the local and the contingent over the absolute. Santayana wrote that America *was* modernism itself, but that it would fully flower only when it got beyond its investment in the idealism of the genteel tradition. His student, Van Wyck Brooks, took up Santayana's analysis and extended it during a crucial period in the teens. However, instead of taking his mentor's lead in championing the possibilities of pragmatism as an antidote to transcendentalism, Brooks instead mounted a harsh and extremely influential critique of it.

Brooks essentially repeated Santayana's observation that America had become divided into two mentalities. However, he replaced the terms of that division with his own formulation, and reversed the allegiances implicit in Santayana's remarks about the genteel tradition. For Brooks, the crucial division in American culture was between a poetic and a pragmatic orientation. Where Santayana saw the future of modern America residing in the possibilities of pragmatism, Brooks argued that pragmatism had improperly stolen away the poet's essential right to legislate individual and social values. In asserting the primacy of the poet over the pragmatist, Brooks attempted to save the Emersonian concept of self-reliance from pragmatists who, he asserts, transformed its motives into purely economic ones. At this point in American cultural thought, the pendulum begins to swing back toward transcendentalism in a reaction against the economic self-assertion of pragmatism. Brooks attempts to refashion for the twentieth century an Emersonian preoccupation with the individual subjective personality, and to marry it to an Arnoldian insistence on the poet's and critic's disinterest. In doing so, he mounts an offensive against pragmatism, and at the same time begins to critique the emergence of the kind of mass culture Horkheimer and Adorno would attack two decades later.

When Santayana and Brooks are read in the context of Emerson's attempt to reconcile metaphysical idealism with instrumental reason, it becomes clear how central the tension between transcendentalism and pragmatism had become in American cultural thought, and how that tension formed the dramatic context for the playing out in America of problems central to the development of modernity. The important challenge of how to define the individual and his or her responsibility to the state, how to formulate a thoroughly secular relationship to nature, and the related problem of how to ground norms and values in a post-metaphysical age, were filtered in America through the competing discourses of transcendentalism and pragmatism. Pragmatism, by the time Santayana was writing, was on the verge of becoming associated in the United States with the triumph of a certain kind of political and material modernity, a triumph be believed was held back on the cultural plane, however, by vestiges of transcendentalism. Santayana therefore endorsed (James's version of) pragmatism as the best hope for America's emergence as a modern culture and nation. Yet, a few years later, Brooks could assert something like the opposite, that is, that modernity had triumphed all too insidiously in the form of an economic and material pragmatism.

Brooks's assertion of the primacy of the poet over the pragmatist was part of a wider, modernist critique of the hegemony of instrumental reason launched by aesthetic modernism. In the late teens and twenties, American cultural criticism's engagement with the problem of modernity became complicated by the emergence of forms of aesthetic and critical modernism. Critics writing in the twenties and thirties had to formulate a response both to the ongoing challenges of modernity and to its developing critique by modernism.[9] I examine those complications, and two different attempts to work through them, in the writings of John Dewey and Kenneth Burke.

Dewey, of course, turned on his early Hegelian orientation to mount a systematic critique of all forms of metaphysical idealism, but his version of pragmatism did not develop in the context of an insular philosophical debate about the ontological status of knowledge and truth. It developed, rather, out of the conviction that American democracy and metaphysical idealism were incompatible, and that such idealism hindered America's industrial and economic expansion. Dewey argued, in effect, that the kind of metaphysical idealism associated with the most visionary strains of transcendentalism asserted the inherent supremacy of some realities over others, whereas a democratic culture must function on the assumption that no realities are inherently superior to others. The metaphysical idealism Dewey attacks formed the foundation of Santayana's "genteel tradition," and in this respect their critical analyses of American philosophical thought merged. Dewey, in effect, saw transcendentalism as a secularized version of forms of religious authority that predated the Enlightenment. The instrumental use of reason central to pragmatism, then, represents an extension of the Enlightenment's critique of metaphysical idealism into early-twentieth-century American philosophy and culture. Dewey's pragmatism is essentially

allied with the dominant values of the Enlightenment, so that his philosophical thought must be understood to be consistent with the project
of modernity it launched.

His relationship to the modernism of his own age, however, was
rather ambivalent. Focusing my attention on his book about art, criticism, and modern life, *Art as Experience,* I argue both that he reintroduces into art the metaphysical idealism he banished from philosophy,
and that he comes near to rejecting the possibility that contemporary
experience can be conducive to the production of art. Dewey's book begins with a materialist critique of the role of industrial and cultural institutions in creating a separation between art and everyday life. However, it does not argue that these institutions block the expression of
modern experience in contemporary art. Rather, it argues that they
have isolated the populace from great art, and contributed to a structure of experience wholly incompatible with its continued production.
At this point, the book turns abruptly away from a materialist critique
of art and its institutions in order to articulate a classical formalism to
which artists and critics ought to return. Dewey yields to the temptation to locate an authentic, essential, intrinsic set of qualities in aesthetic objects and experiences, so that art becomes invested with the
kind of idealism he rejected in philosophy. Indeed, he argues that because it contains a kind of metaphysical authenticity, art is ultimately a
higher form of knowledge than philosophy.

Dewey begins his book in a quasi-Marxist mode, but he ends it having anticipated the critical assumptions of the New Criticism. The book
begins with a novel application of pragmatist thought to the analysis of
the relationship between art and culture, but it ends by rejecting that
mode of analysis in favor of Arnoldian disinterest fused with the metaphysical idealism of transcendentalism. Dewey's commitment to formalist principles moves him steadily away from the book's early critical engagement with the question of the relationship between mass
culture and art (here he anticipates Horkheimer and Adorno), while at
the same time it suggests that there is a fundamental incompatibility
between art and modern experience.

Dewey's work thus gets caught up in the same self-canceling kind of
discourse that marks Emerson's. His wholesale break with European
philosophy parallels Emerson's call for a specifically American literature, and can be construed as a kind of modernist gesture ("make it
new"). Where Emerson asserts the value of metaphysical idealism over
instrumental reason, Dewey asserts the value of instrumental reason
over metaphysical idealism. The enthusiasm for the local, the contin-

gent, and the practical in Emerson (and in Whitman) is ultimately rendered secondary to his investment in a transcendental authority. The same thing happens in Dewey's book on art. He begins with a stress on the role of the local and the contingent in the production of art, but he ends up having recourse later in the book to an idealist discourse that moves in something like the opposite direction, away from the primacy in art of the local and contingent toward a valorizing of art's essence as an ideal, unified, harmonized aesthetic form.

Dewey struggles to come to terms in *Art as Experience* with competing approaches to art and its relationship to culture, the one featuring how the aesthetic *changes* over time, the other featuring that element of the aesthetic that marks its *permanence*. Indeed, near the end of his book he writes that the one "problem" that must be faced by the "artist, philosopher, and critic alike" is "the relation between permanence and change" (322). Dewey wrote these words in 1931, while Kenneth Burke was at work on a book he would later title *Permanence and Change*. Dewey's approach to the problem of permanence and change in the realms of art and culture provides a clear point of departure for Burke. Where Dewey's response to the modern condition in *Art as Experience* seems altogether wary of avant-garde forms of aesthetic modernism, favoring instead a more conservative, New Critical approach to art, Burke's literary and cultural criticism developed in the context of his enthusiastic embrace of (and participation in) avant-garde modernism in the Dadaist and surrealist modes. Burke, unlike Dewey and the New Critics, wanted to transform literary and cultural criticism into an oppositional practice (in both stylistic and political terms). This left him, of course, in a lonely position, situated as he was between New Critics like Ransom, Tate, and Brooks on the right who, while defending the difficulty of aesthetic modernism, had no interest in the kind of politically oppositional practice Burke articulated, and on the left writers and critics who were not terribly interested in avant-garde forms of criticism, even if they were committed to a left politics.[10]

Burke's conception of aesthetic production as an oppositional force working consciously to subvert dominant cultural codes sets him apart from critics like Brooks and Dewey. In his first book, *Counter-Statement*, Burke takes the kind of negative view toward the rise of science and the dominance of business and technology we will find in Brooks. However, where Brooks tended to argue for the aesthetic as a place of withdrawal from these dominant aspects of modernity (falling back on nineteenth-century conceptions of the self and art), Burke insists on the aesthetic as a force for disrupting the social and cultural life of moder-

nity. Influenced in part by Dada and surrealism, and committed as a
creative writer in his early career to the subversion of traditional forms
and styles, Burke worked in the late twenties and early thirties to create a critical style that incorporated the disruptive effects of avant-
garde writing.[11]

For all of these reasons, I argue that Burke is one of America's first
modernist critics, modernist both in the sense that his literary and cultural criticism developed as a strong critique of modernity, and because
he sought to produce criticism informed by modern philosophy and
conceptualized and written in a conscious attempt to incorporate avant-
garde styles. Burke's desire to blend modernist aesthetics with cultural
critique relates to his own personal need to reconcile a tension that he
felt in himself and that he observed in modern society between what he
called an "aesthetic" and a "practical" orientation. His argument about
the development of modernity in *Counter-Statement* hinges on the idea
that a practical orientation toward productivity in social, cultural, and
aesthetic life in America had displaced a fundamentally aesthetic nineteenth-century orientation. The book's early chapters argue for the reassertion of the aesthetic as a kind of antidote to the practical. Aesthetic
modernism, from Burke's point of view, must have as its aim a sustained *critique* of the effects of modernization (which he links to a ram-
pant instrumentality and an emphasis, dictated by science, on the
"practical"). Again, in general terms this analysis tends to parallel
Brooks's (though we will see that Burke increasingly distances himself
from Brooks's position). Burke's concentration on the historic tension
between an "aesthetic" and a "practical" orientation underscores the
extent to which cultural criticism in America had come to be determined by the competing interests of metaphysical idealism and pragmatism.

In my chapter on Burke I explore his attempt to resolve this tension
methodologically. What unfolds, in short, is his steady movement away
from an early kind of aesthetic formalism toward an approach to writing about literature and culture that focuses on its ideological and rhetorical qualities. Where *Permanence and Change* was devoted, in the
main, to articulating a modernist style (and theoretical orientation) for
cultural criticism that begins to break down the dichotomy between
art's aesthetic and "practical" elements, his later book, *A Rhetoric of Motives,* moves even further away from an aesthetic ground for criticism in
its attempt to reclaim rhetoric for the uses of literary and cultural criticism. At this point, as we shall see, Burke has made a complete break
not only with Brooks and Dewey, but with Santayana's genteel tradition

as well. Where these earlier critics tended, at crucial moments, to lapse into a transcendentalist mode informed by a metaphysical aesthetic ideal, Burke employs a revitalized form of rhetorical criticism in an attempt to transform the criticism of art into cultural critique. In doing so he begins to treat subjectivity and its relationship to language, ideology, and institutions in a way that looks forward to the work of poststructuralist theory.

The concluding chapter focuses on the influence poststructuralist theory has had on the work of neopragmatist critics including Stanley Fish, Richard Rorty, and Barbara Herrnstein Smith. Rejecting the kind of nostalgia for a refashioned Emersonian pragmatism we find in Giles Gunn and Richard Poirier (and the polemic against poststructuralist theory that accompanies it), these critics extend pragmatism's critique of metaphysics along lines worked out by Burke and toward the end of articulating a postmodern form of pragmatist cultural criticism. In so doing they stress the degree to which modern philosophy from Nietzsche and Dewey demonstrates how any conception of "reality," knowledge, truth, or value is contingent upon language. This neopragmatist stress on the contingency of language is a stress on the inescapably *rhetorical* nature of everything from "truth statements" to epistemologies and critical methodologies, and is thus linked to Burke's attempt to work out a comprehensive postmetaphysical mode of rhetorical theory. I make this point, first, by discussing John Bender and David E. Wellbery's analysis of what they call "the modernist return of rhetoric" (3), and then I go on to show how Fish, Rorty, and Herrnstein Smith have worked out a neopragmatist form of cultural critique that is rhetorical in just the sense Bender and Wellbery mean. Bender and Wellbery argue persuasively that modernism reversed a whole set of philosophical conditions that, since the late eighteenth century, had "brought the classical tradition of rhetoric to its end" (22). The genealogy of this reversal is the same one invoked by Rorty, Fish, and Herrnstein Smith to explain the emergence of neopragmatism as both a theory of knowledge and a critical methodology.

Recognizing the confluence of the new rhetoric and the new pragmatism is ultimately less important, I argue, than recognizing how both are responding to a set of problems that predate "postmodernity," problems that can be traced back to the emergence of Enlightenment modernity. While neopragmatists like Gunn and Poirier insist that our own "crisis of disbelief" can be traced to specifically *postmodern* forms of thought imported from France, Rorty, Fish, and Herrnstein Smith make it clear that this "crisis" predates our own time and has its roots

in modern philosophy from Kant and Nietzsche through Dewey and
Heidegger. This means that the kind of antifoundationalism critics like
Gunn and Poirier deplore is symptomatic of much more comprehensive and long-standing developments in the history of philosophy than
they allow for, developments fostered to a significant degree by the
very pragmatism they want to embrace. Postmodern neopragmatists
like Rorty and Fish, of course, insist that there is no escaping this antifoundationalism, that we have no choice but to work within the contingencies of language and the representational systems and methodologies we construct with it. What Gunn and Poirier see as a crisis of
disbelief they see as a fundamental and unavoidable condition of intellectual work. Unable to ground their critical positions in something
outside these contingencies, both the postmodern neopragmatist and
the rhetorician attempt to use the *irony* inherent in this situation to
legitimate and even authorize their approaches to cultural criticism.
Rorty's ironist position, for example, stems from the fact that, in his
view, all truth statements, observations about reality, and claims to
"know" the world are (1) only vocabularies, and (2) simply redescriptions of other, older claims. This kind of irony characterizes the condition of rhetoricality as well, since for Bender and Wellbery "rhetoricality . . . manifests the groundless, infinitely ramifying character of
discourse in the modern world. For this reason, it allows for no explanatory metadiscourse that is not already itself rhetorical" (25). Fish's "Rhetorical Man" faces a similar irony, since he must work with the fact that
"the truth of rhetorical operations" is the truth that "all operations . . .
are rhetorical" (215).

While each of these critics attempt to articulate a postmetaphysical
epistemology or critical system devoted to a vigilant critique of all systematic forms of analysis or revelation that claim an absolute or transcendental authority, their positions are ultimately not very satisfying,
since they become preoccupied with policing in a theoretical way the
grounds of discourse. For this reason, I argue that we ought to reject
both of these models in favor of the kind of "border studies" approach
I outlined earlier. In order to explore the rich possibilities (along with
some of the potential pitfalls) of American border criticism, I conclude
this chapter by reviewing a number of different approaches to theorizing "border zones" (Pratt, Anzaldúa, Owens, Krupat), discuss some of
the possibilities and problems that attend explorations of "hybridity"
as a factor in the construction of personal and cultural identities, and
analyze how theorizing a "space between" attempts to locate both a
new kind of geographical/cultural space and a way to resolve the his-

torical tension between an idealist and a pragmatist position for cultural criticism.

In order to foreground some of the differences between neopragmatist criticism and the kind of work border studies critics are attempting, I close by examining Rorty's ethnocentrism and Arnold Krupat's attempt to articulate an approach to literary and cultural studies he calls "ethnocriticism." Both Rorty and Krupat are responding explicitly to the potential charge of relativism facing any critic working with the supposition that all knowledge, truth claims, and explanatory systems are contingent upon the methodologies and systems of representation they employ. Rorty's response to the charge of relativism is to retreat to an ethnocentric position that claims the superiority of his own "ethnos," or group, which he associates specifically with liberal intellectuals of the secular modern West, represented by writers such as Blake, Arnold, Nietzsche, Marx, Baudelaire, Eliot, and Orwell. Krupat, on the other hand, insists that in order to avoid relativism cultural criticism must examine the contested, fluid, border spaces in which cultures are ultimately realized, and that it ought to do so in a way that stresses the element of anthropological description (ethnography) inherent in any form of cultural criticism. Where Rorty's "ethnos" is a homogenizing, limiting, and *centering* term, Krupat's "ethnos" explores the heterogeneous margins of cultures in fluid contact with one another, and stresses an ethno*critical* rather than an ethno*centric* practice. I conclude with this comparison because the differences between Rorty and Krupat clearly dramatize some of the more difficult choices facing American cultural criticism as it nears the end of the twentieth century. I suggest here that something like Krupat's ethnocriticism offers a way out of the philosophical morass of contingency theories we encounter in critics like Rorty and Fish, one that leads to a more complex, heterogeneous concept of "ethnos" rooted in material and social culture.

1

Modernity and Nature in Emerson

The past decade has witnessed a remarkable resurgence of interest in Emerson. Much of this new work has focused to one degree or another on Emerson's relation to pragmatism. This is particularly the case in the work of Giles Gunn (*The Culture of Criticism and the Criticism of Culture* [1987] and *Thinking across the American Grain* [1992]), Richard Poirier (*The Renewal of Literature* [1987] and *Poetry and Pragmatism* [1992]), and Cornel West (*The American Evasion of Philosophy* [1989]). The work of these critics has been driven in part by the development of American studies as a discipline particularly interested in revising and deepening our understanding of America's social and cultural history, and in part by the rise of poststructuralist theory, which has encouraged a new generation of critics to rethink the philosophical and methodological assumptions driving Emerson's writing. While this work has dramatically expanded our basic understanding of Emerson and the contexts in which his work can be understood, it has at the same time produced a number of different Emersons. The versions of Emerson we get in recent criticism tend to divide between Emerson the Transcendentalist (or Idealist or Mystic) and Emerson the Pragmatist. Critics like West, McDermott, Poirier, and Gunn, while acknowledging an idealist strain in Emerson's thought, want to read him as essentially pragmatic in his thinking, since their aim is to place him at the beginning of a line of American philosophical and cultural thought that runs through James and Dewey. Another set of critics, however, emphasize the idealist or transcendentalist side of Emerson's thought. Harold Bloom, Leon Chai, and David Van Leer, for example, each in their own way insist on the fundamentally idealist orientation of Emerson's writing (both Chai and Van Leer reassert the importance of his link to German idealism, while Bloom traces Emerson's idealism back through Gnosticism and various mystical versions of Neoplatonism).[1] Like Emerson's own moods, the versions of Emerson we get from these critics are often utterly at odds with one another. At the extreme end of the idealist position, for example, we find Harold Bloom intoning that Emerson "is best thought of as another mystical shaman" ("Emerson" 110), while John McDermott, wanting to insist on Emerson's commitment to the pragmatic and the practical, maintains that he is a "hard-headed empiricist" (34). Claims for Emerson's pragmatism have a general accuracy, but they are regularly overstated, while attempts like Bloom's to insist on the fundamentally mystical side of Emerson (even while linking him to James and Dewey) routinely ignore the materialist, historical, and political orientation of much of his writing. I am less interested in arbitrating the dispute between these two views than in analyzing the tension between idealism and "pragmatism" in Emerson that gives rise to this debate in the first place. In so doing I will be arguing that Emerson's continual slippage between forms of idealism and a kind of materialism or instrumentalism is the result of his struggle to come to terms with a set of problems specific to the emergence of modernity. Surprisingly little effort has been made to read Emerson's writings in relationship to what Habermas has called the philosophical discourses of modernity. When we do read him in the context of this discourse the contradictory positions Emerson takes toward nature, the self, art, and culture begin to make more sense.

Emerson, Cultural Criticism, and the New Pragmatism

Emerson, probably more than any other American writer, is less written about than *claimed*. He is appropriated by critics as divergent in their interests as Bloom and Poirier in the context of working out a usable past that can redeem a present crisis. Thus, while Poirier's Emerson and Bloom's are quite at odds with one another, Bloom's insistence that Emerson's brand of religious individualism is the "only hope for our imaginative lives" (*Ralph Waldo Emerson* 10) is matched by Poirier's equally passionate insistence that Emerson's essentially pragmatic linguistic skepticism may "point to something beyond skepticism, to possibilities of personal and cultural renewal" (*Poetry and Pragmatism* 8). Poirier and Bloom also share the fundamental fact that they write as "Emersonians." This means two things: (1) they write about Emerson in order to *advocate* their version of Emersonianism, and (2) they insist that we read Emerson in an Emersonian way.[2]

The case for Emerson's pragmatism is made in a variety of ways by critics like Poirier, West, and McDermott. Poirier defines Emerson's pragmatism as a brand of linguistic skepticism. In *The Renewal of Literature*, for example, he grounds his assertion that Emerson was "the father of American pragmatism" (17) in Emerson's skepticism about language, which Poirier wants to distinguish from both modernist and deconstructive forms of linguistic skepticism:

> On the one hand, as against modernist spirituality, the Emersonians want to prevent words from coming to rest and want to dissuade us from hoping that they ever might. On the other, as against deconstructionist theory . . . the Emersonian alternative is more complicated. Emerson may sometimes sound deconstructionist himself . . . ("Every end," he says in "Nature," "is prospective of some other end, which is also temporary; a round and final success nowhere.") But he insists, as did James after him, that this very same temporariness is instigated and perpetuated by the human will. (16)

Poirier links Emerson's pragmatist disposition to his use of a "vocabulary of 'fact,' 'action,' and 'power,'" (16), one that in his view leads to James's preoccupation with a rhetoric of "Cash Value." The "pragmatist" skepticism about language Poirier isolates in Emerson is a skepticism about language's ability to mirror a preexisting reality (hence its loose affiliation with deconstruction). The emphasis in Emerson is, rather, on the will and its ability, through rhetoric, to assert facts, perform actions, and be powerful. Poirier finds Emerson's linguistic skepticism latent in his "great difficulty finding a rhetoric to support the positions he advances, positions having to do with the whole phenomenon of human, including literary, production, and with questions of origin, action, and traces" (177). This difficulty marks something positive for Poirier in Emerson's relationship to language, however. Poirier assumes that because Emerson often cannot locate in reality the entities he refers to, "he intends that they should include and therefore abolish their defining opposite" (177). Emerson's verbal constructs, he insists, do not refer to objects but rather "are surfaces only to be manipulated" (177). There may be the sense in Emerson of a "dilemma" in all this, but Poirier sees him as the father of pragmatism precisely because "William James will eventually turn the Emersonian dilemma into an exhortation on behalf of American pragmatism," which is dedicated in part to the idea that "if you follow the pragmatic method, you cannot look on any such word ["God," "Matter," "Reason," "the Absolute," "Energy"] as closing your quest. You must bring out of each word its practical cash-value, set it at work within the stream of your experience" (quoted in Poirier 178).

Poirier reiterates at the outset of his most recent book, *Poetry and Pragmatism*, that Emerson's linguistic skepticism marks his paternal relationship to pragmatism: "Pragmatism [is] a form of linguistic skepticism, and . . . this skepticism is equally at work, and is indeed a generative principle" (5) in Emerson and the modern poets Poirier discusses who follow in his wake. Poirier is careful not to reduce pragmatism to linguistic skepticism (his version of pragmatism here, he admits, is "partial, at once limited and somewhat biased" [4]). However, it is largely Emerson's linguistic skepticism that marks him in Poirier's view as a pragmatist. This equation, it seems to me, is at once very vague and much too specific. It is vague because the kind of skepticism about language's referential function Poirier finds in Emerson—which may simply reflect Emerson's struggle as a poetic writer to come up with the best word for the ineffable—is a fairly common occurrence, and can hardly be made specific to something called "pragmatism." Indeed, it could certainly be argued that this "skepticism" simply underscores Emerson's belief in the overriding existence of an unnameable metaphysical or transcendental being or truth, a belief that is antithetical to pragmatism as it will develop in James and Dewey. From this point of view, what Poirier calls "linguistic skepticism" would simply be a logical result of Emerson's transcendentalism. Poirier's equation is too specific in the sense that it sets up very narrow criteria for measuring the "pragmatic" strain in Emerson.

Cornel West makes a much broader case for Emerson's pragmatism:

> Emerson's dominant themes of individuality, idealism, voluntarism, optimism, amelioration, and experimentation prefigure those of American pragmatism. His complex articulation of a distinct Americanism grounded on specific interpretations of power, provocation, and personality—that is, both the content of this ideology and the way in which he presented it—deeply shaped the emergence and development of American pragmatism. (35)

West reminds us that Emerson was preoccupied with the question of power, with the operations of market capitalism, and with race and the pressing issue of abolition. He also stresses Emerson's interest in the crucial connections between "ideas and institutions, discourses and infrastructures, intellectual practices and modes of social structuration" (35). In contrast with Poirier, whose interest is in Emerson the poet and literary critic and the role his thought can play in the "renewal of literature," West sees Emerson as a cultural critic engaged broadly with the issues and questions of his time and place. (If Poirier's Emerson is

loosely Derridean, West's is loosely Foucaultian.) West's treatment of
Emerson is a refreshing antidote to the more hermetic and withdrawn
versions of Emerson we get from critics like Bloom, but there is a problem with the sheer sweep of the "pragmatist" qualities West sees in
Emerson. West's Emerson is interested less in the shortcomings of language's referential abilities than in social and cultural problems, and in
the relationship between ideas and institutional structures. However,
these issues are so broad and wide-ranging that they seem to represent
much more than a "pragmatist" vision, or if they do represent a pragmatist vision, it is defined in only the most general of senses. How, we
need to ask, does this constitute a "prehistory of pragmatism" rather
than, say, a prehistory of American liberal humanism, or even of democratic political conservatism? The overspecificity of Poirier's link between Emerson and pragmatism is matched by the too general nature
of the link West draws.[3]

Critics like those I have been discussing, who want to argue for Emerson's pragmatism, do so in the context of mapping out a genealogy of
American cultural criticism that situates Emerson at the beginning of
an essentially pragmatic line of thought running from Emerson through
James, Dewey, Wilson, Burke, and Trilling. I call these Emersonian critics
(particularly Gunn and Poirier) "redemptive" because they believe that
American literary and cultural criticism have entered a period of crisis
brought on by the dominance of poststructuralist thought in America
that can be countered only by a return to "Emersonian" principles and
practices. The "renewal of literature" in the face of this crisis, Poirier argues, will be made possible only by a return to the writing of Emerson,
Thoreau, and Whitman, who together constitute an antidote to "the
dominant modernist and so-called post-modernist ways of thinking"
(Renewal 9). Poirier's conviction that American pragmatism as it develops from Emerson and James through Kenneth Burke offers an "effective alternative to" French writers such as Derrida, Foucault, and Lacan
(192) is developed at length by Gunn. While Gunn finds some poststructuralist criticism "brilliant" and "daring" in a way that can illuminate intellectual and social experience (Culture of Criticism 43), he
invokes Marianne Moore to argue that "there are things important beyond all this fiddle" (43). Gunn wants to "demonstrate that the cogency
of the cultural critique mounted by the deconstructionists, despite the
brilliance of many of its insights, finally undermines its own premises
and thereby forces us back on" a form of "critical interpretation" that is
"pragmatic and loosely hermeneutic" (46).

While Gunn appreciates the brilliance of deconstructive criticism, he insists it has ushered in a form of what Habermas has famously called a "legitimation crisis." While deconstruction undermines the legitimacy or groundedness of all discourses, its own legitimacy is undermined, in Gunn's view, by its failure to apply deconstructive principles to its own discourse. If it did, he insists, we would see that deconstructive critiques are as unstable and arbitrary as those that they critique. This creates a kind of hermeneutic "spiral." The way through it, insists Gunn, is not via the "direction of some deinterpreted or uninterpretable surd of signs, as the deconstructionists presumably suggest, nor in the direction of some reinterpreted or overinterpretable system or [sic] signifiers, as the semioticians sometimes argue" (62). In "an age without absolutes," he concludes, the way through this spiral is "in the direction of a fresh look at experience itself" (62). The grounding of criticism in the examination of "experience itself" lays the theoretical groundwork for Gunn's call to a return to a pragmatic method for cultural criticism.

There is a real problem with this line of analysis, of course. It has to do with Gunn's casual invocation of "experience itself." If deconstructive criticism has taught us anything, it is the necessity of pausing over essentializing terms such as "experience itself." Gunn wants to separate systems of signification and interpretation from a kind of experience that stands outside them. In his view, deconstructive and semiotic approaches to language and literature hopelessly complicate our ability to distinguish the true and the valuable from the false and the trivial. Gunn would save us from what he sees as a crisis brought on by the distance deconstruction and semiotics open up between critical discourse and "experience itself." With its attention supposedly focused on "real" lived experience, pragmatism is supposed to offer us a way to heal this distance and the crisis of belief it has caused. What this position ignores is the extent to which "experience itself" is shot through with the processes we associate with signification and interpretation. There is no "experience itself" that stands before or outside of these processes. Experience is constituted through them, not before or beyond them. When Gunn offers pragmatism as a way out of our "legitimation crisis" he can do so only by suggesting that it is somehow grounded in a category—"experience itself"—that we should already know is purely rhetorical.[4] Complicating this problem is the fact, as we will see below, that Emerson himself insists that the category of "experience" is plagued by contingency, and so inferior to transcendental consciousness.

Emerson, Modernity, and Nature

I want at this point to shift my discussion of the debate about Emerson's "pragmatist" and "transcendentalist" sides away from its contextualization in arguments about the genealogy of American cultural criticism toward a rehistoricizing of Emerson's relationship to an emerging set of philosophical problems specific to the emergence of modernity. I will be arguing that it makes more sense to examine the historical reasons for the tension between "pragmatism" and metaphysical idealism in Emerson than simply to claim Emerson as a pragmatic antidote to the excesses of poststructuralism.

We need first to begin with the fact that, writing in the late 1830s and 1840s on American art and culture and its relation to the past, Emerson was working at precisely the moment Jürgen Habermas delineated in *The Philosophical Discourse of Modernity* when "*temps modems [sic]*" lost its "merely chronological meaning" (designating the period from 1500 to 1800) and began to take on "the oppositional significance of an emphatically 'new' age" (5). Habermas (following Weber) delineates this new age in relationship to a "bundle of processes" characteristic of modernity. While the formation of capital, mechanization, and the development of productive forces were transforming both America and Europe, what Habermas characterizes as "the establishment of centralized political power and the formation of national identities" contributed in a particularly telling way to America's sense of its own modernity. Emerson's was a new age, then, in two related senses: the "oppositional significance" of Emerson's America was rooted both in its break with cultural and political values in place since the sixteenth century in Western civilization and, more specifically, in its attempt to ground itself by breaking free from European culture. In the West in general, philosophical, economic, social, industrial, and institutional change accelerated in the first decades of the nineteenth century in a way that marked its break with the past, but this break was even more emphatic in America, where the birth of a nation coincided with the rise of modernity. Emerson's age fits Habermas's characterization precisely: it "can and will no longer borrow the criteria by which it takes its orientation from models supplied by another epoch; it has to create its normativity out of itself" (7).

Emerson's work as a cultural critic is of course marked by an acute awareness that he was living and writing at a time like the one Habermas delineates. The two characteristics Habermas insists are central to modern thought, the preoccupation with one's age as fundamentally different from, and opposed to, a previous epoch that had become outmoded, and the challenge to formulate a basis for normative standards in place of the rejected the criteria of the past, drive much of Emerson's work during this period. This can be seen with particular force in the oft-discussed opening paragraph of *Nature* (1836):

> Our age is retrospective. It builds sepulchers of the fathers. It writes biographies, histories, and criticism. The foregoing generations beheld God and nature face to face; we, through their eyes. Why should not we also enjoy an original relation to the universe? Why should not we have a poetry and philosophy of insight and not of tradition, and a religion by revelation to us, and not the history of theirs? . . . [W]hy should we grope among the dry bones of the past, or put the living generation into masquerade out of its faded wardrobe? . . . Let us demand our own works and laws and thoughts. (7)

The lines Emerson draws here couldn't be clearer. American culture must turn from a dead and certain past to a living, if uncertain, present. It must choose between history and experience, between mediated and unmediated contact with "the universe," between a poetry of tradition and a poetry of insight. Emerson's modernity lies in his recognition that his age must shift from being "retrospective" to being both "original" and "oppositional." Of course, Emerson is less interested in discarding the products of the past on the junk heap of history than in denying them the power to usurp the creative energies of his own generation. America may have inherited texts, laws, and institutions born out of an original relation to the universe, but he insists they now block the possibility of such a relation for others. The "works and laws and thoughts" of the past can no longer serve as the normative *ground* for personal, social, and political behavior. Such a ground must somehow be generated out of, and for, itself.[5]

Emerson's self-conscious response to these problems reflects an attitude Michel Foucault has argued is central to the emergence of modernity, which Foucault insists is less a period than an attitude, a "mode of relating to contemporary reality," a "way . . . of acting and behaving that at one and the same time marks a relation of belonging and presents itself as a task" (39). This "attitude" has three constituent parts. It involves the problematizing of our relation to the present, a recognition of the necessarily historical nature of our being, and the challenge of constituting ourselves as autonomous subjects. The "thread that may connect us with the Enlightenment" is the necessity of our "faithfulness" not to "doctrinal elements" about which we may (and ought to) have strong debates, but to a "philosophical ethos that could be described as a permanent critique of our historical era" (42).

Foucault associates the beginning of this critique with Kant. Before Kant, philosophical reflections on the present had taken three forms: (1) the present was "represented as belonging to a certain era of the world, distinct from the others through some inherent characteristics, or separated from the others by some dramatic event" (33); (2) the present was "interrogated in an attempt to decipher in it the heralding signs of a forthcoming event" (33); or (3) the present was "analyzed as a point of transition toward the dawning of a new world" (34). Kant, on the other hand, views modernity as an "exit," a "way out" (34), a release from subordination to modes of authority based on belief or faith, rather than reason.[6] This relation to the present is embodied in "a reflection by Kant on the contemporary status of his own enterprise" (38). The shift Foucault locates in Kant's "attitude" is a shift from metaphysics to metacriticism. Arguing that his own historical moment is marked by a shift from faith to reason and critique, Kant formulates a methodology that reasons about and critiques the conditions of its own status as a philosophical discourse. This metacritical attitude, in Foucault's view, virtually defines modern thought as a mode of philosophical interrogation based on "a permanent critique of our historical era" (42).

Written "at the crossroads of critical reflection and reflection on history," Kant's essay on the Enlightenment is in Foucault's view "a reflection . . . on the contemporary status of his own enterprise" (38). Emerson shares this self-consciousness about writing at the crossroads of a thought at once historical and critical. For example, in "The American Scholar" Emerson defines the predicament of his age in terms of its being caught between two epochs. The "discontent of the literary class," he writes, is "that they find themselves not in the state of mind of their fathers, and regret the coming state as untried" (68). Where in *Nature* the age is described as "retrospective," here it is described variously as "reflective" and "philosophical," as an age of "introversion," and as a "critical," even a revolutionary, age. While we will see that Emerson's sense of the modernity of his age seems to parallel the traditional senses Foucault enumerates (the present is separated from the past by dramatic changes or events; the present heralds a forthcoming event or change; the present is a point of transition toward a new world), it is also based on a conviction that the present represents an exit or a way out of subordination to traditional sources and modes of authority. It is this reflective, critical, revolutionary orientation in Emerson's relation to contemporary reality, combined with his continual reflection on the contemporary status of his own enterprise, that links his cultural project with the attitude Foucault associates with modernity. Like Kant,

Emerson attempts to put his "own reason to use, without subjecting it-self to any authority" (Foucault 37). Moreover, he reflects on history and the present in the context of "a particular analysis of the specific moment at which he is writing and because of which he is writing" (Foucault 38).

This is particularly the case in Emerson's writing about nature in *Nature*. Indeed, Emerson was the first American cultural critic to see that modernity was defining itself in terms of a dramatic post-Enlightenment shift in the relationship between humankind and nature. In *Nature*, he attempts to deal with one of the defining experiences of modernity, the emergence of an instrumental relation to nature based on humankind's increasing ability to dominate and subdue nature toward its own in-strumental ends. In so doing, he foregrounded the tension in his work between metaphysical idealism and an emerging pragmatism. Emer-son took up the challenge in *Nature* of theorizing humankind's relation to nature in a way he hoped might reconcile the contradiction between a pragmatic or instrumental and a spiritual relationship to nature, be-tween, that is, a view that sees nature as the repository of spiritual being, and one that sees nature as material to be molded and dominated.

By now it is nearly a cliché to observe that the age we call "moder-nity" is characterized by an increasingly technical and instrumental re-lationship to nature. Here, for example, are Freud's comments on the topic in *Civilization and Its Discontents:*

> During the last few generations mankind has made an extraordinary advance in the natural sciences and in their technical application and has established his control over nature in a way never before imagined . . . But . . . this newly-won power over space and time, this subjugation of the forces of nature, which is the fulfillment of a longing that goes back thou-sands of years, has not increased the amount of pleasurable satisfaction which they may expect from life and has not made them feel happier. (34–35)

Freud's point is a double one. Modernity is the child of science and technology, which have enabled humankind to subjugate nature to its own ends. However, the "progress" it represents has been purchased at considerable emotional and psychological cost. Freud assumes the in-evitability of this cost, believing that it represents a kind of trade-off for progress. He is interested less in the issue of whether or not nature is to be subjugated toward the end of technological and cultural develop-ment, however, than in the kind of balance that ought to be struck be-tween the domination of nature and human pleasure or happiness. He assumes that "the motive force of all human activities is a striving towards the two confluent goals of utility and a yield of pleasure" (41). In the analysis he pursues of civilization's psychological discontents the subjugation of nature modulates into the repression of instinct, so that humankind's necessary domination of nature in the construction of modern civilization has its parallel in the individual's necessary repression of instinct in the formation of the modern ego.

Following up on Freud's analysis of the relationship between the domination of nature and the rise of modern civilization, Max Horkheimer and Theodor Adorno insist in *Dialectic of Enlightenment* that "the fallen nature of modern man cannot be separated" from the forms of "social progress" generated by Enlightenment reason and the ferociously instrumental use of nature (xiv). The "program of the Enlightenment was the disenchantment of the world" (3), a turn away from metaphysical and theological systems toward rationality, a belief in the autonomy of the wholly secularized individual and the unlimited possibilities of instrumental reason. The Enlightenment launches modernity in a philosophical sense because it marks the beginning of the end of metaphysics. "From now on," they write, "matter would at last be mastered without any illusion of ruling or inherent powers, of hidden qualities . . . whatever does not conform to the rule of computation and utility is suspect" (6). The twin poles of modernity thus become positivism and empiricism; science gains an increasingly hegemonic foothold while whatever does not "reduce" to numbers gets written off as "literature" (7).

Horkheimer and Adorno want to "focus understanding more clearly upon the nexus of rationality and social actuality, and upon what is inseparable therefrom—that of nature and the mastery of nature" (xv–xvi). The history of modernity, in their view, is the story of humankind's estrangement from nature, estrangement born of a utilitarian relationship to nature that has emptied it of mystery. The age of reason inaugurates an approach to nature based on calculation, domination, and use, one that attempts to break radically with a pre-Enlightenment, essentially Platonic view of nature based on a fundamental link between nature and human subjectivity.[7]

For Horkheimer and Adorno, this break represents a central moment in the development of modernity. In their view, the Enlightenment's ethic of utility led inexorably to the disenchantment of nature, the emptying out of its mystery, its inherent powers, its hidden qualities and symbolic power, and the fear of uncomprehended, threatening nature that constitutes the sublime. This disenchantment is the result of humankind's concentration on a mode of thought they call "factual mentality," a version of rational thought that becomes increasingly technological, since "technology is the essence" of the kind of knowledge developed out of Enlightenment rationality.

For Horkheimer and Adorno, then, modern history is the story of how myth, enchantment, and superstition turned into enlightenment, and nature into mere objectivity. As a result, humankind paid "for the increase of their power with alienation from that over which they exercise power" (9). The paradoxical result of this transaction underscores their main point. Not only has modernity's domination of nature and its technical expertise been purchased at the cost of happiness (Freud's point), it has brought all of Europe to the brink of barbarism, for by 1940 "the fully enlightened earth radiates disaster triumphant" (3). What "appears to be the triumph of subjective rationality, the subjection of all reality to logical formalism, is paid for by the obedient subjection of reason to what is directly given" (26). The "directly given," the calculable, that which can be observed, measured, and used determines humankind's relation to nature in a way that leads not just to its objectification, but to the objectification as well of the knowing subject in his or her relation both to self and to others.

Horkheimer and Adorno mourn the loss of an irrational, magical, even mystical or superstitious relationship to nature, but they do not call for some kind of wholesale return to such a relationship. They are as wary of the illusionism of a mythic orientation toward nature as they are of a thoroughly pragmatic one: "thought becomes illusionary whenever it seeks to deny the divisive function, distancing and objectification. All mystic unification remains deception, the impotently inward trace of the absolved revolution" (39) (in part, I will be arguing about Emerson that his transcendentalism is linked to the kind of "mystic unification" Horkheimer and Adorno refer to here, and that in the final analysis it supersedes the protopragmatist elements of his thought). Thus while humankind's modern relationship to nature, born of Enlightenment rationality, seems dialectical, it lacks the potential for some kind of new synthesis that will lift the culture of modernity out of the debilitating tension between transcendentalism and pragmatism. It will simply perpetuate—and be perpetuated by—that conflict.

Emerson perceived the possibility of such a debilitating tension one hundred years earlier and tried to resolve it. One of the central aims of Emerson's *Nature* (1836) is to work out a post-Enlightenment orientation toward nature that reconciles an emergent technological approach with a pre-Enlightenment spiritual one.[8] The problem of modernity Horkheimer and Adorno recognize as having come to a *crisis* in the first three decades of the twentieth century can be seen developing in its early stages in Emerson's collection of essays.[9] Emerson understood in the 1830s that science and the fledgling forms of technology it was developing constituted the foundation of America's development as a modern nation. Since he was passionately involved in conceptualizing America's modernity, he could hardly take the kind of stand against the appropriation of nature for the purposes of "man" we have observed in Horkheimer and Adorno (or that one finds in Heidegger's writings on technology). On the other hand, Emerson was deeply committed to a form of idealism that believed in nature's inherent link to a spiritual power and mystery that transcended material reality. His approach to nature had to endorse humankind's instrumental relationship to it while retaining what Horkheimer and Adorno call its "enchantment." In other words, Emerson needed to balance his commitment to a loosely defined "pragmatism" with an even deeper attachment to the notion of fixed and transcendental reality. In *Nature*, Emerson wants to restore a loosely Neoplatonic approach to materiality without rejecting out of hand the idea that nature exists for the use of humankind in its drive toward material and social modernization, and without turning his back on the value of rational calculation, scientific measurement, and quantification. He wants to allow for the possibility of the latter without its leading to a fundamental estrangement between human beings and nature, without, that is, the kind of radical alienation Horkheimer and Adorno find one hundred years later.

Because he wants to insist on both the instrumental use and the spiritual being of nature in a way that avoids nature's domination by humankind's material needs, Emerson balances the stress in some of the chapters on nature's usefulness in the realms of scientific, mechanical, and social development (the side some of his critics link to pragmatism) by the stress in others on its beauty, spiritualism, and idealism. Moreover, the purely material and instrumental uses of nature are theorized in such a way that nature continues to dominate humankind even while humankind appropriates nature to its own ends. Understanding how this can be the case, and how the articulation of such a position relates in Emerson's mind to the specific nature of America's modernity requires a closer look at some of the chapters in *Nature*.

"Nature" is defined at the outset of *Nature* "as the *NOT ME* . . . nature and art, all other men and my own body" (8). "Nature, in the common sense, refers to essences unchanged by man; space, the air, the river, the leaf," while "*art*" involves the "mixture" of humankind's "will with the same things, as in a house, a canal, a statue, a picture" (8). Emerson links the products of technology with those of art under a single category to be distinguished from nature: a canal or a house derives as much from humankind's "art" as does a statue or a picture. At one stroke the collective products of human ingenuity are distinguished in a hierarchical way from nature ("art," he writes a few pages later, cannot rival the "pomp" of nature [16]), and art is linked, as the exercise of will, to cultural production in general. Aesthetic production is implicated in the general act of culture making. The idea that there is a fundamental difference in kind between the making of a painting and a canal becomes questionable. The production of art, in effect, becomes simply a part of the general productive forces of culture. While it would have been awfully difficult for Emerson to envision in 1836 the kind of negative transformation of art into the products of mass culture Horkheimer and Adorno decried one hundred years later, the possibility of such a transformation appears in what he writes here.

This link between the products of art and the products of technology results from the idea that nature embodies a method or economy reproduced by human beings in the exercise of their wills—whether toward the end of constructing a statue or building a canal. Both activities are *taught* by, and are thus dominated by, nature. This is the point of his remarks in "Commodity." The ability to engage in what Emerson calls "useful arts" (12) we "owe to nature" (12), since the useful arts constitute "reproductions or new combinations by the wit of man" (12) of processes he has learned from nature. "Nature," Emerson explains, "in its ministry to man, is not only the material, but is also the process and the result. All the parts incessantly work into each other's hands for the profit of man" (40–41). Mechanical developments including the use of steam, the paving of roads with iron bars, building coaches, "cities, ships, canals, bridges" result from mental and physical processes learned from nature, so that while human beings shape nature for their needs, they do so under the ministry and hence the domination of a nature whose ultimate power is spiritual.

Emerson specifically wants to avoid the kind of relation to nature Horkheimer and Adorno inherit by theorizing an organic instrumentality that preserves nature's domination over humankind. He seeks to formulate a relationship between humankind and nature that allows for the use of nature by human beings in a benign way. Though humankind establishes an instrumental relation to nature, Emerson insists that nature retains its dominant position through its link to the divine. *This is why it is misleading simply to label this instrumentality in Emerson "pragmatism."* When Emerson refers to the instrumental use of nature he is doing so in the belief that those uses are determined, sanctioned, and directed by nature itself, and that nature's processes constitute a divine "ministry." "The Imagination" drives both the production of a picture and the building of a canal, and is "defined to be the use which the Reason makes of the material world" (65). Emerson thus insists that the processes of imaginative reasoning are directed not just at, but *by*, nature.

As I have already noted, Emerson's stress on the *uses* of nature in *Nature* is often invoked by critics who see him as a kind of protopragmatist. "Let us inquire, to what end is nature?" Emerson declares in his introduction (7), and later, in "Commodity," he writes:

> Whoever considers the final cause of the world will discern a multitude of uses that enter as parts into that result. They will admit of being thrown into one of the following classes: Commodity; Beauty; Language; and Discipline. (12)

Kenneth Burke refers to both these passages in arguing that "now that modern pragmatism has flourished long enough to show a course of development we can see the incipient pragmatism in Emerson's idealism" (*Grammar* 277). In his gloss on the above passage from "Commodity," Burke calls attention to the fact that Emerson's investigation of "the final cause of the world" or of nature is not simply an ontological or metaphysical meditation on final causes, but an investigation of the practical uses of nature.

Burke sees this stress on the usefulness of nature as a kind of counterdiscourse to Emerson's stress on nature's divinity, so that there are two principles associated with nature that seem to be in opposition. However, Emerson is actually attempting something more than this. He wants to articulate a fundamental unity between nature's metaphysical and "pragmatic" elements. While he clearly values nature's metaphysical qualities over its mere usefulness, Emerson wants to find a way to link nature's instrumental use to what he believes to be its essential spirituality. The passage about nature's uses from "Commodity" serves as a kind of introduction to the rest of the volume, but only up to a certain point. It ends with "Discipline," leaving out "Idealism," "Spirit," and the conclusion, "Prospects." These omissions are not inadvertent; they structurally reinforce Emerson's conviction that nature's "being" incorporates, yet transcends, its usefulness. Nature's "idealism" and "spirit" are related to its *essence* in a way that demands they be distinguished from the "multitude of uses" discussed in the other chapters of *Nature*, uses foregrounded by recent critics to argue that Emerson's was an essentially "pragmatic vision."[10] For in the final analysis, "all the uses of nature admit of being summed in one . . . it always speaks of Spirit. It suggests the absolute . . . nature is to stand as the apparition of God. It is the organ through which the universal spirit speaks to the individual, and strives to lead back the individual to it" (40).

Here spirit, the absolute, and God are not divided off from instrumental nature. Rather, the "uses" of nature are a part of—and are determined by—its absolute spirit. The essays in *Nature* seem, therefore, to proceed in a roughly hierarchical way, but with what Burke calls the pragmatic uses of nature *linked* to its essential spirituality.[11] This is the "method" of nature Emerson describes in his essay "The Method of Nature" (1841):

> We hear something too much of the results of machinery, commerce, and the useful arts . . . The rapid wealth which hundreds in the community acquire in trade, or by the incessant expansions of our population and arts, enchants the eyes of all the rest . . .
>
> I do not wish to look with sour aspect at the industrious manufacturing village, or the mart of commerce. I love the music of the water-wheel; I value the railway; I feel the pride which the sight of a ship inspires; I look on trade and every mechanical craft as education also. But let me discriminate what is precious herein. There is in each of these works an act of invention, an intellectual step, or short series of steps taken; that act or step is the spiritual act . . . (115)

Emerson's upbeat, even proud embrace of modernization is rooted in his conviction that the progress it represents is born of a spiritual act at the very heart of nature's method. The act of invention or the intellectual step necessary to create a railway, a ship, trade, or any mechanical craft is a spiritual one. While such an act employs reason to use nature as an instrument of humankind's will, because that use is sanctioned and enabled by a spirit that permeates nature, it is not (following Emerson's logic) an act of domination.

The method of nature Emerson outlined in 1841 is a version of nature's "discipline" outlined in the chapter by that name in *Nature*. "Discipline" and "Idealism," which stand back to back in the volume, represent the two poles or modes of thought Emerson seeks to link—what Burke isolates as idealism and an "incipient pragmatism." The stress in "Discipline" is on the *disciplining* function of nature. The chapter opens with the same stress on nature as the very ground of culture found in the passage from "The Method of Nature":

Space, time, society, labor, climate, food, locomotion, the animals, the mechanical forces, give us sincerest lessons day by day, whose meaning is
unlimited. They educate both the Understanding and the Reason. Every
property of matter is a school for the understanding,—its solidity or resistance, its inertia, its extension, its figure, its divisibility . . . Meantime,
Reason transfers all these lessons into its own world of thought, by perceiving the analogy that marries Matter and Mind. (26)

The ministry or method of nature underscores its didactic function (it
gives us "lessons day by day") and thus forges a link between mind
and matter in the creation of culture. The stress here on the marriage of
Matter and Mind captures in capsule form Emerson's commitment to
the idea that nature's being and its uses are interrelated. Because he believes he has avoided emptying nature of its mystification (what Horkheimer and Adorno lament about modernity) by linking organic nature, spirit, mind, and the usefulness of matter, Emerson can embrace
the technological benefits brought by instrumental reason without betraying his belief in its essential divinity. Nature's "ministry" *is* in part
its availability as instrument of humankind's reason, so for Emerson
modernity (at this early date) can look attractive precisely because nature's metaphysical being incorporates, and thus checks, its domination
by sheerly instrumental or pragmatic forces.[12]
    In a way, Emerson's rejection of the Calvinist mystification of nature
as depraved represents an important break with tradition that might be
said to mark his own modernity. That is, Emerson insists on a new relationship to both God and nature, one that tends to banish in one
stroke the deadening principle of sin, the tyranny of an anthropomor-
phic God, and the policing power of a nature (organic and human) defined as the embodiment of evil. This break with a Christian tradition
of thought that had determined the cultural life of the West since the
sixteenth century, especially in the context of Emerson's "New World"
roots, seems to speak forcefully for Emerson's positive relationship to
what we generally call the modern age. However, Emerson's revision of
Calvinism constitutes less a demystification than a remystification of
nature, for he tends, as we have seen, to replace Calvinism's negative
idealization (or mystification) of nature with a positive one. Emerson
defines nature in a way that overcompensates for Calvinism's negative
idealization of it. In so doing, he forces a wedge between nature and
culture and between the individual and society, creating a system of
values in which nature and the solitary, self-reliant soul are valued over
culture and society in a way that leaves both ill equipped for modernity. Indeed, it might be argued that as long as nature remained the

focus, whether in the negative Calvinist sense or the positive Emersonian one, philosophical thought and the culture it helped produce would be incapable of coming to terms with modernity.

While I have been stressing that *Nature* works overtly to lessen or resolve the tension between an instrumental and an idealist orientation toward nature, it would be wrong to suggest that such a resolution actually takes place, or that this tension does not persist in all Emerson's writings. The point is not that Emerson achieves such a resolution, but that his writings at this crucial period dramatize the centrality of this tension. It is more often the case, however, that Emerson's stress on the instrumental or the practical (as we have seen in relation to the question of nature) is subordinated to his stress on the metaphysical. Emerson's transcendentalism almost always ends up as the ultimate ground for value or being—even if the stress has been heavily on the instrumental. This is why a redemptive stress on Emerson's "pragmatism" can distort our understanding of his work. Again, it is not that there aren't "pragmatist" elements in Emerson's writings. The point is that they are constantly qualified or undercut by his transcendentalism in ways that suggest that his own point of view lacked the resolution his critics seem to have.

One of the clearest evocations in Emerson of the tension between metaphysical idealism and materialism comes in the opening passage to "The Transcendentalist" (1842):

> As thinkers, mankind have ever divided into two sects, Materialists and Idealists; the first class founding on experience, the second on consciousness; the first class beginning to think from the data of the senses, the second class perceive that the senses are not final, and say, the senses give us representations of things, but what are the things themselves, they cannot tell. The materialist insists of facts, on history, on the force of circumstances, and the animal wants of man; the idealist on the power of Thought and of Will, on inspiration, on miracle, on individual culture. These two modes of thinking are both natural, but the idealist contends that his way of thinking is in higher nature. (193)

Though the essay from which this passage comes reads in its final pages as a homage to the transcendentalist,[13] Emerson resists associating himself here explicitly with transcendentalism. What is striking about this passage, though, is how explicitly the two "modes of thinking" it treats recall the general tension between idealism and materialism throughout Emerson's writing. Although both these modes of thought are here called "natural," Emerson emphasizes a crucial difference between them.

The idealist "concedes all that the [materialist] affirms, admits the impressions of sense, admits their coherency, their use and beauty, and then asks the materialist for the *grounds* of assurance that things are as his senses represent them" (193, emphasis mine). From the transcendentalist's point of view, the materialist *cannot* "ground" his assurance; for him the world of visible reality is only a world of appearances, it has no ground without recourse to a transcendental one. "The materialist," Emerson writes, thus "is a phantom walking and working amid phantoms" (194). "Ask him," Emerson continues, "why he believes that an uniform experience will continue uniform, or on what grounds he founds his faith in his figures, and he will perceive that his mental fabric is built up on just as strange and quaking foundations as his proud edifice of stone" (194–95). The Idealist, it turns out, has "another measure, which is metaphysical . . . Mind is the only reality, of which men, and all other natures are better or worse reflectors" (195).

It is less important that Emerson underscores in this essay the ultimate value of the transcendentalist position than that he identifies the central philosophical problem that divides idealism from materialism (and later, pragmatism), the problem of *grounding*. The crucial distinction between these two positions, for Emerson, is that the idealist concedes all that the materialist affirms but questions the grounds of the materialist's assurance about the nature of material reality. The problem with the materialist position is that it is mired in contingency. The materialist, without access to a transcendental certainty, must be content with the productions of his own "mental fabric." The idealist, on the other hand, can take the actual "measure" of reality, since "mind is the only reality." The problem Emerson foregrounds here is not only the ontological one represented by the question of whether or not "things" *are* as the senses represent them, but the epistemological and ethical question of how the true and the good can be authoritatively grounded in a world where all assurance has become contingent.

In raising this problem, Emerson anticipates one of the fundamental starting points for what would become pragmatism. For pragmatism, as Richard Rorty points out, foregrounds the fundamental choice "between accepting the contingent character of starting-points, and attempting to evade this contingency" (*Consequences of Pragmatism* 166). The problem for critics like Gunn and Poirier, who want to see Emerson as a pragmatist (Rorty has no interest in making such a connection), is that in the passage on idealism and materialism Emerson locates the advantage of idealism in its ability to avoid the kind of contingency Rorty refers to. The idealist has the edge over the materialist, for Emerson, precisely because he can measure things metaphysically, thus avoiding the kind of contingency he associates with materialism. According to Rorty, on the other hand, the pragmatist "tells us . . . to give up the notion that God, or evolution, or some other underwriter of our present world-picture" can allow us to evade the contingent character of starting points (165–66). Pragmatism, Rorty quite rightly insists (166), requires that we give up the kind of "metaphysical comfort" (the phrase is Nietzsche's) Emerson evokes in the passage quoted above.

The philosophical issue Emerson focuses on in this passage is the same one critics like Gunn and Poirier evoke in their call for a return to Emersonian pragmatism: a concern about contingency. The crisis of belief that sends Gunn back to pragmatism is precipitated in his view by a loss of the kind of comfort Emerson associates with the transcendentalist's "assurance" about the accuracy of his "measure." Gunn wants to return to "experience itself" precisely because it seems to him to offer the solace of a measure beyond the contingencies ushered in by poststructuralism. The irony here, of course, is that while Gunn wants to position himself as something like the materialist in Emerson's passage, he actually ends up taking an idealist position. For the category "experience itself" is nothing if not an essentializing one whose authority is grounded in the transcendental idea of the in-itselfness of "experience." Emerson relates the category of "experience" to materialism, however, precisely because it embodies the kind of contingency this in-itselfness can elide. In the final analysis, of course, he sides with what he regards as the superior value of the transcendentalist position, and he seems to do so precisely because it saves him from the kind of contingency Rorty quite rightly sees pragmatism as embracing. Emerson is able, with remarkable clarity, to sketch out the materialist position that will modulate in James and Dewey into pragmatism. However, as in all of the essays I have been discussing, Emerson's ultimate allegiance is to a set of transcendentalist assumptions he deems higher, because less contingent, than those of materialism.

This is why I have insisted that it is a mistake to claim Emerson as a pragmatist. The simple fact is that while his writings often invoke the "practical" in a way that looks forward to pragmatism, Emerson ultimately grounds his major arguments about nature, the self, literature, and culture in a universal power or transcendental principle. We can at this point fold our discussion of the question of Emerson's pragmatism back into the historical argument we made at the outset of this chapter in our discussion of Emerson's relationship to modernity. As I noted a moment ago, the transcendentalist position is attractive to Emerson precisely because it seems to avoid the kind of epistemological contingency a pragmatist position would require. It offers him "assurance." Emerson's engagement with the tension between contingency and assurance has to be understood in terms of a larger post-Enlightenment preoccupation with the challenge of grounding what Habermas calls the "normative." In Habermas's view, modernity can be characterized by a post-Enlightenment philosophical and ethical preoccupation with the whole challenge of formulating and grounding norms for behavior that do not lie outside of behavior itself and in the past, what he has called the problem of "self-reassurance":

> Hegel was the first to raise to the level of a philosophical problem the process of detaching modernity from the suggestion of norms lying outside of itself in the past . . . [O]nly at the end of the eighteenth century did the problem of modernity's *self-reassurance [Selbstvergewisserung]* come to a head in such a way that Hegel could grasp this question *as a philosophical problem,* and indeed as *the fundamental problem* of his own philosophy. The anxiety caused by the fact that a modernity without models had to stabilize itself on the basis of the very diremptions [or divisions: *Entzweiungen*] it had wrought is seen by Hegel as "the source of the need for philosophy." As modernity awakens to consciousness of itself, a need for self-reassurance arises . . . (*Philosophical Discourse* 16)

The concept of "self-reliance" or "self-trust" in Emerson, articulated specifically in relationship to the conduct of individuals, actually has a much broader set of implications related to modernity's need to generate its own mode of "self-reassurance." Earlier in this chapter I pointed out that Emerson's cultural program was committed to the invention of America as a separate and autonomous entity, one with an "original relation to the universe," building not "sepulchers of the fathers" but "our own works and laws and thoughts." Understood from this point of view, his attempt to theorize a national culture does not have just a local imperative, but is broadly connected to the demands of an emergent Western modernity. This connection is underscored by Emerson's insistence that American culture must reject the whole idea of relying on norms lying outside of itself in the past, that it had to constitute itself, in Habermas's terms, as "a modernity without models." Emerson's philosophical problem was precisely the one of theorizing modernity's self-reassurance in an American cultural context, and we have seen (as other critics have noted) that he moves back and forth between an idealist and a pragmatic ground for that reassurance. While Emerson is passionate in his insistence that America find a ground of assurance beyond tradition and the past, he rejects the contingency of a pragmatic ground for the metaphysical assurance of transcendental norms. This is where the logic of those who argue that Emerson was the father of American pragmatism breaks down. Emerson does confront the central problem of an emergent modernity, but by having recourse to a transcendental ground for knowledge and truth he reintroduces the kind of metaphysical assurance modernity defined itself by rejecting. Emerson attempts to resolve the legitimation crisis of modernity by embracing a transcendentalist position that is at times tentatively harnessed to a commitment to the practical and the utilitarian, and that tries to avoid embracing contingency in the ways twentieth-century neopragmatists will have to do.[14] The tension between these two positions marks the extent to which Emerson's cultural criticism is determined by the demands of working out a post-Enlightenment approach to subjectivity, knowledge, and experience. It is a tension that will continue to determine the lineaments of American criticism through the rest of the nineteenth century.

2

Emerson, Whitman, and the Problem of Culture

In the previous chapter we observed that Emerson's cultural project in general, and more specifically his attitude toward nature, had to be understood as the response to a set of conditions specific to post-Enlightenment culture in Europe and America. Where some recent critics have tried to historicize Emerson by situating him at the beginning of a narrative about the development of American pragmatism, I have insisted that it is more appropriate to see his work as part of a larger response to philosophical, social, and cultural problems specific to the challenges of a newly emergent modernity. In the preceding chapter I focused in particular on how Emerson's writings about nature indicated the form of his engagement with these problems. In this chapter I want to turn to some of his essays on aesthetics and culture, and to pursue the issues they raise in an analysis of Whitman's *Democratic Vistas*.

In *The Philosophical Discourse of Modernity*, Habermas writes that "the problem of grounding modernity out of itself first comes to consciousness in the realm of aesthetic criticism" (8). Both Habermas and Foucault (following Walter Benjamin) locate the emergence of the aesthetic problem of self-grounding in Emerson's French contemporary, Baudelaire. "For Baudelaire," writes Habermas, "the aesthetic experience of modernity fuses with the historical. In the fundamental experience of aesthetic modernity, the problem of self-grounding becomes acute, because here the horizon of temporal experience contracts to the decentered subjectivity that splits away from the conventions of everyday life. For this reason, he assigns to the modern work of art a strange place at the intersection of the axes of the actual and the eternal" (8).[1] Emerson's attempt to deal with the problem of "self-grounding" also af-

42

fects his treatment of art, which, like Baudelaire, he wants to situate at the intersection of the everyday and the transcendent. Emerson, as we shall see in a moment, wants American literature to focus its attention on the conventions of everyday life. However, the aesthetic quality of everyday life, for Emerson, must be informed with and infused by a transcendental spirit. The result is that Emerson works out an aesthetic distinguished by an insistence on intersection and fusion much like the one Habermas finds in Baudelaire:

> The actual present can no longer gain its self-consciousness from opposi-
> tion to an epoch rejected and surpassed, to a shape of the past. Actuality
> can be constituted only as the point where time and eternity intersect. In
> this way, modernity is rescued, not from its infirmity, surely, but from
> triviality . . . (*Philosophical Discourse* 9)[2]

Emerson would agree that the actuality of the present cannot be con- stituted in relationship to the past, but must be grounded in eternity's intersection with the present. Indeed, his specific interest in helping formulate a characteristically American literature is informed by the conviction that his age and place constitute a "point where time and eternity intersect." In essays like "The American Scholar," the actual present represented in art gains its legitimacy or authority not from op- posing the past, but from a form of aesthetic creation that establishes an intersection between eternal spirit and the local and common. However, what happens in Emerson is that contemporary experience, rescued from triviality by eternity, is actually overwhelmed and subsumed by it.

Emerson insists American literature can establish an original, mod- ern, and authentic relationship to reality by turning its attention to "the near, the low, the common," and the everyday (68). An authentic and original culture liberated, in his view, from a tradition that has grown dry and ineffectual can be erected only on the foundations of art con- cerned with "today" (69). Thus at the end of "The American Scholar" Emerson identifies in some contemporary poetry the "sign" of a move- ment that will break with the aesthetic traditions of Europe: "Instead of the sublime and beautiful; the near, the low, the common . . . the litera- ture of the poor, the feelings of the child, the philosophy of the street, the meaning of household life, are the topics of the time. It is a great stride" (68). The long list of contemporary poetic topics that follows will give us "insight into to-day" (68) rather than into "what is doing in Italy or Arabia; what is Greek art, or Provençal minstrelsy" (69).

We can chart from this moment the American beginning of the mod- ern tension between high and popular culture that reached its critical apotheosis in Horkheimer and Adorno's essay on mass culture and the culture industry. On the one hand, the desire to turn the attention of art away from the traditional images and themes of classical and European art toward the common and the everyday constitutes a defining moment in modern Western culture, yet, at the same time, it inaugurates a distinction that eventually leads to a crisis in Western cultural criticism (represented in America, as we shall see in the next chapter, by the distinction Van Wyck Brooks makes between High Brow and Low Brow culture). Creating the kind of national culture envisioned by Emerson (and later by Whitman) necessitated grounding American art in the everyday materials and experiences of a social world linked less to the traditions of high art than to working-class culture.[3]

However, while Emerson insisted American literature find its subject matter in objects and activities we now associate with mass culture, the aesthetic quality of those objects and activities was lent them by a higher, transcendental power. In order to see why, we need to take a look at Emerson's aesthetic criticism, especially his essays on poetics and creativity, which are structured by the same philosophical distinction between idealism and materialism informing his writings about nature and the self.

In "Self-Reliance," Emerson's position on creativity is dominated by a familiar metaphysical idealism. Aesthetic production, he insists, is grounded in the soul—in "Spontaneity," "Instinct," "Intuition," so that *knowing* has its sources in the reception of a transcendental first cause. The "self" here is "Aboriginal"; it "grounds" knowledge in a way that merits "universal reliance" (the twist on the essay's title makes his point). Here, Emerson draws a central distinction between the *involuntary* and the *voluntary*, between "wilful actions" and "native emotions":

> If we ask whence this comes [justice and truth], if we seek to pry into the soul that causes, all philosophy is at fault. Its presence or its absence is all we can affirm. Every man discriminates between the voluntary acts of his mind, and his involuntary perceptions, and knows that to his involuntary perceptions a perfect faith is due . . . My wilful actions and acquisitions are but roving;—the idlest reverie, the faintest native emotion, command my curiosity and respect. (269)

This emphasis on the involuntary over the voluntary, on emotion over will, translates into a valuing of the permanent over the transient, so that intellectual or artistic creation can be rooted in something transcendental. This leads to a theory of creativity weighted toward the passive reception of truth and beauty cut loose from both the will and historical contingencies, whether political or intellectual. "The student," he writes in "Literary Ethics," is "great only by being passive to the superincumbent spirit" (109). Such a theory of aesthetic production views the writer as expressive only to the degree he "resigns" himself to the "divine *aura*" that flows through "the circuit of things" ("The Poet," 459). Emerson's poet is "self-reliant" only in the limited sense that he or she can be grounded in this circuit. The poet's "seeing," according to Emerson, comes not by "study" but by "sharing the path" of this "aura," which "breaths through forms" ("The Poet," 459). Poetry, in effect, *is* nature, or nature's "primal warblings":

> For poetry was all written before time was, and whenever we are so finely organized that we can penetrate into that region where the air is music, we hear those primal warblings, and attempt to write them down. ("The Poet," 449)

The perfect poem, from this point of view, would be an exact transcription of nature's "warblings," for when the poet "attempt[s] to write them down," he inevitably will "substitute something of [his] own, and thus miswrite the poem" ("The Poet," 449). The poem's beauty is thus measured by the accuracy of its transcription from nature.

According to Emerson, genius or thought in its highest and best form has its first cause in permanent, involuntary nature, not in a contingent, voluntary, or wilful intellectual act. This means that "the highest merit we ascribe to Moses, Plato, and Milton is, that they set at naught books and traditions, and spoke not what men but what they thought. A man should learn to detect and watch that gleam of light which flashes across his mind from within, more than the lustre of the firmament of bards and sages" (259). Emerson's position here recalls the familiar conceptual division between inner and outer ("books and traditions" as opposed to "that gleam of light which flashes across the mind from within"), and at a more general level of abstraction, between nature and culture and between metaphysical reception and practical action. (This division essentially replicates the one underlying his distinction between a poem based on a faulty transcription of nature and one more closely allied to its primal warblings.)

Taken together, these essays constitute an aesthetic theory derived from the same commitment to transcendental being that grounded Emerson's approach to nature. However, some of his essays on literature and art have a heavier investment in art's sources in material reality and pragmatic need. In "Shakespeare; or, the Poet," for example, the act of poetic creation seems rooted in the active representation of contemporary forms of material and social culture rather than in the passive transcribing of nature's aura. Here "the greatest genius is the most indebted man," but his debt is not to nature but to other writers, other texts, and to the social life around him. The "general" influence that makes a "genius" great is not an "aura" but "the river of . . . thoughts and events, forced onward by the ideas and necessities of his contemporaries" (710). The theory of poetic creativity Emerson sketches in here is still based on the act of *reception*, even the reception of "spirit," but that spirit is not free of the contingencies of time and history but "the spirit of the *hour*" (711, emphasis mine).[4] The poet's power comes not from a sympathy with the circuit of things flowing through nature, but from a "sympathy with his people"; not from nature as such, but from nature transformed by human labor, with "hills" that have been "sunk," "hollows" that have been "filled," rivers that have been "bridged" (711). Here aesthetic creativity is the function of a sympathy with nature's method. This passage recalls the one we looked at earlier in *Nature* that links such creativity with the kind of cultural efforts and social labor that were transforming the geographical landscape of the continent. The instrumental use of nature surfaces here as a metaphor of aesthetic production.

The rest of the essay links poetic creativity to the world of practical action. "It is easy to see," Emerson writes, "that what is best written or done by genius, in the world, was no man's work, but came by wide social labor, when a thousand wrought like one, sharing the same impulse" (715). Poems are not, from this point of view, the accurate transcriptions of nature's primal warblings, but like hills leveled, hollows filled, bridges built by social labor with practical ends in sight. The theory of poetic creation he elaborates here is grounded in the approach to nature we reviewed in "The Method of Nature." Interestingly, both of Emerson's approaches to poetic creativity stress that "originality" is not at issue, but for different reasons. His idealist side tells him a poet can never be original because what he expresses is already a poem in nature, while his materialist or pragmatic side tells him that poems are always borrowed from other texts and other authors.[5] Where the poet in "The Poet" must eschew tradition as a distraction from nature, Shakespeare is great because he "knew that tradition supplies a better fable than any invention can" (713).

When Emerson seeks to reconcile the tensions between historical and transcendental sources of creativity and art, however, he comes down firmly on the side of the transcendental, a position he shares with Baudelaire.[6] We can see this clearly in the essay "Art." Emerson begins by reiterating that art comes from the poet's being positioned within "the circuit of things," that creation is fundamentally the expression of nature *through* rather than *by* the poet: "the landscape has beauty for his eye . . . because the same power which sees through his eyes, is seen in that spectacle" (431). However, the "creative impulse"—the poetic *act*—is "the abridgment and selection we observe in all spiritual activity, the ability to "convey a larger sense by simpler symbols" (431). Power itself cannot be poetically rendered, but must be shown to be infused through things. Hence, the importance of the "symbol": "the artist must employ the symbols in use in his day and nation, to convey his enlarged sense to his fellow-men. Thus the new in art is always formed out of the old" (431). From here, Emerson begins to launch what will become, by the end of the essay, a plea familiar from essays like "The American Scholar" for an art specifically rooted in American experience and in American things:

> As far as the spiritual character of the period overpowers the artist, and finds expression in his work, so far it will retain a certain grandeur, and will represent to future beholders the Unknown, the Inevitable, the Divine . . . No man can quite emancipate himself from his age and country, or produce a model in which the education, the religion, the politics, usages, and arts of his times shall have no share . . . Above his will, and out of his sight, he is necessitated, by the air he breathes, and the idea on which he and his contemporaries live and toil, to share the manner of his times, without knowing what that manner is. (432)

Emerson wants art to focus on the stuff of everyday experience, but the objects and experience of everyday life are not deemed to be poetic in and of themselves. They symbolize beauty only to the extent that they can stand as contemporary symbols of the "Divine." In effect, they have the same status the poet has in relation to Emerson's circuit, for the poetic has its origin outside of and prior to both the poet and the objects of his or her experience (this goes as well for the self per se, who engages a truth grounded outside and prior to its experience). The stress in the passage above on historical contingency reiterates the point he makes about the creative process in the "Shakespeare" essay. Indeed, the passage calls our attention to what we now call the role of ideology in the construction of both the perceiving subject and the poetry he or she produces: "thoughts" related to the poet's "age," "country," "religion," "politics," and "education" determine the poet's work "above his or her will, and out of his sight." In his "ideas," the poet "shares the manner of his times, without knowing what that manner is."[7]

Having begun with a reference to "the popular distinction" between "use" and "beauty" (431) Emerson concludes near the end of the essay that "nature" does not "permit" the "division of beauty from use," that "beauty must come back to the useful arts, and the distinction between the fine and the useful arts must be forgotten" (439). This is quite like the point Emerson makes about nature when he insists that we not separate its being from its usefulness. In both cases, he insists we see that there is beauty in the useful, and that it is useful to see beauty there. Here we get one of many passages in Emerson that look forward to the poetry of Walt Whitman:

> Beauty will not come at the call of a legislature ... It is in vain that we look for genius to reiterate its miracles in the old arts; it is its instinct to find beauty and holiness in new and necessary facts, in the field and roadside, in the shop and mill. Proceeding from a religious heart it will raise to a divine use the railroad, the insurance office, the joint-stock company, our law, our primary assemblies, our commerce, the galvanic battery, the electric jar, the prism, and the chemist's retort, in which we seek now only an economical use. (440)

All these manifestations of material, local culture have a use for Emerson beyond the sheerly economic. Seeing beauty in local culture, he can situate the transcendental in the everyday by finding a place where the practical and the ideal meet. This brings us back to the symmetry between Emerson's project and Habermas's point about modernity's self-consciousness having to be constituted as the point where "time and eternity intersect." Emerson's aesthetic theory also converges on this point with Baudelaire's, who wrote in "The Painter of Modern Life" that "modernity is the transient, the fleeting, the contingent; it is one-half of art, the other being the eternal and the immovable" (403). The synthesis Emerson envisions here, however, works by an economy that finally shortchanges the local because it grounds beauty in an involuntary investment in "aboriginal Power." Emerson's approach in "Art" privileges the transcendental over the local in the sense that the latter is subservient to, or a vehicle for, the former. The actual or contingent is less "one-half of art" than the empty vessel for a power outside it.

This should not obscure the fact, of course, that Emerson was attempting to formulate a conception of culture grounded in the actual experiences, activities, and tastes of the masses. "Culture" in America, in his view, had to be defined in opposition to the culture of European aristocracy and in relation to an emergent set of working-class interests and values. The problem lay, as I have been arguing, in the theory and rhetoric of Emerson's writings on art and beauty, for together they tended to undermine the value and validity of the conception of culture he was beginning to formulate. Ultimately, Emerson's transcendental-ist metaphysics conflicted with his vision of a truly democratic culture. Indeed, the philosophical tension between materialism and idealism in nineteenth-century America is nowhere more apparent than in the sphere or idea of "culture."[8]

We can observe that conflict reverberating through the "programme" of culture articulated by the writer who did the most to continue the work Emerson began in essays like "The American Scholar," Walt Whitman. In *Democratic Vistas* (1871) Whitman took up Emerson's insistence that America must create its own art and literature, free from European influence and grounded in a specifically American constellation of experiences. The pace of America's modernization measured in material terms was enormous, Whitman acknowledged, but the nation's social and cultural development was static. "I say that our New World democracy," Whitman wrote, "however great a success in uplifting the masses out of their sloughs, in materialistic development, products, and in a certain highly deceptive superficial popular intellectuality, is, so far, an almost complete failure in its social aspects, and in really grand religious, moral, literary, and aesthetic results" (461).[9] Significantly, Whitman adds to Emerson's nationalist rhetoric a stress on the challenge of being *modern,* for the cultural program he lays out is aimed at an "original" and "transcendental" expression of "democracy and the modern" (456). Whitman builds on Emerson, but, writing later in the century, he can see that the destinies of America and of modernity have become intertwined, so that the Emersonian challenge of constructing a specifically American literature or culture has modulated into the challenge of constructing a specifically modern culture. "Our fundamental want today in the United States," he writes, "is of a class, and the clear ideas of a class, of native authors, literatuses, far different . . . than any yet known, sacerdotal, modern, fit to cope with our occasions, lands, permeating the whole mass of American mentality, taste, belief" (457). The stress on "native authors" is Emersonian, but the stress on being "modern" is Whitmanian.[10]

Whitman's stress on the whole issue of modernization marks a difference in emphasis from Emerson, but so too does his very specific focus on "culture" and his desire to sketch out a "programme" for culture in America. Indeed, Whitman writes that "this word Culture, or what it has come to represent, involves . . . our whole theme, and has been, indeed, the spur, urging us to engagement" (479). Whitman's program involves rescuing the word "culture" from its effete, almost aristocratic European connotations and reconceptualizing it in terms grounded in

American working-class social forms. Thus to write about "culture" puts Whitman in "close quarters with the enemy" (479), since the term had begun to take upon itself an elitist association, denoting something restricted to the activities of "a single class alone, or for the parlors or lecture rooms" only (479). The word "culture," as Raymond Williams has pointed out, had by Whitman's time become an "independent and abstract noun which describes a general process of intellectual, spiritual and aesthetic development" associated with exposure to the "fine arts" (90–91).[11] Whitman is reacting not simply to the precious and effete connotations of the term culture, or to its European associations, but to the *class* differences it had come to imply. When Whitman writes that he is insisting "on a radical change of category" for the term "culture," he is clear about his desire to wrest it from its upper-class connotations:

> I should demand a programme of culture, drawn out, not for a single class alone, or for the parlors or lecture rooms, but with an eye to practical life, the west, the working-men, the facts of farms and jackplanes and engineers, and of the broad range of the women also of the middle and working strata, and with reference to the perfect equality of women, and of a grand and powerful motherhood. I should demand of this programme or theory a scope generous enough to include the widest human area. (479)

Whitman, then, is intervening not just in a local debate about culture. He is writing at a time when the forces of modernization had begun to destabilize an earlier, European conception of culture. Moreover, while the "culture" of business and industry had become thoroughly modern, the kind of culture we associate with the arts and with social forms of entertainment had come more and more to be coopted by the advocates of gentility, decorum, and the "fine arts." As Levine has shown, the last half of the nineteenth century witnessed the development of an increasingly hierarchical conception of culture in America. Alarmed by a growing sense of chaos under the pressures of industrialization, urbanization, and immigration, and motivated to a significant degree by their fear of urban violence, politicians and genteel industrialists alike began to conceive of what we now call "high" culture as a refuge and an escape from these pressures, but also as a civilizing instrument. In response to the increasing fragmentation and heterogeneity of a multiethnic and "riotous" working class, Levine writes, the "elites" developed a tripartite strategy:

> to retreat into their own private spaces whenever possible; to transform public spaces by rules, systems of taste, and canons of behavior of their

own choosing; and, finally, to convert the strangers so that their modes of behavior and cultural predilections emulated those of the elites. (177)

With increasing intensity and efficacy during the last three decades of the nineteenth century, this tripartite response drove a wedge between the culture of the elites and that of the working classes, so that by the end of the nineteenth century one of what Levine calls "the cultural consequences of modernization" (225) was the now familiar distinction between high and low (or popular) culture. The hierarchizing of economic classes in the eighteenth and early nineteenth centuries was mirrored and reinforced in the final decades of the nineteenth century by a hierarchizing of cultures. Culture, under the banner of this new hierarchy, is given a civilizing function. It is codified as fine art, and removed to galleries, museums, libraries, and genteel concert halls. The civilizing function of culture became tied to the heirarchizing of culture with the assumption that its positive effects on the upper classes would eventually "trickle down" to the working and lower classes. One could, as Levine points out, pursue one's own cultural interests with the comforting assumption that eventually the value of one's experience would work its way down to the lower classes.[12]

Whitman, writing at the very moment when this move toward hierarchy was beginning to accelerate, attempted to counter it head-on in *Democratic Vistas*.[13] He not only argues in his essay, in Emersonian fashion, for the importance of breaking free from the culture of Europe, but challenges as well the developing dominance of the ruling class and its attempt to control and define "culture."[14] This is clear both in the anticapitalist rhetoric of the essay and in the fact that it was a response to Carlyle's remarks on American democracy in his essay "Shooting Niagara." Whitman's desire to respond to those who, like Carlyle, see a fundamental contradiction between "democracy's convictions, aspirations, and the people's crudeness, vice, caprices" (456) turned quickly into a critique of elite culture and the articulation of a program for culture that resisted the kind of hierarchy Levine analyzes. Where Carlyle might have felt that the crudeness of self-interest would always undercut the viability of democracy, Whitman wants to argue that literature can vitalize individuals into a cohesive union in which self-interest and shared interest meet. "Politics, materials, heroic personalities, military *eclat*, etc., remains crude, and defers, in any close and thoroughgoing estimate, until vitalized by national, original archetypes in literature" (486).

Whitman's critique of the concept of "culture" as it was being reformulated by the ruling classes was based on his insistence that culture be defined in terms of the practical, material experiences of the working class. However, as Betsy Erkkila has pointed out, "in his attempt to give democracy a spiritual base, separate from the institutions of church and state, Whitman came more and more to deny the material conditions of American life" (253). We find in Whitman the same tendency we found in Emerson: to privilege the material and the practical over the ideal, while at the same time locating the very value of the material and the practical in their embodiment of universal or transcendental principles or forces. Thus while Levine is right in pointing out the ways in which Whitman explicitly attempts to counter the elitist hierarchizing of culture in America, he misses how the rhetoric of Whitman's discourse in defense of what we now call "mass culture" is often grounded in a metaphysical idealism that has more in common with the discourse of what was becoming "high culture."

It is important to keep in mind that Whitman's program for culture did not insist on the importance of existing popular cultural forms relative to more genteel ones. It was based, rather, on America's need to produce "American" authors who would write a specifically "American" literature. For example, where Levine demonstrates the extent to which Shakespeare was an integral part of what we now call popular culture in America,[15] Whitman argues that the poetry of Shakespeare and the other major writers of European culture must be rejected in America as a kind of poison.[16] "Powerful and resplendent" as they are, he writes, "ye were, in your atmospheres, grown not for America, but rather for her foes, the feudal and the old—while our genius is democratic and modern" (487). The fact that Whitman was willing to label Shakespeare "poison" even though his drama was popular with the very classes whose culture he wanted to praise suggests he was interested less in championing cultural forms embraced by the working class than in the development of a certain class of writers: "[W]hat finally and only is to make our Western world a nationality superior to any hitherto known, and outtopping the past, must be vigorous, yet unsuspected Literatures, perfect personalities and sociologies, original, *transcendental* and expressing . . . democracy and the modern" (456, emphasis mine). The stress here is on the development of a class of authors characterized by the transcendental nature of their expressions. Whitman is thus calling less for what we might now call "cultural materialism" than for the "spiritualization" of culture: The "tremendous and dominant play of solely materialistic bearings upon current life in the United States," he concludes, "must . . . be confronted and met by at least an equally subtle and tremendous force-infusion for purposes of spiritualization, for the pure conscience, for genuine aesthetics" (500).

Though Whitman stresses the importance of the material culture of the working class, his anticapitalist rhetoric constitutes an argument against materialism that spills over into his program for culture, grounding it in a pure, genuine, spiritual, and transcendental aesthetic. Indeed, the whole of Whitman's argument is grounded in the kind of metaphysical idealism that complicated Emerson's writings on this topic. Following Emerson, Whitman views the poet's role as one in which "the peculiar combinations and the outshows of [a] city, age, or race, its particular modes of the universal attributes and passions," are "passed on to illumine our own selfhood, and its experiences" (486). However, like Emerson, he measures the aesthetic or cultural value of the "peculiar" and the local in terms of its *universal* attributes and passions. Where in Emerson's "Art" "local culture" requires an investment of "aboriginal Power," Whitman finds the "peculiar" and the "particular" of value only to the extent that it is infused with universal, timeless attributes. In arguing for a conception of American culture rooted in the local, the material, and the contingent, Whitman reflects the side of Emerson critics have linked to "pragmatism," since he measures the value of culture by its connection to practical life. However, when his argument follows the structure of the two terms *local* and *universal,* the local always ends up being displaced by, or gaining its authority from, the universal. Whitman's metaphysical idealism, in the end, overwhelms the materialist side of his cultural project. Value, ultimately, is embodied not in the local itself, but in the absolute.

The more Whitman comes to focus on the role literature must play in changing the American "spirit," the more his vision of the ground of culture reverts to the form of metaphysical idealism he absorbed from Kant and Hegel. Whitman tends to locate that ground within the spirit of individual being, but it is a form of Being validated by its connection with the absolute:

> [America is] daughter of a physical revolution—mother of the true revolutions, which are of the interior life, and of the arts. For so long as the spirit is not changed, any change of appearance is of no avail . . . What is independence? Freedom from all laws or bonds except those of one's own being, control'd by the universal ones. To lands, to man, to woman, what is there at last to each, but the inherent soul, nativity, indiosyncrasy [sic], free, highest poised, soaring its own flight, following out itself? (490)

The "self" here is grounded less in the material and social culture of the local than in the "laws" of an "interior life" or being informed by "uni-

versal" Being. The freedom Whitman invokes is not the freedom of the
individual to produce art out of the relationship between interior life
and material experience, but rather the more circumscribed and transcendentalized "freedom" to evoke the "universal" and the "inherent."
This position underscores the tension in Whitman's essay between metaphysical idealism and materialism, but it also raises a question Emerson often grappled with: how to reconcile the demands of the individual with the social body. There is, at best, a delicate balance in both
Emerson and Whitman on this question. On the one hand, the individual is given precedence over the community. However, the individual is
conceived in terms of its access to "universal laws," and so long as each
individual bases his or her actions on those laws, democracy will be
able to function, since in theory each isolated and self-reliant individual will tap into the same transcendent or universal insight. This is, of
course, a kind of trade-off between the idealist and the materialist impulses of each writer. However, the important point I want to emphasize is how value and truth are ultimately grounded on the metaphysical side of the equation.[17]

Like Emerson, Whitman emphasizes the important relationship between creative expression and nature. "Present literature, while fulfilling certain popular demands," Whitman writes, is deficient and must
begin to "tally and express Nature, and the spirit of Nature" (494). In
linking the fulfillment of a thoroughly original and modern literature
in America to the artist's ability to tally and express the spirit of nature,
Whitman grounds his cultural program in a theory of nature much like
the one we found in Emerson. Whitman employs in *Democrative Vistas*
a hierarchical distinction between nature understood as material and
instrument, and nature understood as the very repository and expression of pure spirit. "Nature, true Nature, and the true idea of Nature,"
he writes, have been "long absent" in America (494). By "nature" he
does "not mean . . . only what is entertainable by the physical conscience,
the sense of matter," but "the kosmos . . . that rolls through the illim-
itable areas, light as a feather" (494). This "true Nature" must be "fully
restored" and "enlarged" (494) until it literally becomes the "vista" of
the essay's title, for it is to be both the ground and the height from
which aesthetic production will proceed.

Whitman's "New World metaphysics" ends up constituting the "vista"
or "the heights" from which, "breathing rarest air," the artist produces
under the influence of a pure "Idealism" (595). The irony here, of course,
is that Whitman's ground, figured in the title as a "vista," turns out to
be a metaphysical point of view toward reality, an irony that figures the

slippage in the body of the essay itself between the material and everyday and the transcendental. Whitman argues that we must "take our stand, our ground" on this metaphysical vista because, in order to be truly and vitally creative, "a human being, his spirit" must "ascend above, and justify objective Nature, which, probably nothing in itself, is incredibly and divinely serviceable" (496). Here Whitman relies on something very close to Emerson's theory of the "method of nature" (and approximates what Burke called Emerson's incipient pragmatism), for nature *is* serviceable to the artist, but only to the degree that it provides spiritual "analogies" for his or her use: "Observing, rapport, and with intuition, the shows and forms presented by Nature . . . and seizing what is in them, the poet, the aesthetic worker in any field, by the divine magic of his genius, projects them, their analogies, by curious removes, indirections, in literature and art" (496).

"Nature," like the outward manifestations of everyday culture or the social self, is linked negatively to "shows and forms." Truth and reality exist *behind* the appearances of nature and material and social being, where they must be intuited by the aesthetic worker. Where earlier in the essay Whitman seemed to be grounding his cultural program in the intrinsically aesthetic nature of the local, in a radical valuation of contemporary reality and the contingent, he eventually rejects such a point of view entirely. "The elevating and etherealizing ideas of the unknown," he writes," and of unreality must be brought forward with authority . . . Fearless of scoffing, and of the ostent, let us take our stand, our ground, and never desert it, to confront the growing excess and arrogance of realism. To the cry, now victorious—the cry of sense, science, flesh, incomes, farms, merchandise, logic, intellect, demonstrations, solid perpetuities, buildings of brick . . . fear not . . . to sound out equally determin'd voice the conviction brooding within the recess of every envision'd soul—illusions! apparitions! figments all!" (495–96). Here all the material and rational characteristics of modernity—from science and flesh to merchandise, logic, and "demonstrations"—are dismissed as "apparitions all." The ground he stands on here is emphatically metaphysical, for "the culmination and fruit of literary artistic expression, and its final fields of pleasure for the human soul, are in metaphysics . . . and the question of the immortal continuation of our identity . . . Standing on this ground—the last, the highest, only permanent ground . . . we have peremptorily to dismiss every pretensive production . . . which violates or ignores, or even does not celebrate, the central divine idea of All" (495).

The tension here between what Whitman calls idealism and what he calls realism replicates the one between metaphysical idealism and an incipient pragmatism or instrumentalism in Emerson. In each case, the tension dramatizes a double impulse: to insist on the aesthetic value of a specifically American "reality" while at the same time subordinating that reality to a transcendental one. American culture is to be distinguished from previous ones because it develops, literally, out of its own ground and in reaction against an inappropriate European tradition. Yet, Whitman insists, his cultural program for America is rooted in the conviction that "in all ages, the mind of man has brought up here [in the mysteries of the spiritual world] and always will. Here, at least, of whatever race or era, we stand on common ground" (495). This tension can be captured in the double sense we have of the term "ground" here, for while Whitman and Emerson want American culture to develop in its own peculiar and democratic way out of an American cultural ground, each is tied to an idealist commitment to the *metaphysical as ground*. The significance of American "being" is ultimately tied to its particular showing through of Universal Being.[18] Whitman's cultural program builds on Emerson's interest in the particular and the local. However, in both writers, the modernist character of this interest is finally checked by a transcendentalism rooted in pre-Enlightenment forms of metaphysics. This insight, as we shall see in the next chapter, was the point of departure for George Santayana's influential critique of the genteel tradition's inability, by the end of the nineteenth century, to deal with modernization in its cultural and social complexity.

3

George Santayana and Van Wyck Brooks
Pragmatism and the Genteel Tradition

> America . . . is a country with two mentalities, one a survival of the beliefs and
> standards of the fathers, the other an expression of the instincts, practice, and
> discoveries of the younger generations . . . [O]ne-half of the American mind, that
> not occupied intensely in practical affairs, has remained . . . slightly becalmed; it
> has floated gently in the backwater, while, alongside, in invention and industry
> and social organization, the other half of the mind was leaping down a sort of
> Niagara Rapids . . . The one is all aggressive enterprise; the other is all genteel
> tradition.
>
> George Santayana, "The Genteel Tradition in
> American Philosophy" (1911)

Santayana's complaint in his famous essay on the genteel tradition that
American productivity in the "practical affairs" of industry and social
organization had far outrun its productivity in philosophical, cultural,
and aesthetic affairs repeats the one we have just traced in Emerson and
Whitman. Writing over forty years after Whitman's *Democratic Vistas,*
Santayana still finds American cultural and philosophical thought wanting. The promise of a distinctly American form of cultural expression
remains in his eyes mortgaged to an enthusiasm for invention and industry in the sphere of material culture. Santayana's assessment contains the same problematic tension between tradition and modernity
Emerson and Whitman complained about. On the one hand there is a
"traditional mentality" tied to "the beliefs and standards of the fathers," and on the other hand a contemporary mentality wholly preoccupied with material production. Left undeveloped between the two,
so his assessment goes, is culture.

Santayana's general argument, then—that in the world of "practical
affairs" America has developed into a thoroughly modern society, but

57

that its culture has floated gently in the backwater of modernity—parallels those we have just been discussing. Emerson, Whitman, and Santayana all insist on the need for America to break with a debilitating cultural and philosophical tradition linked to the past, to overthrow the "beliefs and standards of the fathers." However, by Santayana's time the beliefs and standards that had arrested America's cultural development could be traced less to the "courtly muses of Europe" than to an ossified form of Emersonian transcendentalism. Structurally, Santayana's analysis of the slow pace of American cultural thought mirrors Emerson's (the development of an original, national, and vital culture requires a fundamental break with tradition and the past). However, in his view Emerson's project had atrophied into a new and paralyzing gentility. Transcendentalism, grounded by Emerson in metaphysical idealism, self-reliance, and a wariness about mass culture, was meant to form the cornerstone of America's modern cultural development during the mid-nineteenth century. However, by the end of that century, according to Santayana, it represented the greatest threat to that development.[1]

Santayana's criticisms of nineteenth-century American philosophy were made easier by the fact that he was a citizen of Spain, someone, that is, who did not have the kind of nationalist orientation we find in Emerson, Whitman, or James. Rorty has noted the double advantage of this position. On the one hand, he "was able to laugh at us without despising us," and on the other hand (and more important) "he was entirely free of the instinctive American conviction that the westering of the spirit ends here . . . that our philosophers have only to express our national genius for the human spirit to fulfil itself" (*Consequences of Pragmatism* 60). In Rorty's view, Santayana's contribution was his gentle chiding of American philosophy's provinciality, his criticism of the Emersonian idea that literature or philosophy in America had to describe or evoke something that was uniquely American. Santayana saw that this kind of provinciality severely limited American philosophy in its attempt to come to terms with modern culture. So Rorty praises his ability to "avoid the conviction that America is what history has been leading up to, and thus that it is up to American philosophy to express the American genius, to describe a virtue as uniquely our own as our redwoods and our rattlesnakes" (69). This kind of provinciality, which in his essay on the genteel tradition Santayana traces back to Emerson, represented what Rorty calls a "mild chauvinism," a chauvinism that, while it suffered a serious setback after World War I, still persists in the minds of some critics.

It was a strange genealogy that put the Spanish-born George Santayana at the center of an important turning point in American cultural
criticism. Through his teacher at Harvard, William James, Santayana
learned philosophy from a pragmatist philosopher who had early in his
life sat at the feet of the transcendentalist Emerson. The critique of
American culture Santayana developed under the influence of James at
Harvard was in turn passed on to Van Wyck Brooks. Brooks's more
pointed and polemical attack on the genteel tradition (and the kind of
pragmatism associated with James) in turn ignited a host of young
modernists intent on remaking American literature and American culture by turning their backs on nearly everything that had come before.
Santayana thus played a pivotal role in generating a critique of nineteenth-century American philosophical and cultural thought. While he
was at the same time supportive and condescending toward what he
called these "young radicals," Santayana's own critique of the genteel
tradition helped lay the critical groundwork for the positions they took.

Santayana's critique of the genteel tradition principally focuses on
Calvinism and transcendentalism, which, he insists, together contributed most significantly to the development of American philosophical
thought. It is not hard to see how Calvinism (defined broadly by Santayana so as to include philosophical principles he finds in the Koran,
Spinoza, Carlyle, and Josiah Royce) would be profoundly incompatible
in Santayana's eyes with the development of secular, industrial modernity. "Calvinism," he writes, "asserts three things: that sin exists, that
sin is punished, and that it is beautiful that sin should exist to be punished. The heart of the Calvinist is therefore divided between tragic
concern at his own miserable condition, and tragic exultation about the
universe at large . . . Human nature, [the Calvinist] feels, is totally depraved" (38). Calvinism emerges here as a kind of psychotic and paralyzing response to the very condition of modernity. It possesses an insistent, almost elegant negativity, a dark metaphysics that produces an
intricate kind of paranoia absolutely antithetical to the kind of secularized, instrumental use of reason we associate with Enlightenment progress. In Santayana's view, Calvinism produces a premodern check on
America's emotional, material, and philosophical development, one
that left it ill equipped to deal with the pressing practical problems of
modernity.[2]

When at its founding the nation was isolated and tiny, living "under
pressure and constant trial," the "vigilance" associated with Calvinsim
had a kind of logic to it, and so could be perpetuated in various versions by leaders like Franklin and Washington (39). However, with the

expansion the nation experienced in the first three or four decades of the nineteenth century this logic ceased to make sense. The age required a new and more positive vision of nature and the self. To the degree transcendentalism emerged in opposition to Calvinism it of course represented a necessary corrective. "The sense of sin," Santayana observes, "totally evaporated" in the transcendentalist scheme of things (39). Transcendentalism banished evil from nature and erased the fundamental depravity of human behavior, liberating humankind from the agonized cycle that led from sin, punishment, and redemption to more sin. "Nature," Santayana writes, "in the words of Emerson, was all beauty and commodity; and while operating on it laboriously, and drawing quick returns, the American began to drink in inspiration from it aesthetically" (39). However, Santayana also observes a complicity between Calvinism and transcendentalism that tended to mitigate their opposition to one another and to fuse the two systems into his "genteel tradition." This complicity is grounded in the movement's investment in metaphysical idealism. Santayana, working with what he calls a distinction between "theological" and "philosophical" Calvinism, argues that "philosophical Calvinism" fused with transcendentalism to dominate "traditional metaphysics" in America (41).

Santayana's attitude toward transcendentalism itself is equivocal, for in his view while it offers a *method* of thought with the potential to overcome the genteel tradition, it helps perpetuate a form of *idealism* that serves to strengthen and reinforce it. Santayana's discussion of transcendentalism turns on a distinction he makes between transcendentalism conceived as a *system*, and transcendentalism conceived as a *method*. Santayana associates transcendentalism as a system with myth and idealism, and in this respect it fuses with the idealism in Calvinism to help produce the genteel tradition. As a method, however, transcendentalism constitutes "the chief contribution made in modern times to speculation" (42). "Transcendentalism proper," he writes, is a "method, a point of view, from which any world, no matter what it might contain, could be approached by a self-conscious observer . . . Knowledge, it says, has a station, as in a watchtower; it is always seated here and now, in the self of the moment" (41).

Santayana, in effect, wants to separate out what Burke calls the "incipient pragmatism" in Emerson's transcendentalism from his Neoplatonic idealism, call that incipient pragmatism the "method" of transcendentalism, and play down Emerson's systematic idealism as an aberration of transcendentalism that eventually fed into the genteel tradition. In Santayana's view transcendentalism falters when it begins to ask, "What exists; in what order is what exists produced; what is to exist in the future?" (42). When the transcendentalist asks these questions, Santayana insists, he abuses the transcendental method and creates myth (42). When the methodical "self-conscious observer," the self as "watchtower . . . seated in the here and now" applies transcendentalism to these questions, he creates "systems of the universe" based on a "transcendental self" as the very "centre" of "reality" (42). This kind of "systematic subjectivism" (41), Santayana warns, turns the method of transcendentalism toward the creation of "metaphysical fables" (43). "We must therefore distinguish sharply," he concludes, "the transcendental grammar of the intellect . . . from the various transcendental systems of the universe, which are chimeras" (42).

Santayana's rhetorical strategy—to indict transcendentalism for its role in perpetuating the genteel tradition while placing Emerson outside that tradition as a possible counter to it—gets bogged down in a number of contradictions and questionable assertions. In the first place, his distinction between method and nature is a distinction not in kind but in degree, and in the second place it makes at least as much sense to understand Emerson's transcendentalism as a system as to understand it as a method. That the difference between these two terms is a difference in degree rather than in kind is made clear in *Webster's New Collegiate Dictionary*, for the entry on "method" warns that "*system*" is "very much like *method*," often simply suggesting "a more fully developed or carefully formulated plan of procedure." The *OED* defines "system" as

> A set or assemblage of things connected, associated, or interdependent, so as to form a complex unity; a whole composed of parts in orderly arrangement according to some scheme or plan . . .

"According to some scheme or plan" insists on the *methodical* nature of any system, of course. This sense of the word is emphasized later in the entry when "system" is defined as "a comprehensive and regularly arranged exposition of some subject," an "orderly or regular *method* of procedure," an "established scheme or *method*," and as an "orderly arrangement or *method*" (emphasis mine). On the other hand, the *OED* defines "method" as a "pursuit of knowledge" and a "mode of investigation," a "way of doing anything," and as a "*systematic* arrangement" or "order," an "orderly arrangement of ideas and topics in thinking and writing."

This close link between method and system undercuts the absolute distinction Santayana wants to make. We need only, for example, recall our discussion of Emerson's "The Method of Nature" to realize that what Santayana calls transcendentalism's "sham system of nature" (42) is explicitly rooted by Emerson in its method, which works systematically and in a comprehensive way. In this essay method and system are conflated and work interchangeably, for nature, spirit, and the human mind all participate methodically in a single, whole, unified system that does in fact seek to answer the questions "what exists; in what order is what exists produced," etc. Moreover, we saw in the previous chapter how Emerson's metaphysical idealism (the side of transcendentalism Santayana consigns to "system") systematically informs his approach to nature, subjectivity, creativity, and aesthetic theory. The element of system in Emerson's idealism—and the fact that nature's method is subservient to it—simply belies the distinction Santayana wants to work with.

Indeed, the aspect of Emerson's thought Santayana associates with his methodical transcendentalism, the concept of "self-trust," veers close to the kind of subjectivity he regrets in both German and American transcendentalism. Santayana points out how practical the idea of self-trust was for "a pioneer who is actually a world-builder" (43). However, such self-trust has a methodical value for the pioneer not because of some empirical attribute it has, but because it represents the application of what Santayana calls a "metaphysical fable": "Self-trust, like other transcendental attitudes, may be expressed in metaphysical fables. The romantic spirit may imagine itself to be an absolute force, evoking and molding the plastic work to express its varying moods" (43). Self-trust, then, turns out to be applied metaphysics, the methodical use of a fable that, in turn, is based on a system. There seems, in the final analysis, no difference in kind between metaphysics and method in Santayana's formulation, just degrees of difference in the methodical application of metaphysical fables. In this way even Santayana's attempt to isolate out an element of pragmatism in Emerson does not really succeed.

The chief danger in transcendentalism, in Santayana's view, is its "starved and abstract quality," its tendency to foster "a sort of inner play," to be "self-indulgent," to be limited to "a play of intra-mental rhymes" (40). Santayana attributes this sensibility to American romanticism, to the work of Poe, Hawthorne, and Emerson. Santayana, echoing Henry James's observations about the deficiencies of American writing in his *Nathaniel Hawthorne*,[3] complains that these writers, "not being fed sufficiently by the world," were "driven in upon" their "own resources" (40). They were too "keen" and "independent" to "retail the genteel tradition," but "life offered them little digestible material" (40).

They had to "feed on books," indulge in "inner play" in a "refined labor" that "was subjective" (40–41). "In their persons," he concludes, "they escaped the mediocrity of the genteel tradition, but they supplied nothing to supplant it in other minds" (41). This is just the kind of subjectivism Santayana links to the form of German idealism that bred systematic transcendentalism, a subjectivism that inevitably made the transcendentalist's "own knowledge" the "centre of the universe" (42).

Santayana argues that in spite of developing transcendentalism as a method, Emerson could not successfully "escape from the genteel tradition" (46), since his transcendentalism remained wedded to a systematic metaphysics. That Santayana would want to clearly distinguish between transcendentalism as system and transcendentalism as method, and then opt for the methodical over the systematic side, underscores the influence of his pragmatist mentor, William James. Simply put, the metaphysical idealism in transcendentalism leaves it unable to cope with modernity in Santayana's view. Since modernity requires "method" and an engagement with "practical affairs," the only way Emerson can be incorporated into Santayana's vision of American modernity is to foreground his methodical side and link it to pragmatism. Santayana's effort serves to underscore my earlier point, that Emersonian transcendentalism, to the degree it remained fundamentally invested in metaphysical idealism, was unable to come to terms with the complex material and social challenges of modernity.

Santayana identifies two potential alternatives to the genteel tradition in American philosophical thought: the "bohemianism" of Walt Whitman, and the pragmatism of William James. He charts in both writers the potential for a break with the genteel tradition that might make American philosophical thought more responsive to the problems of modernity. In his discussion of Whitman, he follows much the same strategy we have already seen in his discussion of Emerson, playing down the extent to which Whitman's thought was saturated with the kind of romantic transcendentalism that would link it to the "genteel tradition," and playing up the modernist possibilities of what he calls Whitman's bohemianism. The potential for a break with the genteel tradition in Whitman's thought lies in his rejection of the removed and abstract subjectivity of transcendentalism. His was "not the polite and conventional American mind," for it expressed the "spirit and the inarticulate principles that animate the community" (47). While Santayana links Emerson to a tradition that concentrates on a kind of self-absorbed meditation that remains aloof from community, he sees Whitman preoccupied with the ragged and eccentric multiplicity as it forms a community against all rational possibility. In what would become a familiar reading of Whitman, Santayana insists that Whitman's poetry is "democratic" in the sense that "the various sights, moods, and emotions are given each one vote; they are declared to be all free and equal, and the innumerable commonplace moments of life are suffered to speak like the others" (47). In Whitman, Santayana observes, "Bohemia rebelled against the genteel tradition" (47).[4]

Though he was fascinated with Whitman's bohemianism, Santayana in the final analysis felt Whitman did not chart a "reconstruction that alone can justify revolution" (48). This is related to the common observation that Whitman's poetry is infused by a "pantheism" that is "unintellectual, lazy, and self-indulgent" (47). According to Santayana, Whitman felt that in his poetry, "everything real was good enough, and that he was good enough himself" (48). It is Whitman's tendency to accept, embrace, and celebrate what is simply *because it is* that both marks his "bohemianism" and limits what Santayana calls its "constructive" potential. Because, in Santayana's view, Whitman "reduced his imagination to a passive sensorium for the registering of impressions . . . no element of construction remained in it, and therefore no element of penetration" (48). Structurally, Whitman and Emerson have a similar orientation toward modernity, for where the progressive element of Emerson's thought is checked by his reaction against culture and society, in Whitman that element is checked by a commitment to sweeping affirmation, an absence of critical discrimination.

Santayana insists that James's pragmatism offers a more promising countertradition to the gentility of American philosophical thought. He sees in James the same bohemianism he celebrates in Whitman. The bohemian mentality is linked in Santayana's mind to an expansively democratic vision, to a reorientation away from gentility that marks a necessary break with ossified tradition. Santayana writes that "convictions and ideas came" to James from "the subsoil" (48), that he "had a prophetic sympathy with the dawning sentiments of the age, with the moods of the dumb majority" (48). Because he drew from this "true America," James "represented in a measure the whole ultra-modern, radical world" (49). He "gave a sincerely respectful hearing to sentimentalists, mystics, spiritualists, wizards, cranks, quacks, and impostors . . . He thought, with his usual modesty, that any of these might have something to teach him" (49). In becoming "the friend and helper of those groping, nervous, half-educated, spiritually disinherited, passionately hungry individuals of which America is full," Santayana's James seems to mirror the bohemian side of Whitman.

Santayana begins his discussion of James by foregrounding his bo-hemianism because for him it is the *blend* of bohemianism and prag-matism in James that is significant. Whitman's bohemianism is a sign of his democratic vision, and in Santayana's view it mitigates his tran-scendentalist impulses. James's bohemianism, fused with his funda-mentally pragmatic philosophical orientation, has the same effect. San-tayana praises James's pragmatism because of his conviction that "theory is simply an instrument for practice, and intelligence merely a help to-ward material survival" (49–50). It is not so much that Santayana sees pragmatism as the modern answer to transcendentalism as that he sees in it the fulfillment of the "method" of transcendentalism. Counter to what Santayana called the subjectivist "metaphysical fable" of tran-scendentalism, James believed "intelligence . . . is no miraculous, idle faculty, by which we mirror passively any or everything that happens to be true, reduplicating the real world to no purpose" (50). "Creeds and theories," in his view, do not mirror a universal or absolute over-soul, but rather constitute "a local and temporary grammar of action . . . To know things as a whole, or as they are eternally, if there is anything eternal in them, is not only beyond our powers, but would prove worth-less, and perhaps even fatal to our lives" (50). Where Emerson insisted that the value of the local and the temporary was grounded in the eter-nal, Santayana embraces James for his conviction that creeds and theo-ries gain their value in terms of the efficacy of their response to local concerns. The idea of an eternal or transcendental power is a "fatal" mystification. In Santayana's view, James's bohemianism counters the gentility of transcendentalism, and begins to move modern American critical thought out of its paralyzing idealism. It also adds an instru-mental theory of knowledge to Whitman's bohemian orientation, in-fusing it with the kind of reconstructive potential Santayana found wanting in Whitman.[5]

For Santayana James is the harbinger of a contemporary worldview that would seem outrageous to those schooled in the genteel tradition. "William James . . . has given a rude shock to the genteel tradition. What! The world a gradual improvisation? Creation unpremeditated? God a sort of young poet or struggling artist?" (52). James represents for him the combined modern revolt of the "Bohemian temperament" and the "poetry of crude naturalism" (54). James's privileging of the "local and the contemporary" over the absolute begins to reverse the tradi-tional hierarchy he inherited from both Emerson and Whitman. More-over, unlike Whitman, Santayana's James does not simply embrace or celebrate the local and the contemporary for itself, or because it is "good enough." He wants to put philosophy to work there, to make it function in a way that does not transcend, but responds directly to, the pressing needs of contemporary life, what James calls the "local . . . grammar of action." Santayana's critique of the genteel tradition, then, leaves him favorably disposed—if not enthusiastic about—the possibilities of pragmatism, which he views as a potentially attractive alternative to the gentility of Emerson's transcendentalism.

One of Santayana's most significant (if oblique) criticisms of Emersonian transcendentalism comes in his closing speculations about the possibility of a "revolution" (54) in American intellectual thought that might break absolutely with the genteel tradition. Here he turns to the subject of nature. He outlines a set of contemporary assumptions about reality that postulate a view of nature directly at odds with an older, Emersonian one: "When you transform nature to your uses, when you experiment with her forces, and reduce them to industrial agents, you cannot feel that nature was made by you or for you, for then these adjustments would have been pre-established" (54–55).[6] The mystical or spiritual side of nature (one that assumes nature has its own intentions) has all but dropped away. Emerson attempts to balance a transcendentalist view of nature with an instrumentalist one, but Santayana simply lets the transcendentalist side of his equation go. Nature becomes wholly subservient to, and defined by, the ends to which humankind puts it. Nature has "no transcendental logic" to teach us, it gives "no sign of any deliberate morality seated in the world" (55). While there is beauty in nature, there is "nowhere permanence, everywhere an incipient harmony," but "nowhere an intention, nor a responsibility, or a plan" (55). It is hard to conceive of a more absolute break with the concept of nature promulgated by Emerson and perpetuated by the genteel tradition. Nature no longer has its own intentional logic, and "man" is no longer conceived to be its "centre" (55). Embracing a pragmatic orientation toward nature, Santayana endorses a philosophical system "very different from what those systems are which the European genteel tradition has handed down since Socrates; for these systems are egotistical; directly or indirectly they are anthropocentric, and inspired by the conceited notion that man, or human reason, or the human distinction between good and evil, is the centre and pivot of the universe" (55).

Santayana comes close to deconstructing the logical structure of Emerson's conception of nature. Earlier in his address he states that transcendentalism went off track when it tried to turn a "conscientious critique of knowledge" into a "sham system of nature" (42). Santayana's is a decentering refiguration of nature that dislocates both its logocentric and its anthropocentric logic. The logocentric logic of this earlier system called "nature" was embedded in the idea that it contained a "transcendental logic," "plan," or "intention," a *ground* that stood outside the local and the contingent. The center of nature, finally, is *not* reason. Nor is it "man." Divested of its anthropocentric and logocentric logic, nature for Santayana becomes "wild" and "indifferent," a "non-censorious infinity" (56). Such a conception of nature breaks sharply with Emersonian nature, begins to refigure reality in a way consistent with modern philosophers from Bergson and Bradley on, and, not insignificantly, clears the way for its pragmatic use, since it divests nature of the kind of Holy Being transcendentalism attached to it. In doing so, of course, Santayana veers toward the kind of disenchantment of nature Horkheimer and Adorno will come to associate negatively with modernity.

We have seen, then, that by 1911 Santayana understood the necessity of an American intellectual revolution against the genteel tradition, which he linked to both Calvinism and transcendentalism. Though not wholly convinced by pragmatism, he seemed pretty certain that such a revolution would need to be rooted in a pragmatic conception of knowledge applied to contemporary, local problems. At any rate, transcendentalism was in his view an outmoded form of philosophy that was increasingly hindering America's ability to come squarely to terms with its own modernism. Indeed, Santayana made no distinction between America and modernism. "Americanism," he wrote, "apart from the genteel tradition, is simply modernism—purer in America than elsewhere because less impeded and qualified by survivals of the past" (189). When, ten years after his essay on the genteel tradition, Santayana turned his attention to a new generation of cultural critics who had come of age in America after his departure from Harvard, he was impressed with the extent to which they had rejected that tradition in favor of a more pragmatic or instrumentalist position. In "America's Young Radicals" (1922), an essay about the popularity of socialism among college students, he wrote that he was

> not at all surprised that the life of the ancients, although alone truly human and addressed to a possible happiness, should not appeal to young America. It is too remote, too simple; it presupposes the absence of this vast modern mechanical momentum, this rushing tide of instrumentalities on which young America is borne along so merrily. (185)

The tone here is a bit tongue-in-cheek, of course, but clearly in Santayana's eyes America's young radicals have displaced Whitman and James as the best hope for countering the genteel tradition in America.

While they mirror the Emersonian and Whitmanian conviction that America must break absolutely with the courtly muses of Europe, they do so in the context of a head-on critical engagement with modernity seemingly unfettered by the metaphysics of transcendentalism.

Santayana is sympathetic with the idea that cultural and political theory in America has to grow out of a direct response to the exigencies of "modern mechanical momentum," in response to industrial, commercial, and urban life. Although "The Genteel Tradition in American Philosophy" laments the absence of modern cultural expression in America in the face of its expanding productive forces, Santayana basically thinks of modernity as a reflection of these forces. Modern forms of cultural expression must develop not by rejecting the new state of practical affairs, but by positively responding to it.[7] This is why, though he clearly senses a form of idealism in the socialism of the young radicals, it is the *instrumental* aspect of their attraction to socialism he seeks to emphasize—just as he chose in discussing Emerson to emphasize the so-called methodical side of his transcendentalism.

It is a *critical* preoccupation with the present that distinguishes this generation, in Santayana's eyes, and thus marks the modernity of their intellectual point of view:

> I call it socialism for short, although they are not all advocates of socialism in a technical sense, but style themselves liberals, radicals, or (modestly) the *Intelligentsia*. The point is that they all proclaim their disgust at the present state of things in America, they denounce the constitution of the United States, the churches, the government, the colleges, the press, the theaters, and above all they denounce the spirit that vivifies and unifies all these things, the spirit of Business. Here is disaffection breaking out in what seemed the most unanimous, the most satisfied of nations: here are Americans impatient with America. (186)

Santayana, in effect, locates two modernisms in America, one related to the "spirit of business," the other developing in the young radicals' critique of that spirit and the culture it had produced. The first simply characterizes the general condition of America, where "only the present situation counts . . . the present task, the present state of business, and present fashion in pleasure that create the hearty unity and universal hum of America" (189). The second is a *critical* modernism, impatient with the traditions, values, and institutions of the first. As an Old World self-described "Tory" who has returned to his native Spain, Santayana can take a kind of detached attitude of sympathetic bemusement toward both manifestations of America's modernity. The telling point about Santayana's equating Americanism with modernism is that the equation works only when the genteel tradition has dropped away. America's modernism is in fact dependent upon its ability to remove the impediment in that tradition, a cornerstone of which was the metaphysical idealism of transcendentalism.

Van Wyck Brooks and the Rise of Critical Modernism

One of the leading young radicals of the generation Santayana referred to was his former student, Van Wyck Brooks. Brooks took Santayana's critique of the genteel tradition and gave it a sharper, more polemical edge. In doing so, he helped rally a generation toward the kind of intellectual revolution Santayana envisioned in his essays on American philosophy.[8] Brooks infused Santayana's polite, sometimes tongue-in-cheek assessments of Calvinism (or Puritanism), Emerson, transcendentalism, and Big Business with an American kind of brashness that made his Spanish professor's writings about America seem, well, genteel. Brooks's analysis of American intellectual life was also invested with a keen sense of nationalism Santayana could of course never have felt.

In the opening chapter of Brooks's influential *America's Coming-of-Age* (1915), he translates Santayana's genteel tradition into the term "High Brow" culture, and replaces its vague antithesis in Santayana's bohemian Whitman with the term "Low Brow" culture. Brooks was writing at a time, Levine points out (225), when the division between genteel and popular culture, which emerged in the last half of the nineteenth century, had become so common that there seemed no middle ground between them. Like Santayana, Brooks wants to identify two competing *traditions* in American intellectual thought, an impulse that leads him to trace the first back to Jonathan Edwards, and the second to Benjamin Franklin.[9] However, Brooks is interested less in tracing genealogies than in mounting a dialectical analysis of American culture, a kind of Hegelian drama without Hegelian terminology, one that attempts to forge a synthesis between highbrow and lowbrow culture. Where Santayana identified a genteel "tradition," Brooks finds highbrow and lowbrow "attitudes," "values," "ethics," and "culture." Where Santayana tried to identify in Whitman and James a nascent countertradition in American philosophy and cultural criticism, Brooks envisioned (in a poetic gesture wholly appropriate to his argument about the role of poetry in cultural thought) the emergence of a new, middle, or third way that unified the other two.

Brooks's analysis in *America's Coming-of-Age* contains a near-dizzying array of binaries that are worth charting at the outset. Using the central categories of "High Brow" and "Low Brow" as our points of orientation, we get something like this:

HIGH BROW	LOW BROW
Theory	Practice (2)
God	Action (5)
Puritanism	Opportunism (4–5)
Desiccated culture	Stark utility (7)
New England	Chicago (9)
The University	Business (13–14)
Metaphysics	Bare facts (38)
Spiritual	Economic (43)

Brooks's categories generally replicate the two modes of thought we traced in Emerson's essay on transcendentalism (highbrow there was linked to idealism and metaphysics, lowbrow to materialism and the pragmatic). However, where Emerson asserts that the transcendentalist orientation is of a higher order than the materialist, Brooks sets out to debunk both orientations. Highbrow and lowbrow represent, for Brooks, "two attitudes of mind . . . on the one hand, a quite unclouded, quite unhypocritical assumption of transcendent theory ('high ideals'), on the other a simultaneous acceptance of catchpenny realities" (3). He writes with equal disdain about both highbrow and lowbrow "attitudes," about the preoccupation either with "metaphysics" or with "bare facts." His complaint is simply that each is oriented too radically in its own direction; between the two "there is no community, no genial middle ground" (3). He finds these "two main currents in the American mind running side by side," and "both equally unsocial":

> on the one hand, the transcendental current, originating in the piety of the Puritans, becoming a philosophy in Jonathan Edwards, passing through Emerson, producing the fastidious refinement and aloofness of the chief American writers, and resulting in the final unreality of most contemporary American culture; and on the other hand the current of catch penny opportunism, originating in the practical shifts of Puritan life, becoming a philosophy in Franklin, passing through the American humorists, and resulting in the atmosphere of our contemporary business life. (4–5)

Refined aloofness and "catchpenny opportunism": Brooks captures in these terms his utter dissatisfaction with Emerson's metaphysical idealism and James's pragmatism. This dissatisfaction, however, is not so much with the philosophies per se as with their appropriation by the vulgar interests of Big Business. This position echoes the one we saw Whitman take in *Democratic Vistas*. Like Whitman before him, Brooks sees literature (specifically, poetry) as the third and saving term in the tension between highbrow and lowbrow culture:

> Human nature itself in America exists on two irreconcilable planes, the plane of stark intellectuality and the plane of stark business; and in the back of its mind lies heaven knows what world of poetry, hidden away, too inaccessible, too intangible, too unreal in fact ever to be brought into the open, or to serve, as the poetry of life should serve, in harnessing thought and action together, turning life into a disinterested adventure. (15)

Brooks underscores this position in his sequel to *America's Coming-of-Age, Letters and Leadership* (1918). Here he laments the "fact" that poetry's place in determining cultural values has been effectively displaced by pragmatism. We will see in a moment how the Arnoldian note in the passage above ("turning life into a disinterested adventure") comes to dominate *Letters and Leadership*. At the very moment Brooks rejects the transcendentalism of Emerson because it could not withstand the challenge of pragmatism, he turns "disinterest" into a transcendental principle to counter the philosophy of William James.

Emerson and Whitman stand as central figures in Brooks's analysis. On the one hand, Brooks views Emerson as a central conduit between Puritanism and the genteel tradition, and on the other hand he builds on Santayana's comments about Whitman in characterizing him as the "precipitant" of a "new tradition" that "effectively combines theory and action" (*America's Coming-of-Age* 59). "We have in America," Brooks writes, "two publics, the cultivated public and the business public, the public of theory and the public of activity" (58). Whitman's value as a poet lies, for Brooks, in the public, active nature of his engagement with America's social fabric, in what Brooks calls his "contact with actuality" (58). What Whitman precipitates, in essence, is a merging of the idealism of transcendentalism and the "rude feeling" of actual "human experience" (59). In Whitman, Brooks writes,

> the hitherto incompatible extremes of the American temperament were fused. The refinement of the Puritan tradition, . . . able to make nothing of a life so rude in its actuality, turned for its outlet to a disembodied world, the shadow-world of Emerson . . . Whitman was the Antaeus of this tradition who touched earth with it and gave it hands and feet. (59)

Whitman precipitates an engagement with the body, with the material world. In him, Brooks argues, the disembodied shadow world of transcendentalism gives way to an embodied earth (with hands and feet), to the possibility of an engagement with "actuality." "All those things that had been separate, self-sufficient, incoordinate—action, theory, idealism, business—he cast into a crucible," and so "precipitated the American character" (62). Brooks praises here Whitman's "democratic" vision, his forging of a "harmonious and molten . . . fresh . . . whole personality" (62). In so doing, Whitman "laid the cornerstone of a national ideal capable . . . of releasing personality and of retrieving for our civilization, originally deficient in the richer juices of human nature, and still further bled and flattened out by the 'machine process,' the only sort of 'place in the sun' that is really worth having" (63–64).

In attempting to forge a usable past out of Whitman by foregrounding the poet's desire to precipitate a synthesis between idealism and materialism, Brooks plays down the extent to which Whitman's transcendentalist side (which would link him to what Brooks sees as the most debilitating side of Emerson) undermines that synthesis by becoming the ultimate ground for his cultural program (as we saw in chapter 2). Brooks's characterization of Emerson is weakened by a related problem: his inability to recognize how the very idealism he condemns in Emerson informs *his own* cultural theory. Brooks criticizes Emerson for having unfolded an "immense, vague cloud-canopy of idealism which hung over the American people during the nineteenth century," one that "was never permitted, in fact, to interfere with the practical conduct of life" (23). Brooks insists that Emerson's thought was weighted so heavily toward an engagement with *spirit* and the transcendental that it severely restricted the practical value of his doctrine of self-reliance. "Emerson's really equivocal individualism on the one hand asserted the freedom and self-reliance of the spirit," Brooks writes, "and on the other appeared to justify the unlimited private expediency of the business man" (23–24).[10]

Brooks actually complains less about Emerson's thought per se than about how he perceives it was appropriated by future generations, how it turned into a justification for sheer acquisitiveness. In effect, Brooks laments that the valuable current in Emerson's concept of self-trust as a spiritual principle became short-circuited as it was picked up by the world of commerce and applied as a business ethic, finally playing itself out in Norman Vincent Pealism. Brooks praises "Emerson's position in the world of the *spirit*," for "he alone appears to me to have proved the reality of that world and to have given some kind of basis to American Idealism" (42, my emphasis). However, "Emerson's idealism was double-edged" (42). While he was concerned both with the spiritual life and the *conduct* of life, it was, according to Brooks, the latter aspect of his thought that became dominant in the nineteenth century. "If the logical result of a thorough-going, self-reliant individualism in the world of the spirit is to become a saint," he insisted, "it is no less true that the logical result of a thorough-going, self-reliant individualism in the world of the flesh is to become a millionaire" (43).

Brooks cannot forgive the apparent fact that Emersonianism came to sanction economic self-assertion. "There is," he writes, "a world of difference between individualism on the spiritual plane and individualism on the economic plane" (43). In Brooks's view, Emerson's concept of individualism was just equivocal enough for it to have been appropriated by the latter. For this reason, Brooks wants to recapture Emerson for the life of the spirit, and to energize and revitalize American poetry. Dramatizing his famous call for a usable past, Brooks attempts to turn Emerson into a philosopher who will lend his name to Brooks's own project. He hopes that when economic opportunities play themselves out in an orgy of individual greed based on a misappropriated Emersonianism, Emerson will come to take his rightful place again as the father of "self-reliance in the spirit itself":

> For as the scope of practical enterprise and self-reliance becomes with every generation more limited, as the generality of men are caught with both feet in the net of economic necessity, and are led thereby to seek scope for their initiative in disinterested activity, just so the Emersonian doctrine comes into its own, the Emersonian virtues mount upward and create a self-reliance in the spirit itself. Emersonianism, in short, can only begin to be itself when it has taken its final place on the plane of poetry. (43)

While Brooks complains about Emerson unfolding a cloud canopy of idealism over American thought, he invokes a similar idealism here in the name of a disinterested poetry that might mount upward and away from "practical life." Moreover, though Brooks identifies in Emerson's thought the dramatic tension between metaphysical idealism and pragmatism we reviewed in the preceding chapters, his vision of American character ends up endorsing a personalism as thoroughly invested in idealism as was Emerson's commitment to "self-trust." Once again the Arnoldian idea of disinterest (which of course had its roots in Kant) becomes crucial, for Brooks's aim is to return the Emersonian notion of "self-reliance" to an aesthetic sphere defined as disinterested. In Brooks's view, the Emersonian doctrine of self-reliance can "come into its own" only when the scope of its exercise is limited to the disinterested sphere of poetry. Something rather pathetic has happened to "Emersonianism" at this point: "Self-reliance" has been thoroughly absorbed, according to Brooks, by the ideology of capitalism. However, instead of reasserting Emersonianism in the interests of some other social or political vision, Brooks wants to appropriate it for a completely disinterested aesthetic activity. Emersonianism thus ends up being emptied of significance from both sides—the instrumental and the aesthetic.

Beneath the surface of his celebratory rhetoric about Whitman's engagement with practical affairs, then, Brooks's reliance on Emersonian idealism suggests that Emerson stands as the true precipitant of the kind of cultural change Brooks argues for. His relationship to Emerson bears many of the marks of the anxiety of influence Harold Bloom has popularized. Brooks's attempt to become a "strong" cultural critic depends for its success on his rebellion from Emerson, but that rebellion (which Bloom interprets as a kind of necessary killing of the father) is only an ostensible swerve away from Emerson; it really serves to mask Brooks's own Emersonianism. (This is what makes Brooks's engagement with Emerson so much more highly charged than Santayana's.) Brooks swerves away from Emerson by strategically misreading him (Bloom's "clinamen"), antithetically completes Emerson by retaining his terms but meaning them in another sense (Bloom's "tessera"), and yet at the same time attempts to affect discontinuity with him (Bloom's "kenosis").[11]

This phenomenon is clearest in Brooks's continual emphasis in both *America's Coming-of-Age* and *Letters and Leadership* on the primary importance of the individual personality. When Brooks writes about the relationship of the individual to society early in the first book he invokes the ideal of "self-fulfillment" as the "working out of one's own personality . . . through forms of activity that are directly social" (17), but as he goes on to elaborate the importance of personality ("one cannot have personality, one cannot have the expressions of personality so long as the end of society is an impersonal end like the accumulation of money" [18]), the self emerges more and more, as it did in Emerson, at war with society and the state. Moreover, for all of his criticism of the "cloud-canopy of idealism" let loose by Emerson, Brooks's concept of the self turns out to be no less metaphysical than his precursor's.

Brooks is clear enough at the outset about the kind of synthesis he wants to achieve:

> The only serious approach to society is the personal approach, and the quickening realism of contemporary social thought is at bottom simply a restatement for the mass of commercialized men, and in relation to issues

> that directly concern men as a whole, of those personal instincts that have been the essence of art, religion, literature—the essence of personality itself—since the beginning of things. It will remain of the least importance to patch up politics, to become infected with social consciousness . . . unless, in some way, personality can be made to release itself on a middle plane between vaporous idealism and self-interested practicality . . . (*America's Coming-of-Age* 18)

This passage, with its setting of the individual over against a threatening mass culture, is Emersonian through and through. This is underscored by the fact that the nature of the blend on this "middle plane" between a personal and a social orientation (or between what he calls in his chapter on Whitman theory and action) remains obscure. In its place is the thoroughly Emersonian notion that if we each turn within to "instinct"—which is "the essence of personality itself"—we will find those truths that have been truths "since the beginning of things." Self-reliance for Brooks must, as it did for Emerson, come prior to "politics" and "social consciousness." This may not be as "vaporous" a form of idealism as Emerson's, but it serves to invoke the same hierarchical relationship between the self and society we observe in Emerson. We get in Brooks's observation less the possibility of a synthesis between vaporous idealism and self-interested practicality than the endorsement of a kind of self-interested idealism.

Like Emerson before him, Brooks turns toward the personal and the "instinctive" in reaction to the conditions that define the modernity of his own age, in reaction, that is, to material institutions and popular culture. "Self-fulfillment" becomes "the immemorial compensation" (the echo of Emerson's famous essay is telling) for the price one pays for living in the modern world. More than compensation, really, it becomes a bulwark against that world:

> Self-fulfillment is the immemorial compensation for having eaten of the fruit of good and evil, and under the conditions of modern life self-fulfillment has to be a somewhat artificial thing. In a world of instincts blunted by trade, system and machinery, the sweat of the brow, the resurgence of the seasons, the charm of perfect colour and of pure form are not for the generality of men sufficient . . . In that world the majority are lost and astray unless the tune has been set for them, the key given them, the lever and the fulcrum put before them, the spring of their own personalities touched from the outside. (*America's Coming-of-Age* 83–84)

Here Brooks insists on a clear distinction between natural instinct and socially constructed desires, a distinction that functions in a more general economy determined by the demarcation between inside and outside (with "instinct" being the ground for moral and ethical positions). "Instincts" constitute, in his view, the very center and essence of personality or being in what becomes the negative drama of modernity. "Trade, system and machinery" have become the conditions of modern life, and together (with the state) constitute an "outside" that has "blunted" instinct. The problem for Brooks is that modernity has altered the very terms of "self-fulfillment." Where formerly self-fulfillment, with its source in "the spring" of individual personality, served as a kind of knowledge that compensated for humankind's having eaten from the tree of good and evil, modern life has now made self-fulfillment an "artificial thing," since it is rooted in economic and material achievement. The ideology of industrialism, not just its culture, has in Brooks's view set the tune for the modern individual. It has established what we now call a hegemonic influence over the self, for the ideology possesses the very keys and springs that control personality.

While Brooks begins to grasp the complex way in which personality and behavior are socially constructed, and while he develops the outlines of what would become, in Horkheimer and Adorno, a critique of capitalism as mass culture, he persists in the squarely Emersonian notion that the essence of subjectivity is grounded above such forces, in "instinct" and nature. Modernity, for Brooks, thus constitutes a fallen condition in which systems of trade and the rise of machine technology have fundamentally altered an earlier harmony between the individual and more simple economic and cultural forms. Face to face with the material conditions of late capitalist modernity, Brooks turns away from formulating a cultural theory that will engage those conditions directly, endorsing instead an earlier Emersonian notion that the proper role of the intellectual is to pursue knowing rather than doing, directing attention "above" the planes of politics and social consciousness to the pursuit of poetry as a "disinterested adventure" (*America's Coming-of-age* 15). Having rejected the capitalist appropriation of Emerson, Brooks ends up embracing what Santayana defined as Emerson's genteel side.

In so doing, as we noted earlier, Brooks mixes Emerson's reaction to the problems of modernity with Matthew Arnold's, whose ideas clearly influenced his own during this period.[12] Brooks's cultural theory, grounded in Emerson's metaphysical conception of subjectivity, is also heavily invested in Arnold's insistence that the essential quality of criticism is disinterestedness (see "The Function of Criticism at the Present Time"), and that the study of poetry ought to avoid an engagement with the practical, the political, and the historical (see "The Study of

Poetry"). Criticism, for Arnold, must operate independently of the practical spirit and interested social action and pursue the criticism of literature, which will lead to the kind of spiritual perfection Arnold locates in "the serener life of the mind and spirit" ("Function" 263).[13] Brooks's continuity with Arnold represents another aspect of what I earlier called his negative drama of modernity; the ostensible absorption of disinterested art and philosophy by economic and technological systems marshaled in the interests of "trade":

> Just those elements which in other countries produce art and literature, formulate the ideals and methods of philosophy and sociology, think and act for those disinterested ends which make up the meaning of life; just that free, disinterested, athletic sense of play which is precisely the same in dialectic, in art, in religion, in sociology, in sport—just these, relatively speaking, have in America been absorbed in trade.

The problem with Brooks's cultural theory is that it retreats from the challenge of coming to terms with the economic, mechanistic, and institutional sides of modernity. It tends, rather, to reject the possibility of either self-fulfillment or aesthetic experience in these realms, and to fall back on nineteenth-century myths about both the self and art.[14] Since Brooks holds to the idea that the realms of commerce and material production alone embody interested activity, while forms of cultural production do not, his cultural criticism is hampered by a serious (if familiar) theoretical flaw. Brooks's call for a wholesale break from the genteel tradition of American thought struck a real chord among a generation of young intellectuals tired of things as they were, but his conviction that the cure for an overly technological and crassly material modernity was a return to instinct and a reassertion of the notion that art, literature, and philosophy determined the "meaning of life" through disinterested play left him with precious little ability to affect real change.

This left Brooks—paradoxically enough—inspired less by the possibilities of a modern democratic culture than by the achievements of culture that flourished under life at court in prerevolutionary France: "Why did the existence of the court" in France "make so much difference?" Brooks asks. "Because the court, removed as it was from the influences of the market-place, kept alive in France the free, the non-acquisitive, in short the creative conception of life; and this conception, permeating thence downward the whole fabric of society, linked the artistic expressions at the top with the common consciousness of the race beneath" (*America's Coming-of-Age* 132–33). Brooks contrasts a "creative conception of life" with an *interested* one, but "interest" seems to refer only to motives having to do with acquisition in a capitalist mode (in the "market-place"). Brooks fails to see (or at least to acknowledge) that those at court have "interests" that the literature, art, and philosophy they encourage and sanction serve to uphold. Again, Brooks's cultural theory seems hampered by the nostalgia for a mythic condition that never was (when art and philosophy were "disinterested").

The oppositional terms structuring Brooks's discussion of culture are telescoped in his pivotal chapter on American cultural criticism, "Our Awakeners," into pragmatic criticism and poetic criticism. The kind of cultural criticism Brooks espouses here has its basis in poetic thinking. It is not analytical but visionary—in the specific sense of seeking to chart and direct the future through the power of the creative imagination rather than by using the analytic tools of sociological thought. The problem that preoccupies Brooks is a crucial one: the determination of value in the modern age, that is, in a world where foundationalism has begun to collapse. Here Brooks writes in the guise less of Emerson or Arnold than of Shelley, for the claims he makes about the cultural power of poetry echo the "Defense of Poetry," except that reason, Shelley's protagonist, becomes pragmatism, Brooks's antagonist, in the American scheme.

In his view, American "criticism" is unable to awaken the intellect because it is dominated by an "academic tradition," which is "colonial in essence" and therefore "remote from the springs of" national life (*America's Coming-of-Age* 139). American criticism in the second decade of the twentieth century remains in the same paralyzed and subservient condition as Emerson found American literature almost one hundred years earlier. With criticism thus marginalized, sociologists "purport to be" our "real awakeners," Brooks observes. They are hampered, however, by their pragmatist orientation, their concern with "adaptation," and their "narrow efficiency" (139). Under pragmatism the "whole spirit of our life" has been rationalized (139), so that we "stand in mortal fear of letting loose the spiritual appetites that impede our pursuit of a neat, hygienic and sterile success" (140). Brooks's position here recalls his earlier criticism of acquisitiveness and his insistence on the importance of personality and the creative will.

Indeed, it is only because of "the impotence of our poetical tradition" (140) that pragmatism has been able to take hold in America at all, in Brooks's view. Pragmatism has "attempted to fill the place which poetry alone can adequately fill," that place being "the right to formulate the aims of life and the values by which those aims are tested, aims and values which, we are led by history to believe, can be effectively formulated only by individual minds not in harmony with the existing fact but in revolt against it" (140–41). This usurpation by pragmatism of poetry's proper function is a central element in Brooks's negative drama of modernism. In this drama, reason, rationalization, and the will to practical action (always associated with the values of the marketplace and mechanization) continually assault instinct and nature.[15] "The natural order of things" (141) requires that "the imagination" discover "new and more vital ideals" (141) than reason ever can. Moreover, it is creative or poetic imagination (not reason) that stands as "the value-creating entity."[16]

The problem of modernity for Brooks has ultimately to do with the problem of determining value, the problem of finding a normative ground for value in an age in which all forms of foundationalism seem to have been swept away. In this respect Brooks has inherited from Emerson and Whitman one of the challenges Habermas identified as central to the philosophical condition of modernity. Despite his strong criticism of transcendentalism, Brooks attempts to solve the problem of grounding value by recourse to a metaphysical aesthetic not far from the one Emerson worked out. Unwilling to accept the pragmatist approach to truth and value, Brooks opts for a position here that can be traced through Emerson all the way back to German idealism, to philosophers like Schiller and Schelling who insisted on making a clear distinction between rational cognition and the imagination, and on privileging poetry as a superior, redemptive mode of knowing. The problem with pragmatism, Brooks insists, is that it "turn[s] the natural order of things inside out when it accepts the intelligence instead of the imagination as the value-creating entity" (141). This position leads him inexorably down the road to a romantic valuation of art's redemptive function. Like Schiller before him, who believed the "wound" of modern civilization (resulting from a split between imagination and reason) could be healed through the "play-drive" rooted in aesthetic experience, Brooks insists that only "the poetic view of life" (150) can begin to alter the plight of *his* modern civilization.[17]

Where Santayana tended to value pragmatism because it presented an alternative to the genteel tradition, Brooks rejects it out of hand as an instrumentalist and materialistic usurper that has smothered America's poetic and spiritual sensibilities. By Brooks's time, pragmatism in America had emerged in a loose fashion as the philosophical counterpart to industrial, corporate, and bureaucratic modernity. Brooks's reaction against pragmatism, then, is a reaction against a philosophically refined form of what had begun in the Enlightenment as instrumental reason. Of course Brooks's break with pragmatism is part of the more general break with Enlightenment rationality we have historically associated with the aesthetic modernism of Baudelaire and the philosophical modernism of Nietzsche, though Brooks's modernism is grounded less in Baudelaire or Nietzsche than in an earlier form of opposition to Enlightenment rationality: the transcendentalism of Emerson.

Given the logic of Brooks's critique of pragmatism, we might expect to find its chief proponent in the teens, twenties, and thirties, John Dewey, taking a position about art and modernity diametrically opposed to Brooks's. This is not the case, however. While Dewey develops a trenchant critique of metaphysics in his discussions of the history of philosophy, metaphysics resurfaces in his aesthetic theory as the very ground and mode of being in art. Dewey's critique of metaphysical idealism did help lay the groundwork for the kind of instrumentalist philosophy Brooks criticized under the name pragmatism in *Letters and Leadership*. For in his work in philosophy Dewey developed a mode of rationality that extended the hegemony of instrumental reason into the twentieth century. His response to the tension we have been tracing in American cultural theory between metaphysical idealism and pragmatism, of course, was to side firmly with the rational over the transcendental. However, his attitude toward modernity turns out to be rather ambivalent. In both his critique of metaphysics and his working out of a thoroughly pragmatic approach to philosophical problems, Dewey extends the project of modernity begun in the Enlightenment. However, when he turns his attention to art and modern culture in *Art as Experience* (1934), he invests art and aesthetic production with the very metaphysical properties he tried to banish from philosophical thought. This, coupled with a concept of "experience" that borrows heavily from Emerson's transcendentalism, leaves Dewey's approach to art and culture as divided as Emerson's. Moving back and forth between a pragmatic and an idealist approach, he dramatizes a surprisingly conservative response to modern experience in his own time. His trenchant critique of metaphysics promises to bury the transcendentalism of the genteel tradition for good, but the transcendentalist bent that resurfaces in *Art as Experience* underscores how persistently the legitimation crisis continued to haunt modern American criticism.

4

John Dewey

Pragmatism, Modernism, and Aesthetic Criticism

> The attempt to divorce philosophy from metaphysics will always, I suspect, be
> merely a protective screen for the setting up of metaphysical assumptions.
> Kenneth Burke, a review of John Dewey's *Liberalism and Social Action*

John Dewey's pragmatism developed out of his attempt to demystify philosophy by questioning its self-conception as the systematic discovery of fixed, universal truths (though Dewey by no means contradicted Brooks's assertion that the imaginative or poetic faculty was a "value-creating entity"). As such, his work, together with that of James and Peirce, constituted a thoroughgoing critique of American transcendentalism. Indeed, by the end of the nineteenth century pragmatism seemed to resolve the debate between idealism and instrumentalism or materialism we traced earlier in Emerson's thought, and to insure the end of what Santayana called "the genteel tradition." In turning to Dewey's critique of metaphysics and his long book on aesthetics, *Art as Experience*, however, I want to question this assumption. To be sure, Dewey *does* insist on turning philosophy away from its traditional commitment to forms of metaphysical idealism, and in so doing he articulates a program for American philosophy that marks a clear break with Emersonian transcendentalism. However, as Richard Rorty has argued, Dewey's work, sometimes in spite of itself, often retains a strong metaphysical bent. Picking up on Rorty's point, I want to show how forms of metaphysical idealism persist in Dewey's philosophical writings, and how they emerge in a particularly insistent way in his writings on aesthetics and art. I will be arguing that in the very context of trying pointedly to resolve the tension between metaphysical idealism and materialism Dewey often ends up reproducing that tension, especially when he turns to the relationship between art, aesthetic experience, and mass culture.

Dewey's systematic critique of metaphysics was based on the conviction that metaphysics was in many ways incompatible with democracy.[1] The central point of "Philosophy and Democracy," for example, is that American "democracy . . . must in time justify itself by generating its own" philosophy (855). This point comes at the end of a historical demystification of philosophical thought that argues that philosophy is always generated in specific places at specific times to justify and perpetuate collective, national interests. Dewey begins his analysis by foregrounding two competing "assumptions" about philosophy. The first "is that philosophy ranks as a science, that its business is with a certain body of fixed and finished facts and principles," that "as a form of knowledge" it seeks "apprehension and acknowledgment of a system of truths comparable in its independence of human wish and effort with the truths of physics" (841–42). The second assumption denies that "philosophy is in any sense whatever a form of knowledge" (843). It argues, on the other hand, that we view philosophy as "a form of desire," as an "effort at action . . . an aspiration subjected to rational discriminations and tests, a social hope reduced to a working program of action" (843). Dewey insists, then, that the traditional conception of philosophy as metaphysics must give way to a materialist and ethical rhetoric aimed at achieving individual or collective aims.

Beginning with the observation that "economic, political and religious differences manifest themselves in philosophy" (844), Dewey argues that philosophy develops not out of "colorless intellectual readings of reality" but out of humankind's conscious attempts to articulate, justify, and perpetuate "basic beliefs about the sort of life to be lived" (844). Philosophical thought therefore does not refer to a fixed and universally valid reality or set of truths, but develops out of "a choice about something to be done, a preference for living this sort of life rather than that" (845). Dewey insists that philosophy is a historically specific, national, pragmatic, and suasive discourse. This means that in philosophy " 'reality' is a term of value or choice" (846).

Dewey returned to this point in 1931 in his book *Philosophy and Civilization*. Again rejecting the idea that philosophical discourse reveals transcendentally valid truths, Dewey insists that "philosophy, like politics, literature, and the plastic arts, is itself a phenomenon of human culture. Its connection with social history, with civilization, is intrinsic" (175). This point is both the result of Dewey's historical analysis of the history of philosophy and a reflection of the function he thinks philosophy must have in contemporary culture. His conflation of the philosophical, political, and aesthetic realms here is not casual, for the origin and effect of each implicate it in the others. Philosophy and politics are intrinsically connected. It is easy to see how politics always has a philosophy, but Dewey insists as well that philosophy has a politics, and that, as modes of representation, figuration, and persuasion, both are related to literature and the plastic arts.

This insistence goes to the heart of Dewey's argument in "Philosophy and Democracy," where he finds metaphysical idealism incompatible with democracy. "The traditional conception of philosophy . . . which identifies it with insight into supreme reality or ultimate and comprehensive truth, shows how thoroughly philosophy has been committed to a notion that inherently some realities are superior to others, are better than others" (852). For this reason, Dewey finds metaphysical idealism fundamentally incompatible with democracy, for democratic values cannot be grounded in *inherently* (or transcendentally) superior realities. The problem as Dewey sees it is that "any such philosophy inevitably works in behalf of a regime of authority, for it is only right that the superior should lord it over the inferior. The result is that much of philosophy has gone to justifying the particular scheme of authority in religion or social order which happened to exist at a given time" (853). These lines concisely summarize Dewey's critical analysis of the history of philosophy and its *function* for culture. He does not condemn that function, however. He condemns the metaphysical rhetoric that covers over or mystifies it. The problem with democracy in relation to philosophy is that it has tried to sustain itself by adhering to a form of philosophy not very far removed from "a metaphysics of feudalism" (852). "Modern philosophy began when man, doubting the authority of revelation, began a search for some authority which should have all the weight, certainty and inerrancy previously ascribed to the will of God" (853). The problem with that search is that it retained a structure of belief grounded in traditional metaphysics, the belief in and the valuation of ultimate, fixed, transcendental categories of truth and reality, but transferred from God and church to man and nature. "The men who questioned the divine right of kings," Dewey observes, "did so in the name of another absolute. The voice of the people was mythologized into the voice of God" (853).

Of course, this was just the kind of mythologizing we observed in Emerson. Indeed, Dewey's critique of the kind of metaphysical idealism Emerson endorsed, one that claimed the kind of "insight into supreme reality or ultimate and comprehensive truth" Dewey refers to in

"Philosophy and Democracy," makes the recent claims for Emerson's pragmatism rather difficult to sustain. As we saw in our analysis of Emerson's approach to both nature and art, the local and the contingent are continually subordinated in his thinking to an absolute and transcendental force or first cause. The only thing that allows Emerson's transcendental system to function alongside democracy is his belief that when each individual looks within, he or she will intuit the same transcendental truth, so that there will be a kind of democratic agreement about things because each citizen has the same access to what Dewey refers to as a "superior reality." The glue that holds this arrangement together is not democracy, but metaphysics. Indeed, Dewey's central complaint about American transcendentalism is that "it has tried to achieve a philosophy" that "clothed itself in an atomistic individualism," that "makes equality quantitative, and hence individuality something *external* and *mechanical* rather than qualitative and unique" (854, emphasis mine). In Dewey's view the transcendentalist version of subjectivity lodges truth in an "external" being or force, and makes the discovery of truth a purely "mechanical" process of intuiting a fixed and superior reality.[2]

Near the end of *Philosophy and Civilization*, Dewey writes that "the presence and absence of native born philosophies is a severe test of the depth of unconscious tradition and rooted institutions among any people, and of the productive force of their culture . . . If American civilization does not eventuate in an imaginative formulation of itself, if it merely rearranges the figures already named and placed—in playing an inherited European game—that fact is itself the measure of the culture which we have achieved" (10–11). At first glance Dewey seems to echo Emerson's and Whitman's vision of an American literature freed from the inappropriate and debilitating traditions of European culture. For Dewey's claim that philosophy can produce an imaginative reformulation of America recalls Emerson's conviction that literature has a central role to play in the constitution of American culture, that it has the power to instigate a second revolution of the spirit. Dewey, Emerson, and Whitman seem to be making the same double claim, the one for philosophy, the other two for literature: that America embodies a set of unique conditions that demand the transformation of philosophy and literature into vital instruments in the ongoing attempt to define American culture.

As I have noted in chapter 1, recent critics writing in an attempt to delineate a pragmatist tradition in American literature and cultural criticism have stressed this kind of continuity between Emerson and

Dewey. While it would be wrong to deny Dewey's admiration of Emerson, and to ignore the general influence he had on Dewey's thinking, we have seen that these critics have tended to play down Emerson's fundamentally transcendentalist orientation in making the case for Dewey's Emersonianism (just as they have in making the case for Emerson's pragmatism). This tendency is a variant of what I have called the tendency of these critics to *claim* Emerson for a particular tradition in American cultural thought. Emersonian pragmatists who tend to mute his transcendentalism in favor of underscoring an instrumentalist or pragmatist strain in his thinking go on to insist on too intimate a genealogical continuity between Emerson and Dewey.

Cornel West sums up the relationship between Emerson and Dewey in a balanced and subtle way. While he implicitly agrees with critics like Poirier, Gunn, and McDermott that Dewey's work is in part an inheritance from Emerson, his emphasis is less on the continuity between them than on the extent to which Dewey marks a point of departure from Emerson:

> John Dewey is the greatest of the American pragmatists because he infuses an inherited Emersonian preoccupation with power, provocation, and personality—permeated by voluntaristic, amelioristic, and activistic themes—with the great discovery of nineteenth-century Europe of a mode of historical consciousness that highlights the conditioned and circumstantial character of human existence . . . Dewey is the first American pragmatist who *revises* Emersonian motifs of contingency and revisability in the light of modern historical consciousness. (69–70, emphasis mine)

West rightly emphasizes Dewey's *revisions* of Emerson, and he sees the intellectual relationship between the two not in terms of a shared interest in the instrumentality of thought but in their larger interests in forms of social, cultural, and institutional power. Moreover, the stress in West is less on Emerson's "pragmatism" defined specifically in terms of the instrumentality of thought than on how Dewey's interest in historical consciousness revises Emerson's vision of "history as heroic autobiography" (70). Dewey builds on Emerson, in West's view, by displacing Emersonian self-reliance in favor of considering "the larger structures, systems, and institutions" of culture (70). West's treatment of the Emerson/Dewey connection resembles Santayana's critique of the "genteel tradition" in that he sees Dewey's pragmatism as revitalizing an American mode of philosophical thought that had become too turned in on itself. The kind of attention Dewey pays to the relationship between systems, institutions, and cultural forms could never have been developed by Emerson since he "enacted a poetic evasion of modern philosophy" (95) grounded in the (transcendental) self's supposed autonomy from society.

West explains Dewey's sympathetic essay on Emerson (often cited by those who want to stress the connection between them) with the observation that "Dewey could not avoid or candidly jettison Emerson" (72). In West's view, Dewey's is a "creative misreading" of Emerson that reveals how "desperate and determined Dewey is to convince his audience that a figure like Emerson is not alien to his own pragmatic perspective and project" (74).[3] What we get in the essay, West concludes, is Dewey's attempt to "dress himself in Emersonian garb by dressing Emerson in Deweyan garb" (85).

For all of these reasons we ought to be very cautious about drawing a clear genealogical line between Emerson and Dewey's pragmatism. When West points out that "Dewey's rejection of the epistemological problematic of modern philosophy leads him to cast aside all metaphysical inquiries into the 'really Real' . . . [since] such inquiries promote the conception of philosophy as a form of knowledge with access to a more deep and fundamental Reality than that of the sciences and arts" (93–94), he underscores the difference between Dewey's pragmatism and Emerson's transcendentalism, a difference that ought to complicate any discussion of Emerson's "pragmatism" and its relation to Dewey.

To begin with, Dewey calls for a transformation of American philosophical thought that would undermine the metaphysical ground of Emerson's literary and social vision, a ground that, we have seen, cannot really be separated from his interest in the pragmatic. Dewey's desire to rid philosophy of an "inherited European game" based on the metaphysical idealism of "figures already named and placed" in Western philosophical thought from Kant to Hegel actually makes his position a radical departure from Emerson's (who, though he insisted on this same break, relied heavily on German idealism). The position Dewey articulates in "Philosophy and Democracy" isn't "Emersonian." It follows the line of Santayana's analysis of American philosophical thought in "The Genteel Tradition." The philosophical tradition Dewey critiques is in large measure the one Santayana found genteel and outdated. His pragmatist reformulation of philosophy extends the hopeful work of William James, which Santayana praises in his essay, though in a way that brought down upon Santayana the wrath of his student, Van Wyck Brooks. There is agreement among all three that transcendentalism, as the fundamental cornerstone of American philosophical thought, left the country ill equipped to respond to the pressures of modernity. Each, however, comes down on different sides of the question of what role pragmatism will play in the vacuum left by the genteel tradition. Santayana was sympathetic to James, we recall, praising him for having "broken the spell of the genteel tradition" (53). However, he was less convinced about the "truth" of pragmatism, warning that it "may prove no less alluring than" the philosophy of the genteel tradition (53). Brooks, on the other hand, was adamant that pragmatism was dangerous, since its rhetoric and methods had been appropriated by capitalism. Dewey, it goes without saying, took upon himself the job of a massive articulation of pragmatism that would prove Brooks wrong and overcome the skepticism of the more sympathetic Santayana.

It is important to recognize the extent to which Dewey's critique of metaphysical idealism came from his conviction that it had become anachronistic in the modern industrial world. Emerson's ideal of self-reliance, for example, born of a post-Enlightenment preoccupation with the individual subject, wedded to a belief in transcendental and universal laws, and developed at a time when America's social, economic, and political life was still rooted in the relatively simple needs of an agrarian society, had, in Dewey's view, become an outmoded and idealistic concept by the 1880s. Dewey's critique of the kind of individualism associated with Emerson's thought, as David Marcell has pointed out, developed from his assessment of the economic and political realities of an emerging industrialized and urban America. Dewey realized that

> Democracy in America had been shaped in the eighteenth and nineteenth centuries as a system wherein individuals, exempted from feudal or aristocratic restrictions, might freely exercise their natural rights and privileges. Such a society, guided by the invisible hand of a beneficent nature, would inexorably progress as individual wants and needs were gratified. But with the coming of industrialism, economic and technological consolidation, and conglomerate capitalism in the late nineteenth and early twentieth centuries, the social environment was radically transformed—often with tumultuous consequences for the individual. (Marcell 241–42)

Marcell here outlines some of the reasons why Dewey is so intent on exposing the rhetorical and strategic implications of metaphysical idealism. In so doing Marcell inadvertently underscores the historical necessity of Dewey's shift away from Emerson. Emerson's self-reliant transcendentalism developed in response to the demands of a subject attempting to theorize "natural" rights and privileges, and their exercise, in a postfeudal, postaristocratic era. Dewey, on the other hand, was writing at a time of industrial, economic, and technological consolidation, a historical moment in which the Emersonian self (this is Santayana's point, of course) had become an anachronism, if not altogether obsolete.

I want to come back to Richard Rorty's reading of Dewey, which I briefly referred to at the outset of this chapter. Rorty's discussion of "Dewey's Metaphysics" (chapter 5 of *Consequences of Pragmatism*) adds another twist as well to the discussion of Dewey's connection to Emerson. Where West sees Dewey's form of philosophy-as-cultural-criticism as revising Emerson's more poetic approach to philosophy, Rorty reminds us that while Dewey "sometimes described philosophy as the criticism of culture," he "*wanted* to write a metaphysical system" (73). Rorty identifies a tension in Dewey that, structurally, is not unlike the one between instrumentalist thought and idealism in Emerson. On the one hand, in Rorty's view, Dewey wanted to use philosophy "as an instrument of social change" (the side West emphasizes), but on the other, he wanted to inhabit "magisterial neutrality" that would allow him to describe "generic traits of existence of all kinds" (74). Rorty reviews Dewey's interest in "naturalistic metaphysics," and demonstrates how at odds it is with the postfoundational side of his thinking and his interest in philosophy as a mode of social and cultural criticism (the side Westbrook emphasizes). In Rorty's view "Dewey himself saw perfectly well except when he was sidetracked into doing metaphysics . . . that we can eliminate epistemological problems by eliminating the assumption that justification must repose on something other than social practices and human needs" (82). Oddly enough, Rorty's emphasis suggests that there *is* some sense to drawing a line of continuity between Emerson and Dewey, but the implication here is that the line would follow from Emerson's transcendentalism to Dewey's metaphysics, rather than from Emerson's pragmatism to Dewey's.

I want to pursue Rorty's general point with a reading of Dewey's *Art as Experience*, one that foregrounds the extent to which, in attempting to banish metaphysics from philosophy, Dewey ends up displacing it into art and aesthetic criticism. This is not only a significant instance of the tendency Rorty finds in Dewey to get "sidetracked into doing metaphysics" (thus underscoring how the tension in Emerson between "pragmatism" and metaphysics continues to play itself out in Dewey). We also will see that when Dewey turns to the subjects of art, contempo-

rary society, and mass culture, his position in some significant ways begins to anticipate the one taken by Horkheimer and Adorno in their
essay on the culture industry. *Art as Experience* is a particularly divided
text. On the one hand, Dewey mounts in the opening pages of his book
a strikingly progressive materialist and institutional critique of what he
calls the "museum conception of art." On the other hand, there are important moments in later portions of the book where Dewey falls back
on a familiar kind of metaphysical formalism, one that tends to undermine his earlier position by complicating his arguments about art, aesthetic experience, and their relationship to contemporary culture. We
will see that Dewey, in trying to negotiate the complex relationship between the local and the transcendent in art, tended like Emerson to
ground art in a form of experience that transcended and overwhelmed
the local and the particular. Where Emerson gravitated at times toward
the pragmatic relation between art and experience but ultimately conceived aesthetic experience in terms of transcendence, Dewey was firmly
committed to a pragmatic approach to aesthetic experience, but he nevertheless at key moments also conceived aesthetic experience in terms
of transcendence.

While Dewey's early essay on philosophy and democracy takes a decided stance against metaphysical idealism and seeks to reorient philosophy in America toward an "instrumentalist" engagement with "practical" human problems, his book *Art as Experience* tends to bear out
Burke's warning. For metaphysics, purged in these early essays, tends
to reassert itself (as Rorty points out) throughout Dewey's writing, but
especially in his theories about art, aesthetics, and the practice of criticism. While Dewey clearly sets out in the early chapters of his book to
offer a detailed materialist critique of the rift between art and popular
culture, that project is continually qualified in subsequent chapters by
formalist and metaphysical formulations about the "essence" of art. As
this happens, the book reproduces the same kind of tension between
a transcendentalist and a pragmatic orientation we observed in both
Emerson and Brooks.[4]

At the book's outset, Dewey's concerns about art mirror the ones he
had about philosophy in the two essays we have been discussing. Wor-
ried about the extent to which art has become a rarefied practice wholly
dissociated from the material world of everyday experience, he wants
to "restore continuity" between art and experience (hence, the title of
his work). Dewey insists that while "the actual work of art is what the
product does with and in experience," once that product "attains clas-

sic status, it somehow becomes isolated from the human conditions under which it was brought into being and from the human consequences it engenders in actual life-experience" (3). Classicism stands in Dewey's thought for what Emerson and Whitman labeled "tradition," for classicism has the same effect of estranging art from the local as tradition did for these writers. What gets lost in any classical approach to art, Dewey points out, is a work of art's culturally specific, pragmatic function. The classical conception of art invests it with a kind of transcendental essence that separates art from the conditions that brought it into being. Under forms of classicism, "art is remitted to a separate realm, where it is cut off from the association with the materials and aims of every other form of human effort" (3). The task of the pragmatist critic writing on "the philosophy of the fine arts" is "to restore continuity between . . . works of art and everyday events, doings, and sufferings" (3).

Up to this point, Dewey's remarks seem to echo Emerson's on the need for establishing in America an organic relationship between art and everyday life. This link is restored by recognizing the place of the aesthetic in everyday objects and experiences. Here, Dewey's claim suggests a thoroughly Whitmanian view of poetry:

> In order to *understand* the esthetic in its ultimate and approved forms, one must begin with it in the raw; in the . . . sights that hold the crowd—the fire-engine rushing by; the machines excavating enormous holes in the earth; the human-fly climbing the steeple-side; the men perched high in air on girders, throwing and catching red-hot bolts . . . the delight of the housewife tending her plants, and the intent interest of her goodman in tending the patch of green in front of the house . . . (4–5)[5]

Dewey's imagery updates Emerson's,[6] but the point is essentially the same: that aesthetic beauty and meaning are inherent in the everyday labor of common American men and women, and that this beauty is the "raw" form of the "ultimate and approved forms" of beauty termed "aesthetic." When we forget or repress this connection in criticism, Dewey wants to remind us, we begin to separate art from everyday experience.

There are two chief causes of this separation, in Dewey's view: the institution of the museum, which has bred a dominant "museum conception of art" (6), and "capitalism," which has "been a powerful influence in the development of the museum as the proper home for works of art, and in the promotion of the idea that they are apart from the common life" (8). Here, Dewey's Whitmanian impulse to celebrate the aesthetic qualities of common experience, his pragmatist view of the nature and function of art, and the influence of Marxism meet in the service of a powerful materialist critique of aesthetic criticism. Dewey writes in reaction to the legacy of late-nineteenth-century "art for art's sake" aestheticism (8), and his brief analysis implies a connection between this form of aestheticism and capitalism. "The rise of the compartmental conception of fine art," which separates it off from ordinary life, has its roots in a fetishizing of the "spiritual" in art directly connected to museums and galleries, which, in Dewey's view, are the extensions of nationalism and imperialism (9). "An instructive history of modern art could be written in terms of the formation of the distinctively modern institutions of museum and exhibition gallery . . . Most European museums are, among other things, memorials of the rise of nationalism and imperialism" that exhibit "the loot gathered by its monarchs in conquest of other nations" (9).[7]

In Dewey's view, the "connection between the modern segregation of art and nationalism and militarism" (9) has been accelerated by the effects of capitalism. Individual collectors contribute to art's segregation from social life (and to its commodification).[8] Moreover, capitalism has created what he calls "industrial conditions" for artists:

> Industry has been mechanized and an artist cannot work mechanically for mass production. He is less integrated than formerly in the normal flow of social services. A peculiar esthetic "individualism" results. Artists find it incumbent upon them to betake themselves to their work as an isolated means of "self-expression." In order not to cater to the trend of economic forces, they often feel obliged to exaggerate their separateness to the point of eccentricity. (9)

For Dewey, the kind of art-for-art's-sake ideology we associate with someone like Oscar Wilde has its corollary in the eccentric aesthetic individualism he describes here. As everyday life becomes flooded with commodities, and as experience becomes tied up with the processes of commodification, artists become less and less integrated into social life, reacting against the economic forces that have marginalized them (or capitulating altogether to commodification). Thus, isolation contributes to their sense that aesthetic creation is an individual form of self-expression, a condition that perpetuates the very separation between art and society that caused their marginalization in the first place.[9]

If market forces work to separate the artist from society, they also work, in Dewey's view, to separate "ordinary" from "esthetic" experience:

> The gulf which exists generally between producer and consumer in mod-
> ern society operate[s] to create also a chasm between ordinary and es-
> thetic experience. Finally we have, as the record of this chasm, accepted
> as if it were normal, the philosophies of art that locate it in a region in-
> habited by no other creature, and that emphasize beyond all reason the
> merely contemplative character of the esthetic . . . Criticism is affected.
> There is much applause for the wonders of appreciation and the glories
> of the transcendent beauty of art . . . (10)[10]

The divorce between the life of the artist and common social life, and
between art exhibited in museums and galleries and the experiences of
those who view it, tends in Dewey's view to reinforce the Platonist idea
that the essence of art is something transcendental. In a move that has
crucial implications for the turn his study will take, however, Dewey
does not propose the decentering of traditional aesthetic values or criteria. He wants, rather, to call our attention to how aesthetic theories
and the criticism they produce have become a mere simulation of effects produced by market forces. "The pleasure of collecting, of exhibiting, of ownership and display, simulate esthetic values," reinforcing "theories which isolate art and its appreciation by placing them in
a realm of their own, disconnected from other modes of experiencing"
(10). "The trouble with existing theories," he continues, is that they
start from a "ready-made compartmentalization, or from a conception
of art that 'spiritualizes' it out of connection with the objects of concrete
experience" (11). Again, Dewey's impulse is not to replace aesthetic
criticism with materialist or ideological criticism (along the lines of a
critic like Raymond Williams, for example) but rather to find a *more
authentic* ground for aesthetic inquiry. "Even a crude experience," he
writes, "if *authentically* an experience, is more fit to give a clue to the *intrinsic* nature of esthetic experience than is an object already set apart
from any other mode of experience" (11, emphasis mine). The point I
want to underscore here is that this preoccupation with the authentic
and the intrinsic in aesthetic experience reveals a latent idealism in
Dewey's thought that works to undermine the materialist and pragmatic orientation of his project. For it will turn out (as we will see in just
a moment) that "the alternative" to the aesthetic theories he criticizes
here is "a conception" of aesthetics "that discloses the way in which"
works of art "*idealize* qualities found in common experience" (11, emphasis mine). The main lines of contradiction in *Art as Experience* are
built quite concisely into this phrase, and they mirror the ones we saw
in Emerson. Dewey's preoccupation with linking art and the aesthetic
to "common experience" begins to take him in one direction, but his

countervailing preoccupation with the *idealized* nature of that experience leads him in another.

While Dewey's pragmatist and Marxian preoccupation with material, historical, economic, institutional, and ideological forces, then, leads him toward the formulation of a materialist approach to art and its criticism, his interest in reformulating art's authentic and intrinsic elements tempts him more deeply into aesthetics. Yielding to a desire to articulate how art idealizes the stuff of common experience, Dewey ultimately produces a text about art based on a form of idealism that invests art with the very metaphysical qualities he earlier wanted to purge from philosophy. In doing so, his book on art dramatizes the same tension between metaphysical idealism and pragmatism familiar from our discussions of Emerson and Brooks.

There is a tendency among recent (usually very sympathetic) critics writing on Dewey to play down his metaphysical idealism by stressing the sections of *Art as Experience* concerned with the more "pragmatic" question of art's relation to everyday life and with critiquing a museum conception of art. As I will point out in a moment, the first two or three chapters do begin the book with a refreshingly materialist kind of institutional critique of art's place in society, one that looks forward to the contemporary work of cultural critics like Hal Foster. However, the point I will be making is that after these chapters the book heads off in a completely different direction, articulating an approach to art and criticism grounded in rather traditional aesthetic categories. Critics like Gunn and Westbrook simply ignore these chapters. Gunn, for example, stresses only how Dewey wants to "reestablish the continuity between the energies of art and the normal processes of everyday life" (*American Grain* 86) leaving out any discussion of the other two-thirds of the book (he quotes only from the first sixty pages), which tend to undermine his reading. Westbrook follows much the same strategy. In his discussion of *Art as Experience* he stresses the progressive nature of the early sections of the book (his citations, too, are overwhelmingly from these early sections, and thus tend to mischaracterize the overall work). While he does cite the Pepper-Croce debate, it doesn't much disturb his assertion that the book's progressive treatment of art fits Dewey's radical politics (see 390–401). While some of these critics note Dewey's tendency toward idealism or organicism, they fail to see the extent to which Dewey's approach to art anticipates the formalism of the New Criticism, a relation that is deeply ironic. Gunn does take note of Dewey's general preoccupation with form (this is impossible to miss) but insists that Dewey is not "a strict aesthetic formalist" (*American Grain* 88). Westbrook, too,

stresses Dewey's interest in "organic form" (392), but neither critic makes
a connection between this organicism and Dewey's reliance on traditional aesthetic categories that are strikingly at odds with the more
pragmatic discussion of art in the book's first two chapters.

The tension in *Art as Experience* between the early materialist sections
and the later ones grounded in a kind of aesthetic formalism can be observed in the way Dewey writes about aesthetic objects. Although early
in chapter 1 he complains about "classical" definitions of art, by the end
of the chapter, in his attempt to begin to sketch in a more "authentic"
concept of the aesthetic than those he has been criticizing, he tends to
ground his own definition of art in classical terms. He sees in the "biological commonplaces" of organic life, for example, "the roots of the esthetic in experience" (14). "Here in germ," he writes, "are balance and
harmony attained through rhythm" (14). "Form" in nature, he continues, "is arrived at whenever a stable, even though moving, equilibrium
is reached . . . Order is not imposed from without but is made out of the
relations of harmonious interactions that energies bear to one another"
(14). Here, formal beauty results from a stable internal equilibrium;
"order is not imposed" from without in the context of an experience
had with the formal object by a subject. It is a property of what Arnold
termed the "object as in itself it really is." In the context of articulating
an aesthetic theory that defines art as *experience*, Dewey invokes a thoroughly classical vision of aesthetic *form* as the internal harmonious balance and harmony of parts in a stable whole. Art, for Dewey, may be the
experience of union (15), but that union is a function of the fundamental harmony and internal equilibrium of the object of contemplation.
The tension between his attempt, on the one hand, to conceive art as an
experience, and on the other to ascribe traditional formal qualities to
the aesthetic object, begins to lead Dewey away from a focus on art's
materialist and historical orientation and toward the formulation of an
idealist aesthetic that in telling moments responds defensively to his
own modernity. This puts Dewey in the paradoxical position of producing a book that calls for the reintegration of art with social life, while
at the same time invoking classical values to ward off art's contamina-
tion by the social life of his own time.

This often leads Dewey to construct a thoroughly formalist approach
to the criticism of art, and to a conviction that modern experience is antithetical to the production of art. Let me be clear about the point I am
trying to develop: Dewey intends to articulate a theory of art rooted in
experience in order to break down the historical division between (high
or fine) art and more "popular" forms of aesthetic experience. On this

point I do not disagree with Richard Shusterman and other of Dewey's critics. What I think these critics fail to acknowledge, however, is how often Dewey's intention is complicated and undercut by a kind of counterdiscourse in his text, the discourse of a classical aesthetic formalism that cuts against the grain of his pragmatic approach to art and aesthetic experience.[11] That this happens seems all the more peculiar because it is preceded by a critique of the Kantian ideal of disinterest usually associated with a formalist aesthetic (and which we saw foregrounded in Brooks). Dewey traces back to Kant the idea that solitary "contemplation" is the essence of the aesthetic experience, and examines the role it had in defining beauty in a way that separates art from the stuff of everyday experience. "Kant," he writes, "was a past-master in first drawing distinctions and then erecting them into compartmental divisions. The effect upon subsequent theory was to give the separation of the esthetic from other modes of experience an alleged scientific basis in the constitution of human nature" (252). The specific separation Dewey has in mind is that between Truth, Good, and Beauty, and Kant's insistence that Beauty is linked to pure feeling, that its experience comes from intuition rather than reflection, remaining "free from any taint of desire" (253). "Thus," he continues, "the psychological road was opened leading to the ivory tower of 'Beauty' remote from all desire, action, and stir of emotion" (253).

Dewey insists that as a mode for both casual appreciation and studied criticism disinterested contemplation leads to a "thoroughly anaemic conception of art" (253), for even "taken at its best . . . contemplation designates that aspect of perception in which elements of seeking and of thinking are subordinated . . . to the perfecting of the process of perception itself" (253). Beauty becomes defined simply as the perfected aesthetic object; its perception is limited to a perception of, or commentary on, its formal beauty divorced from any desire or interest in the object. Thinking and seeking, of course, are linked to interested desire, and the problem with "disinterestedness" (beyond the fact that it always masks a certain kind of interestedness) is, in Dewey's view, that it precludes an intellectual engagement with subject matter, with "all the attendant reverberations" (254) of a work of art's ideas and assertions.

Dewey's critical approach to contemplation and disinterest is compatible with the pragmatic, materialist, and historical orientation of the early chapters of his study, and would seem to lead away from the kind of analysis usually associated with formalism. However, in his chapter on literary criticism, "Criticism as Perception," Dewey embraces formalism in reaction to what he perceives to be the faults of certain kinds of interested criticism. One of the great "fallacies of esthetic criticism,"[12] Dewey insists here, is the kind of "reduction" associated with "criticism made from a historical, political or economic point of view" (315). Here he insists that the very points of view that dominated his discussion of art in chapter one—the historical and the economic—get in the way of aesthetic experience.

> Historical and cultural information may throw light on the causes of their production. But when all is said and done, each one is just what it is artistically, and its esthetic merits and demerits are within the work. Knowledge of social conditions of production is, when it is really knowledge, of genuine value. But it is no substitute for understanding of the object in its own qualities and relations. (316)

With this thoroughly Arnoldian formulation, Dewey both essentializes art and reintroduces the very separation between art and social life his study means to overcome (the last two sentences could have been written by any of the New Critics). According to this passage, the local and contingent circumstances surrounding the creation of a work of art tell us only about its production, which Dewey here wants to distinguish from the work itself. Knowledge of "social conditions," Dewey implies, and knowledge of what a work of art is "artistically," are two different things; to understand a work of art we must, in the final analysis, set aside what we know about the social conditions of its production and look "within the work," for it "is just what it is artistically." The ontological emphasis of the vague "is" in this phrase suggests the ultimate essence or being of a work of art has its sources in something outside time and history; it is something contained "within" the work itself. The function of the critic in this context is radically circumscribed compared with Dewey's vision in the earlier chapters of the book. The quoted passage, for example, seems quite at odds with Dewey's earlier warning about "theorists and literary critics . . . still largely in the thralls of the ancient metaphysics of essence according to which a definition, if it is 'correct,' discloses to us some inward reality that causes the thing to be what it is" (216).

The kind of division Dewey insists on here recalls the "compartmental divisions" he criticized in Kant. Moreover, the kind of aesthetic experience he outlines comes close to the disinterested contemplation Kant endorses. It is in passages like these that Dewey resituates in art the metaphysics he banished from philosophy, privileging art over philosophy precisely because it comes closer to embodying some essential, spiritual totality. In his chapter "The Common Substance of the Arts,"

for example, he insists that a work of art has a "total and massive quality" that lends it its "uniqueness; even when vague and undefined, it is
just that which it is and not anything else" (192, emphasis mine). This
uniqueness (in Kantian fashion) is something that "runs through all the
parts of a work of art and . . . can only be emotionally 'intuited'" (192).
What is intuited is a "totality": "There is no name to be given it. As it
enlivens and animates, it is the spirit of the work of art. It is its reality"
(193). Dewey's metaphysical idealism here echoes Emerson as well as
Kant. Like Emerson, Whitman, and Brooks, Dewey seems to be arguing for the importance of the local and the actual, but ultimately the
value of the local and the actual has its ground in a transcendental or
universal spirit. "The 'spiritual,'" he writes in a passage that Emerson
could have written, "gets a local habitation and achieves the solidity of
form required for esthetic quality only when it is embodied in a sense
of actual things" (198). Although the stress here is on the local and the
actual, both remain, as in Emerson, subservient to the transcendental
spirit that inhabits them and lends them their beauty.

Dewey's metaphysical idealism manifests itself in passages like these
even when he seems to be arguing against it and for the primacy of "actual things." In his chapter on art's "Challenge to Philosophy," for example, he argues for the primacy of experience over metaphysics in art,
but in a way that ends up implying the primacy of metaphysics over
experience after all:

> Instead of fleeing from experience to a metaphysical realm, the material
> of experiences is so rendered [in works of art] that it becomes the preg-
> nant matter of a new experience. Moreover, the sense we now have for es-
> sential characteristics of persons and objects is very largely the *result* of
> art, while the theory that is under discussion [metaphysical essentialism]
> holds that art depends upon and refers to essences already in being, thus
> reversing the actual process. If we are now aware of essential meanings,
> it is mainly because artists in all the various arts have extracted and ex-
> pressed them in vivid and salient subject-matter of perception. (294)

If persons and objects *don't* have in their "being" essential characteristics, then what does Dewey mean when he writes that the artist extracts
essences or "essential meanings" from what he or she perceives? He
wants to argue against essence as a metaphysical quality of being, but
the example he cites implies just the opposite—that there *are* essences
inherent in being. They may be promulgated in a social way by art and
artists, but they have their being, Dewey implies, apart from and above
the workings of a cultural economy.

Dewey's tendency to resituate metaphysics in art leads inexorably to the aesthetic formalism he endorses in his chapter "Criticism and Perception." Dewey begins this chapter by reviewing the familiar distinction between "judicial" and "impressionist" criticism. Both are faulted in a way that seems to lead to an "objective" and "intrinsic" approach to criticism. The problem with forms of judicial criticism (Dewey cites as an example the neoclassical reliance on models) is that they are too strict; tradition becomes rigidified into a set of technical rules for judging the literary value of new works in a process that makes criticism unable "to cope with the emergence of new modes of life—of experiences that demand new modes of expression" (303). "Impressionist criticism," on the other hand, tends to the "opposite extreme," the "assertion that judgment should be replaced by statement of the responses of feeling and imagery the art object evokes" in the critic (304). The impressionist critic can drift off into what Dewey terms "irrelevancies and arbitrary dicta" uncontrolled by "subject-matter" (306). Such a critic tends to "dwell in a world apart" from the artist or the work he or she is criticizing (306).

However, it turns out that Dewey is not against objective values in criticism per se. Rather, his complaint is about the "false notions of objective values" and standards of judicial criticism that make it all the easier for the impressionist critic to assume "there are no criteria of any sort" (306). Dewey insists that making judgments about art by analyzing formal elements will return a proper kind of objectivity to its criticism. He steers criticism toward the "intrinsic" qualities of a work of art, that is, in reaction against both politically interested forms of criticism and the pitfalls of a purely impressionistic criticism:

> Criticism is a search for the properties of the object that may justify the direct reaction. And yet, if the search is sincere and informed, it is not, when it is undertaken, concerned with values but with the objective properties of the object under consideration—if a painting, with its colors, lights, placings, volumes, in their relations to one another. (308)

The formalist orientation of the critic's task here is striking; indeed, Dewey's passage conjures up the whole history of aesthetic formalism from Kant to the New Critics. Particularly important is Dewey's insistence that criticism needs to avoid being concerned with values. Values contaminate each of the three modes of criticism he indicts in this chapter. Politically interested criticism is contaminated by social and political values; judicial criticism by moral and conservative values; impressionist criticism by idiosyncratic "personal" values. The ostensible virtue of the kind of aesthetic formalism Dewey endorses in this chapter is that it is "objective" in the sense of being free of values that predispose the critic toward certain judgments.

Of course the same observation can be made about Dewey's warning here as has often been made about the position taken by the New Critics: to take the position that the critical analyses you produce are "objective" in the sense of being value-free is to endorse a certain value and at the same time deny that you are involved in ascribing value. To define the aesthetic as somehow outside the social or cultural realms of interest and value, and then to restrict critical analysis to the aesthetic as a set of "objective properties," is to intervene in the analysis of art from an ideologically interested position with clearly identified values. The metaphysical assumptions that ground the aesthetic theory Dewey is working with here serve to mystify the interested relationship between criticism and values, no matter how "objective" the critic feels. (I will take up the larger question of pragmatism's approach to value, and to normative standards, a little later in this study.)

The ultimate irony in all this is that because art, in Dewey's view, gives us access to whole and spiritually essential realities, it challenges the primacy of philosophy. In his essays on the relationship of philosophy to democracy and civilization, as we have already seen, Dewey wanted to turn the discourse of philosophy away from metaphysics. The argument in *Art as Experience*, however, is that art challenges philosophy precisely to the extent that it gets us closer to metaphysical realities. The "uniqueness" of art in this respect is a "challenge to . . . that systematic thought called philosophy. For esthetic experience is experience in its integrity" (274). He continues:

> Had not the term "pure" been so often abused in philosophic literature, had it not been so often employed to suggest that there is something alloyed, impure, in the very nature of experience and to denote something beyond experience, we might say that esthetic experience is pure experience. For it is experience freed from the forces that impede and confuse its development as experience; freed, that is, from factors that subordinate an experience as it is directly had to something beyond itself. To esthetic experience, then, the philosopher must go to understand what experience is. (274)

Dewey's desire here to describe "an experience" as a "pure" experience has left him open to the criticism that his whole approach to experience veers too close to idealism.[13] Dewey wanted to formulate a philosophical approach to experience that avoided the excesses of both idealist and realist approaches.[14] Subjectivist philosophy since Locke had come to conceive of reality as what the individual subject experienced, while "realist," materialist, or positivist philosophy over the course of the nineteenth century had come to view reality as separate from, and prior to, experience.[15] Dewey, in effect, wanted to synthesize a third approach to experience that stressed the link between nature and experience. In *Experience and Nature* Dewey insists that, on the one hand, "it is not experience which is experienced, but nature," but that, on the other hand, "things interacting in certain ways *are* experience; they are what is experienced" (4a). Thus, when we experience nature we experience objects "out there," but how they interact with each other and with the subject who experiences them *is* what they are. This approach to experience is meant in one stroke to avoid the idealist reduction of reality to our experience of it and the realist's denial that the nature of reality is mediated by experience. However, as Thomas Alexander succinctly points out, Dewey "seems paradoxically to assert that things are what they are experienced as, and that *some* things are experienced as existing prior to being experienced" (82).

Dewey's temptation in the passage about "pure" experience quoted above to characterize aesthetic experience as a form of experience "freed from . . . factors that subordinate an experience as it is directly had to something beyond itself" is related to a distinction he makes between primary and secondary (or refined) experience. *Primary* experience, for Dewey, is the qualitative experience of the phenomenal world as it is. It denotes something like our immediate experience of nature.[16] Refined experience refers to the processes of reason, analysis, and speculation that follow from our primary experiences, forms of intellectual, metaphysical, or scientific inquiry that attempt to synthesize knowledge from primary experience. Primary experience, as Westbrook stresses (327–46), supposedly provides knowledge of "generic traits of nature." Aesthetic experience, for Dewey, is a form of primary experience and is thus linked to the *unmediated experience of generic qualities*. This is why Dewey is tempted to call it "pure" experience.

Thus when Dewey distinguishes between experience per se and "an" experience in *Art as Experience*, he is, in effect, invoking the earlier distinction he made between primary and refined experience, insisting that aesthetic experience has the kind of consummatory or immediate character that allows the subject to intuit primary, generic qualities. Experience per se, according to Dewey, is "inchoate" and disconnected (35), while "an experience" is characterized by wholeness, integration, and fulfillment (35).[17] "An experience," he continues, "has a unity that gives it its name . . . The existence of this unity is constituted by a single *quality* that pervades the entire experience in spite of the variation of its constituent parts" (37). "For Dewey," Alexander observers, "aesthetic or consummatory experience is . . . ultimately intuited, which is to say that the pervasive qualitative whole is realized throughout the whole developing experience as the binding or grounding of all the phases so that they belong together—they are all parts of *an* experience" (11). Primary experience, as Westbrook emphasizes, is for Dewey a *noncognitive* or precognitive form of experience, so that, as Dewey writes, "things in their immediacy are unknown and unknowable . . . because knowledge has no concern with them. For knowledge is [only] a memorandum of conditions of their appearance" (*Experience and Nature* 74–75). The "quality" of a thing one experiences in "an" experience exists in a pure and whole form prior to the knowledge we begin to have about it as we muse afterward about the experience. It is not therefore hard to see why Dewey's stress on a priori qualities and the immediate experience of pure formal harmony struck some of his critics as idealist and metaphysical through and through.

In *Art as Experience* Dewey clearly *wants* to reconnect art and the aesthetic to experience. The distinction he makes between experiences per se and "an" experience is meant to link the aesthetic with the concrete and everyday in a way that connects the argument in the first chapter of the book with the ideas about experience worked out in *Experience and Nature*. He ends up, however, taking a position much like the ones taken earlier by Emerson and Whitman, one in which the significance for art of the ordinary and the everyday is emphasized, but where its import is ultimately grounded in the extraordinary and the transcendental. "Absolute experience," Dewey writes in *Experience and Nature*, "is 'real' just long enough to afford a spring-board into ultimate reality and to afford a hint of the essential contents of the latter and then it obligingly dissolves into mere appearance" (61). This Platonic distinction between "ultimate reality" and "appearance" is hard to square with a pragmatic naturalist metaphysics, and so leads critics like James Gouinlock to observe approvingly that for Dewey "experience as art is then freed of the irrelevant, the casual, or the discordant which so characterize our usual experience" (151).

Dewey clearly wants to *avoid* our coming to this kind of conclusion. That is, the last thing he would want would be for us to conclude, as Gouinlock does, that his theory of art separates us from usual experience, since the whole point of the first part of the book is to lament just this separation. But the conclusion Gouinlock comes to is, I think, inevitable, and it underscores the way in which Dewey's theory of the aesthetic is unable to accommodate the casual and discordant qualities of contemporary experience. The problem with Dewey's conception of aesthetic experience has to do with the fact that it is grounded, like his approach to form, in a set of assumptions that are ultimately classical. If we recall for a moment the classical theory of form Dewey outlines in chapter 1 of *Art as Experience*, we will see how close it is to the idealist conception of experience we have just been reviewing. There, Dewey writes that the "roots of the esthetic in experience" are in our organic disposition to overcome "conflict," our ability to achieve "equilibrium," to generate "balance and harmony attained through rhythm" (14). Form, in this classical sense of the term, is what distinguishes "an" experience from experience per se, and only "an" experience, as we have seen, can qualify as the grounds for art. This "form is arrived at" only when "a stable, even though moving, equilibrium is reached . . . Order is not imposed from without but is made out of the relations of harmonious interactions that energies bear to one another" (14). Thus, what qualifies as "an" (aesthetic) experience does so by virtue of inherent qualities that exist prior to and above the flux of experience per se. Here again, Dewey compartmentalizes in a way that reinscribes the very split between art and social life his study means to overcome, for he has created two levels of experience, one base because it is formless (in relation to a certain theory of form), the other absolute because it manifests transcendental qualities.

One of the problems with this approach to aesthetic experience is that it subordinates specifically modern or contemporary forms of experience to a classical conception of experience. In so doing, it tends to disqualify contemporary experience as a source for art. "Experience" per se, Dewey writes,

> occurs continuously, because the interaction of live creature and environing conditions is involved in the very process of living . . . Oftentimes, however, the experience had is inchoate. Things are experienced but not in such a way that they are composed into *an* experience. There is distraction and dispersion; what we observe and what we think, what we desire and what we get, are at odds with each other . . . (*Art as Experience* 35)

Experience per se is characterized by "dispersion." It lacks the teleological element that constitutes "an experience." "An experience," in Dewey's view, is one in which "the material experienced runs its course to fulfillment. Then and then only is it integrated within and demarcated in the general stream of experience from other experiences . . . [A]

problem receives its solution; a game is played through; a situation . . .
is so rounded out that its close is a consummation and not a cessation.
Such an experience is a whole and carries with it its own . . . self-suffi-
ciency" (35). "An experience," we should note, is very much like an aesthetic object, for it is "whole" and self-sufficient. It is, tellingly, something that is "composed." The values here carry over from his aesthetic
theory. "An experience" is based on the value of closure, consummation, a rounded-out solution. The problem is not so much in Dewey's
making a distinction between different kinds of experience, but in his
insistence that only one kind of experience can form the basis for art.
The idealist or classical conception of "an experience," based as it is on
an inherent balance and harmony between parts that leads to a sense of
unity and fulfillment,[18] excludes the possibility that what Dewey calls
"dispersed" and "miscellaneous" experiences can be the point of departure for art. Dewey's insistence on linking art to experience is a step
forward. However, in linking it to "an" experience, he links it to experience so essentialized and formalized that he seems to revert back to an
earlier idealism.

He insists, in fact, that such experiences are actually "the enemies of
the esthetic."[19] Given this compartmentalization of experience, and the
way it is employed to narrow the scope of experience deemed appropriate for aesthetic production, it is not surprising that Dewey goes on
to insist that contemporary experience actually falls outside the pur-
view of the aesthetic. "Zeal for doing, lust for action," he writes,

> leaves many a person, especially in this hurried and impatient human en-
> vironment in which we live, with experience of an almost incredible
> paucity, all on the surface. No one experience has a chance to complete it-
> self because something else is entered upon so speedily. What is called ex-
> perience becomes so dispersed and miscellaneous as hardly to deserve
> the name. (45)

Contemporary experience is so removed from the idealist standards
Dewey invokes to define aesthetically productive experience that it is
nearly disqualified as experience altogether. This theme, taken up in his
chapter on "experience," is sounded throughout the rest of the book,
and is invoked in a powerful way in the book's final chapter, "Art and
Civilization." In "The Common Substance of Art," for example, Dewey
argues that modern experience as such has made the production of
contemporary "art" nearly impossible. "The bustle and ado of modern
life," with its "rapid . . . incidents too crowded to permit of decisive-
ness," have made defective contemporary "architecture, drama, and

fiction alike" (212). "The very profusion of materials and the mechanical force of activities get in the way" of the kind of "effective distribution" necessary for aesthetic production (212). The contemporary arts, in Dewey's view, are ruined by "recurrent overstimulation" (212).

Dewey's essentially classicist approach to both art and experience, then, leaves him unable to reconcile his own aesthetics with the products of mass culture. The position Dewey takes on modernity, art, and culture anticipates in some significant ways the one taken by Adorno and Horkheimer in their famous essay "The Culture Industry." Dewey shares with his Frankfurt School contemporaries the conviction that both art and mass culture have been debased by the standardization, routinization, and commodification characteristic of modern Western industrial societies. The nostalgia in Dewey for the recovery of a prior kind of art linked to classical values, a recovery conceived as an *antidote* to modernity, parallels the nostalgia in Horkheimer and Adorno for a kind of pure art unsullied by the values and images of popular culture and unaffected by the processes of mass reproduction. All three, finally, have a fundamental ambivalence toward modernity rooted in their antipathy toward the social and cultural effects of industrialization, mechanization, and standardization, an ambivalence that manifests itself in their discussions of art in a tendency to privilege the products of so-called high culture over popular culture.[20]

Like Horkheimer and Adorno, Dewey blames "the conditions of the market" for the withdrawal of the aesthetic from everyday experience (5). As we have already seen, Dewey argues not so much that this withdrawal is manifested by our inability to recognize the aesthetic possibilities of modern experience or popular art forms as that it is a function of the sequestering and commodification of great art by collectors and museums. His analysis is thus guided by the hierarchical distinction between high art and popular culture Levine has charted. "When what we know as art," Dewey writes, is "relegated to the museum and gallery, the unconquerable impulse towards experiences enjoyable in themselves finds such outlet as the daily environment provides" (6).[21] With art set on "a remote pedestal . . . the movie, jazzed music, the comic strip, and, too frequently, newspaper accounts of lovenests, murders, and exploits of bandits" fill the vacuum (5–6). Although Dewey suggests that these popular media have an "esthetic quality" often missed by the consumer (5), his conflation of movies and jazz with the sentimental and sensationalistic excesses of tabloid journalism is telling. While Dewey's goal is to find a way to reintegrate art and everyday experience, the reintegration he proposes has more to do with making art with traditional formal properties available for experience than with allowing for the possibility that contemporary forms of entertainment *are* modern art. "When, because of their remoteness," he writes, "the objects acknowledged by the cultivated to be works of fine art seem anemic to the mass of people, esthetic hunger is likely to seek the cheap and the vulgar" (6).[22]

This conclusion essentially anticipates the one Horkheimer and Adorno come to in their analysis of art and mass culture. In their view, art has become debased in the modern age not because it has been removed from social life and relegated to the museums, but because the culture industry has conflated high art and popular culture in a way that empties contemporary aesthetic forms of their legitimacy. Their argument is more complex (and paradoxical) than Dewey's, but it is based on the same distinction he makes between high art and the products of popular culture. They write that "anyone who complains that" what they call "light art" is "a betrayal of the ideal of pure expression is under an illusion about society":

> The purity of bourgeois art, which hypostatized itself as a world of freedom in contrast to what was happening in the material world, was from the beginning bought with the exclusion of the lower classes . . . Serious art has been withheld from those for whom the hardship and oppression of life make a mockery of seriousness, and who must be glad if they can use time not spent at the production line just to keep going. Light art has been the shadow of autonomous art. It is the social bad conscience of serious art. (135)

In their view, light art does not betray the bourgeois ideal of pure expression because such a category is necessary in order to hypostatize "serious" art. The structure of antithesis is what keeps the whole system in operation. The light art that appeals to the lower classes cannot be subsumed into high art without making a mockery of that art *and* disrupting the class system. When the modern culture industry tries to reconcile the two by "absorbing light into serious art, or vice versa" (136) it merely creates the "eccentricity" of "the circus, peepshow . . . brothel" and Benny Goodman's appearance with the Budapest String Quartet (136).

This kind of absorption creates a "fusion of culture and entertainment," which "leads not only to a depravation of culture, but inevitably to an intellectualization of amusement" (143). Amusement (or "light" art) necessarily displaces "the higher things" (or serious art) (143). Horkheimer and Adorno match Dewey's working distinction between art and popular media with the distinction they make between light and serious art. While they stress the complicity of bourgeois art with a system that keeps the lower classes in their places, and while they identify "amusement" culture as a necessary creation of the class structure, they remain committed (as many commentators have pointed out) to the products and the aesthetic of traditional high culture. One of the central problems with modernity, from their point of view, is that it fosters light at the expense of serious art. For Dewey this is reflected in the withdrawal of art into the private and corporate worlds, while for Horkheimer and Adorno it is related to the broader demands of the culture industry as it works hand in glove with the state to keep the masses in their place.

I have been arguing that Dewey's insistence on adhering to a classical definition of both the aesthetic *per se* and the kind of experience appropriate for aesthetic production makes him resistant to modern experience as such, or to envisioning the legitimacy of art that grows out of it. His position at key moments relies on a romanticizing of the premodern relationship between art and experience, a relationship he characterizes as organic and seamless, a time before the fall of art into its dissociation from everyday life (6–9, 146–49). This position modulates in the final chapter of his study into a nostalgic and redemptive mode. Returning to his initial focus on the split between art and social life, he again takes a kind of primitivist/organicist position in which art in earlier ages is assumed to have had an immediate, functional, organic relationship to culture, a relationship destroyed in the modern age by industrialization and commodification. "The connection of art with community life" in previous ages, he writes, "contrast[s] with present conditions" (337). The contemporary moment marks for Dewey the development of a fissure or fall, one in which the complex forces constituting modernity have undermined the possibility of aesthetic production altogether: "the absence of obvious organic connection of the arts with other forms of culture is explained by the complexity of modern life, by its many specializations, and by the simultaneous existence of many diverse centers of culture in different nations that exchange their products but that do not form parts of an inclusive social whole" (337). The nostalgia here is for a kind of relationship between art and culture that has become mythologized into something "organic." No one would argue that art is not connected to "other forms of culture," but we should pause over Dewey's idealization of premodern art as organically related to culture.

The biological relationship suggested by Dewey's organic metaphor suggests that at some point in time the substance of art was part of the substance of culture, that there was a systematic relationship of interdependence between the two much like the interdependence between two organs in a single body. Dewey argues that owing to the increasingly complex and commodified nature of modern society, that organic relationship was severed. He blames this break on the rise of "natural science" and the proliferation of mechanical, "non-human" modes of energy and production (337). These new forces, in Dewey's view, are a "manifestation of the incoherence of our civilization," and represent the "widespread disruption" that has accompanied the split in modern experience between the "physical world" and the "moral realm," which stood united in both ancient Greece and the medieval age (337). The "problem of recovering an organic place for art in civilization" is tied up with the necessity of reforging a union between the "spiritual" and the "physical" (338), what Dewey envisions as an "organic synthesis" (340). On the one hand, he sees a "permanent gain" in science's having helped "to diversify" the "materials and forms" of contemporary art, so that "matter that was once regarded as either too common or too out of the way to deserve artistic recognition" now receives it (340). But, on the other hand, such art represents a "diffuseness and incoherence" in contemporary aesthetic production that are the direct result of a "disruption of consensus of beliefs" (340). Thus the aesthetic "integration of matter and form" depends on civilization's recapturing this consensus of belief.

The problem with this analysis is that it measures the ("organic") relationship between modern art and culture using classical aesthetic norms and standards. Since much of the art produced in Dewey's own time does not embody or reflect those norms, it can be dismissed as art and cited as evidence of the breakdown of art's organic relation to culture. However, one could certainly argue that the cultural forms Dewey tends to write off as "cheap and vulgar" do in fact have what he calls an organic relation to culture. It is not so much that the intimate relationship between art and culture has changed, but that Dewey dismisses the legitimacy of some of the art forms produced in contemporary culture. On the one hand, he faults criticism for "its inability to cope with the emergence of new modes of life—of experiences that demand new modes of expression" (303)—but on the other hand his definition of significant experience precludes modern experience from forming the basis for aesthetic production. Modernity will produce significant art, in Dewey's view, only when it has been redeemed by a set of standards and values that predate it.

Near the end of *Art as Experience*, Dewey writes that "there is one problem that artist, philosopher, and critic alike must face: the relation between permanence and change" (322). "The bias of philosophy" so far, he continues, "has been toward the unchanging," toward an iden- tification of the "unified and 'total,'" the "'universal'" (322). This ob- servation is of course another way of criticizing the preoccupation of metaphysics with *being* at the expense of *becoming*, and is therefore con- sistent with Dewey's essays on the history and function of philosophy. In his essays on philosophy and his book on aesthetics Dewey traces the tension between permanence and change as it structures both the dis- course of philosophy and the production and criticism of art. Thus, he has followed his own injunction about the necessity of treating the re- lation between permanence and change as a central problem in both philosophy and art. In his essays on philosophy Dewey comes down on the side of change and becoming in the sense that he argues persua- sively that philosophy always has a strategic and pragmatic relation to culture, that it continually changes and becomes what it needs to be, even if it couches its discourse in the rhetoric of permanence and be- coming. However, in *Art as Experience* the position he takes is more com- plicated and ambivalent. He wants to come down on the side of change here as well to the degree he argues that art, like philosophy, is inti- mately related to cultural, social, and political forms, and that it changes over time given shifts in these forms. Indeed, criticism must account for and judge art in the context of change and becoming. Yet the underly- ing assumptions that drive his argument about both art and experience are related more to permanence and being than to change and becoming.

While Dewey was writing *Art as Experience* Kenneth Burke was tak- ing up the specific challenge Dewey presents to philosophy and criti- cism in a book he would call *Permanence and Change*. Burke is a central, if somewhat neglected, figure in the rise of modern American literary and cultural criticism, and his intellectual relationship to Emerson, Whitman, and Dewey is a complex one. As we will see in the next chap- ter, Burke's work unfolded in the context of a continuing struggle to mediate the theoretical or philosophical tension in cultural criticism be- tween the ideal and the pragmatic, between permanence and change. His work is important both because it responds to the tradition of cul- tural criticism we have been tracing in this study, and because it repre- sents a complex and nuanced response to the problems of his own modernity, one that will turn our attention away from pragmatism and toward rhetoric.

5

Kenneth Burke

Modernism and the Motives of Rhetoric

One of the central points I emphasized in the previous chapter was that Dewey demonstrates a marked ambivalence about the modernity of his own age. On the one hand, his historical analysis of philosophy constitutes a major reappraisal of the very nature and function of philosophical discourse. Both his mode of analysis—critical historicism—and the insights it yielded about the cultural and political work of "metaphysics" constituted a radical break with conventional philosophical discourse. In this context, his work was self-consciously modern, for it sought to inaugurate a new beginning for contemporary philosophy that became part of what Thomas Kuhn would call a "paradigm shift" in contemporary thought. After Dewey, the whole concept of "normal" philosophy would be rethought. On the other hand, as a cultural critic writing about art and its separation from so-called ordinary life, we saw that he often fell back on a premodernist set of aesthetic assumptions that reinforced the very breach between art and contemporary experience he wanted to bridge. While Dewey was busy recasting philosophy in a way that would make it more relevant to modern life, he often seemed ambivalent about the cultural modernism of his own age.

It was his ambivalence about his own modernity that led him to take different positions toward the problem of permanence and change. His commitment to reformulating philosophy so that it might respond to the real needs of twentieth-century life led him to embrace change, while his critique of modern experience and its cultural forms became translated into nostalgia for the "permanent" values of classicism in art *and* experience. Ultimately, it is the inability to grant legitimacy to expressive forms related to radically new and seemingly discordant kinds of experience, experience that seems in its distance from the past to be inferior or even debased, that leads to Dewey's ambivalence toward contemporary culture, and to his adherence to what had become a conventional methodological distinction between high art and popular culture. Instead of exploring the realignment of aesthetic and cultural forms in their response to transformations in the way life is conducted, Dewey laments that the conduct of life is no longer conducive to the production of "art."

Before we begin to look at the ways Kenneth Burke seeks to get beyond the problems we have located in Dewey, I want to clarify some of the issues I have been discussing by comparing Dewey's approach to the problem of permanence and change with Gertrude Stein's. Her essay "Composition as Explanation" (1926), first delivered as a lecture at Cambridge and Oxford, is one of the most striking modernist meditations on the relationship between permanence and change in the arts and philosophy. The essay resonates on a number of different levels. Most specifically, it attempts to explain the emergence of what she calls the "modern composition" in twentieth-century literature and painting, and as such constitutes a meditation on the disruptive advent of nonrepresentational literature and painting. However, Stein's remarks about how and why radical changes in the arts take place lead to the formulation of a general theory of change that sees what we call "modernism" as a phenomenon that can occur (and recur) over time in any given century (in this respect she recalls the theories both of Russian Formalism and, later, of Paul de Man).[1] This general theory assumes a "modern composition" can occur whenever artists produce work in reaction to the aesthetic paradigms dominant at the time. Her conception of the "modern," that is, is not limited to the period of classical high modernism, but rather designates any moment at which there is a revolt against the dominant aesthetic tradition.

At an even more general level, however, Stein attempts to explain aesthetic and philosophical change in terms of changes in the "conduct" of life:

> Each period of living differs from any other period of living not in the way life is but in the way life is conducted and that authentically speaking is composition. After life has been conducted in a certain way everybody knows it but nobody knows it, little by little, nobody knows it as long as nobody knows it. Any one creating the composition in the arts does not know it either, they are conducting life and that makes their composition what it is, it makes their work compose as it does. (517)

Where Dewey tends to see a disjunction between modern experience and the possibility of art, Stein sees the modern "conduct of life" as a form of composition that makes the artistic composition of the time "what it is." The crucial difference here is in the way they view so-called ordinary life. In Dewey's view it is not conducive to the production of art because it lacks the structure of experience defined classically, while in Stein's view ordinary life is an always changing composition that continually finds legitimate expression in art. The "modern composition," in her view, takes its legitimacy and its beauty from the way in which "each period of living differs from any other period of living." The legitimacy of modern art stems from its response to the *difference* of its age, not from its adherence to a set of permanent aesthetic norms. The point is not to cultivate ordinary experience until it can lead to the appreciation of high culture, but to see how new forms of ordinary experience lead to the composition of new forms of art.

Stein attributes significant changes in art and philosophy to shifts in *what* people look at and *how* they look at it. "The only thing that is different from one time to another," she writes, "is what is seen and what is seen depends upon how everybody is doing everything. This makes the thing we are looking at very different and this makes what those who describe it make of it, it makes a composition, it confuses, it shows, it is, it looks, it likes it as it is, and this makes what is seen as it is seen" (516). The term "composition" in Stein's equation refers to the act of seeing, what is seen, and to descriptions of what is seen. A "composition" is what we create when we see and describe something, whether it is one of the objects described in a text like "Tender Buttons," or the cultural phenomenon of modernism she is concerned with in the essay. Moreover, both compositions are explanations, and all explanations are compositions.

In stressing the *composed* and therefore contingent nature of "what is seen," Stein articulates a philosophical position about knowledge and representation consistent with the central insights of modern philosophy. Her analysis, for example, insists that "reality" (what we look at or see) does not simply appear as it is in some fixed and absolute sense, but is a composition that depends upon how the perceiving subject looks at things and conducts his or her life. To say that what is seen in any given historical epoch depends upon how people *look* at things and how they *do* everything is to insist that "reality" is contingent upon culturally specific modes of perception and historically determined sets of norms and values that determine behavior. That is to say, it is to look at philosophy historically and critically in much the same way as Dewey did. Stein's position, like his, breaks absolutely with metaphysical foundationalism. The point Stein makes about change is that it evolves in relation to shifts in perspective and value; the "modern composition" sees, describes, and explains reality the way it does not so much because reality has changed, but because what people choose to look at—and how they choose to look—has changed.

The epistemological theory Stein articulates in her explanation of modernism reflects positions staked out by modern philosophy. Her essay makes clear the connection between the modernist break with representation and critiques of representational positivism in philosophy we associate with philosophers as various as Nietzsche, Dewey, James, and Bergson. Modernist art breaks with the idea that literature or the visual arts can or should mirror reality at the same time that the idea of philosophy as a mirror of nature is being undermined.[2] In this respect, Stein's modernism breaks with the same Enlightenment values William James questioned in his critique of traditional epistemological theories. "Up to about 1850," James wrote in 1904, "almost everyone believed that sciences expressed truths that were exact copies of a definite code of hon-human realities. But the enormously rapid multiplication of theories in these latter days has well-nigh upset the notion of any one of them being a more *literally* objective kind of thing than another . . . [E]ven the truest formula may be a human device and not a literal transcript . . ."(40, emphasis mine). Here, James begins to develop a strain of modern philosophy based on a critique of the rationalist and scientific assumptions of modernity.

Stein's modernist epistemology insists on both distinguishing between theoretical or conceptual models of "reality" and "reality" itself, and on the interdependence between them. Stein locates the real in the flux of sensory experiences rather than in either an ideal, transcendental realm or the seemingly objective reality reported by scientific measurement. The point she makes is not that there is some elusive but "real" reality beneath or beyond metaphysical and scientific realities, but that what we call reality is always relative to the way we compose and explain it—whether theoretically or artistically. In this respect she has less in common with someone like F. H. Bradley, who insists upon an absolute reality beyond the realm of fragmented experiences, or like Henri Bergson, who tends to transcendentalize immediate experience into a metaphysical category, than with Nietzsche, who insists that all explanations are interpretations that lack recourse to any absolute or fundamental realm of the real.[3]

To say that a composition is an explanation is to insist that any composition is also a rhetorical act. This means that Stein intercedes in the dispute between idealism and pragmatism roughly on the pragmatic side via a theory of rhetoric that is not far from Dewey's. Stein's general theory of change in the arts is based on the same theoretical position that informs Dewey's general theory of change in philosophy. Both understand change to result from socially and historically contingent shifts in the way we look at things. Indeed, the conception of philosophy that emerges from Dewey's critique of metaphysics can stand as representative of such shifts, and is therefore just the kind of composition as explanation Stein analyzes. Philosophy changes because Dewey looks at it in a radically different way. He stops *participating* in its epistemological project, analyzes that project in a historical and critical way, and thus begins to decenter its metaphysical and epistemological orientation. His historical and rhetorical analysis of philosophy informs the philosophical practice he espouses, which is based on the idea that philosophy is always a strategic intercession on behalf of a social, moral, or political position.

Kenneth Burke developed something like the same aim for literary and cultural criticism in the increasingly speculative work he produced in the '20s, '30s, and '40s. Burke, as we shall see, embraced in its general outlines the philosophical position Stein took toward the dispute between idealism and pragmatism, and it led him to focus his attention on what Stein identified as the compositional elements of perception and language. He did so, moreover, in the context of a sustained examination of the modernity of his own age. Burke began his career as a writer near the end of World War I immersed in the aestheticism of modern European writers like Flaubert, Dostoevski, Pater, and De Gourmont. However, under the influence first of modernist writers associated with European avant-garde movements, and later of Freud, Nietzsche, and Marx, he developed an incisive critique of this earlier aestheticism. This critique led him, as it had Dewey, to systematically rethink the connection between the aesthetic and the social as it specifically pertained to modernity. Reviewing the evolution of that critique, we will be able to see why and how Burke developed a position toward modernity that was much different from Dewey's.

Burke's early characterization of the challenges to culture presented by modernity is, in its general outlines, not far from those of Dewey and Brooks. In his first book, *Counter-Statement* (1931), he took a decidedly negative view toward the rise of science and the dominance of technologies of information. Burke identifies modernity here with mechanization, industrialization, applied science, and a pervasive preoccupation with material acquisition and consumption. "In contemporary America," he writes, "the distinguishing emergent factor is obviously mechanization, industrialism, as it affects our political institutions, as it alters our way of living, as it makes earlier emphases malapropos or even dangerous . . ." (107). Like Brooks and Dewey, he sees art, or what he calls "the aesthetic" (110–11), as a force that has the potential to oppose mechanization, but that has been continuously and dangerously displaced by it. However, whereas Brooks and Dewey turn to art nostalgic for a mythical time when it had a supposedly "organic" relationship to society, Burke turns to the aesthetic for its oppositional possibilities, envisioning it as a force that can be used to disrupt the very "cultural code behind . . . economic ambitiousness" (121). As we saw in chapter 2, Brooks tended to retreat from the challenge of developing a progressive role for art in its relation to the economic, mechanistic, and institutional character of modernity. Instead, he fell back on nineteenth-century myths about the self and art, insisting in a thoroughly Arnoldian way on the pursuit of art as a wholly disinterested activity the civilizing effects of which would eventually trickle down to the middle and lower classes, buoying them up spiritually in a way that would somehow translate itself into social change. Likewise, we have seen that for Dewey art's ability to affect the modern condition lies wholly in its ability to recapture a classical kind of balance, harmony, and equilibrium, one that is quite at odds with the very nature of modern experience. In *Counter-Statement*, Burke begins to move away from both Brooks's disinterestedness and Dewey's classicism, embracing an oppositional aesthetic for both literature and criticism that recognizes its ideological engagement in cultural struggles, and that departs thoroughly from the classical formalism in Dewey that all but disallows the possibility of a specifically contemporary art that moves beyond—and even critiques—classical norms.

Burke's interest in how the aesthetic can intervene in the practical affairs of the world outside art suggests an affinity between his critical orientation and pragmatism. However, while we will see that Burke was influenced by James and Dewey, and that there are indeed pragmatist elements in his work, the relationship between Burke and pragmatism can be overstated in ways that distort his long and complicated critical project. Gunn, for example, is generally correct in pointing out that there is an insistently pragmatist strain in Burke's thinking, but his tendency to lump together Burke's entire critical project under the term "critical pragmatism" can be misleading. With Lentricchia's reading of Burke as his point of departure, Gunn focuses on the "Program" chapter of *Counter-Statement* in order to stress the "political coloration of his own pragmatism" (*Culture of Criticism* 75). This is true in a very general sense, but the problem here is Gunn's conflation of the "political" with the "pragmatic." Nowhere in his discussion of Burke does Gunn make a specific case for Burke's *philosophical* pragmatism, whether in his discussion of *Counter-Statement* or of Burke's later book on "dramatism." Instead, Burke's focus on the social and political *function* of language and art is invoked to define his pragmatism. This leaves the specific sense of the relation of Burke's critical project to James or Dewey rather obscure.[4] It makes more sense, I will be arguing, after acknowledging Burke's debt to Dewey, to stress how the "practical" or the "pragmatic" manifests itself in Burke's work in the realm of *rhetoric*, not pragmatism. Gunn plays down Burke's relationship to a future poststructuralism in order to stress his connection with a critical tradition running from Emerson to Dewey, and he leaves out how important rhetoric became for Burke after the publication of *A Grammar of Motives*.[5] On the other hand, I want to insist on the extent to which Burke anticipates both poststructuralism and the New Rhetoric. In this way I will be stressing how Burke breaks with both the genteel tradition and Deweyan and Jamesian pragmatism.

Burke worked out the critical position in *Counter-Statement* over the course of the 1920s, a time when his early aestheticism began to give way in response to political, social, and intellectual changes to a more practical and oppositional approach to writing and criticism. Burke's critical position in 1931 resulted from on the one hand his rejection of an early Kantian strain in his thinking and on the other an acceptance of certain elements of Marxism. This shift in allegiance from Kantianism to a version of Marxism can be traced in the differences between the early and late essays in *Counter-Statement* (1931), differences that mark a shift in his interest from aesthetics and literature to a new, much broader interest in culture and communication. This transformation was precipitated by a real crisis in his career, one that began as he was finishing *Counter-Statement*. Just at the moment when he had worked out a formalist aesthetic based on art as self-expression, many of his good friends and acquaintances (including Malcolm Cowley, Matthew Josephson, Granville Hicks, and Robert Cantwell) became increasingly engaged with Marxism. They and other Marxist-oriented literary intellectuals were becoming interested in the "practical" relation between literature and the material conditions of its production, and had begun to discuss literature in terms of its relationship to the dominant values of the ruling class. Burke, however, had just finished nearly a decade of work elaborating a theory of literary form based on the conviction that literature was fundamentally rooted in self-expression. To continue along the lines of the early essays in *Counter-Statement* would have been to pursue a line of thinking about literature he now saw as limited and isolating, but simply to "convert" to the Marxism popular among his associates would risk betraying convictions about the nature of art that ran deep. In a letter to Cowley on 3 October 1932 Burke outlines his predicament, without ever indicating explicitly that it is his particular predicament:

> The "practical" frame of reference is now catching up with the "esthetic" which was valiantly maintained in opposition to the "practical" for over a century . . . [T]he imminent catching up of the practical frame would seem to put many valiant protesters out of a job . . . What does the "esthetic" do next? If it celebrates the marriage of the practical and esthetic frames by "conforming" it risks violating the basic patterns of character out of which it arose . . . If he sings the joys of merger, he must quiet something very much like the most adventurous portions of his former self.[6]

Burke's plight as a modern critic is how to come to terms with the shifting balance between these two forces or frames. During most of the previous decade, Burke had identified himself with what he called the "aesthetic frame," the same "frame" or orientation we have already observed in Brooks and Dewey, who both ultimately maintained an aesthetic orientation "in opposition to the 'practical.'" The early essays in *Counter-Statement* were written within what Burke calls the "aesthetic frame," while the last essays mark a shift toward what he called the "practical." They reflect a shift away from purely aesthetic concerns toward an interest in literature's relation to ideology and the role of the aesthetic as an oppositional cultural force.

The "catching up" Burke refers to in the passage above recalls the rise of sociological and Marxist criticism in the late '20s and early '30s, and the "valiant protesters" include critics like himself who invested heavily in an aesthetic frame only to be put out of a job with the rapid rise of a practical frame rooted in Marxism. Criticism's growing "practical" preoccupation with art's relationship to society and its potential role in a revolutionary movement was, of course, part of a broad response among intellectuals to the Depression, to what seemed like the end of the capitalist system. In an interview with the author about this period Burke observed that by the late '20s the New York avant-garde movement seemed to him to have run its course, and the growing economic depression created a desperate situation that seemed to signal the very bankruptcy of capitalism. Burke recalled that he "really . . . had invested in a big way in the theory of art as self-expression," and that he was "forlorn when . . . the Marxist movement was coming in." Soon, however, he became "convinced that they had a point," that "Marxist criticism was the only one that was really, directly, on the point."[7]

The problem Burke had to face as he turned toward writing cultural criticism in the early '30s is suggested in his letter to Cowley: he had somehow to come to terms with Marxism, shifting his allegiance away from art as a form of self-expression toward art as a form of communication actively mediating—and mediated by—social forces. At the same time, however, he had to be careful not to "quiet something very much like the most adventurous portions of his former self." The strategy he developed was twofold. On the one hand, he took his commitment to the disruptive possibilities of modernist aesthetic principles (which had informed his earlier book of stories, *White Oxen* [1924]) and shifted them to criticism, articulating a critical style inspired by Nietzsche, James Joyce, and Dada. On the other hand, he began to develop a theory of cultural interpretation out of his critical engagement with Marx. These two projects produced an approach to cultural criticism in America that constituted a radical departure from anything envisioned by Santayana, Dewey, or Brooks. To trace the development of these two projects, we need to review some of the key essays that compose *Counter-Statement*.

The essays in *Counter-Statement* can generally be divided between those written between 1921 and 1925 ("Three Adepts of 'Pure' Literature," "Psychology and Form," "The Poetic Process," and "The Status of Art") and those written between 1926 and 1931 ("Thomas Mann and André Gide," "Program," "Lexicon Rhetoricae," and "Applications of the Terminology"). The earlier essays are preoccupied with literature from a predominantly aesthetic perspective. They are concerned with literary expression as self-expression, and with elaborating a theory of form. The later essays, on the other hand, begin to stress the social and ideological forces mediating "self" expression in art, modify the Kantian elements of Burke's formalism, and begin to treat aesthetic practice as a politically oppositional force. Thus, by the time he came to write his next work of criticism, *Permanence and Change* (1935), Burke (here he is writing about himself) "stressed interdependent, social, or collective aspects of meaning, in contrast with the individualistic emphasis of his earlier Aestheticist period" (214).

Burke's early aestheticism is best represented by "Psychology and Form" (begun in 1921), which contains his well-known definition of literary form as "the creation of an appetite in the mind of the auditor, and the adequate satisfying of that appetite" (31). The question of form is tied to *psychology*. However, "the psychology here is not the psychology of the *hero*, but the psychology of the *audience*" (31). This definition develops in the context of his discussion of the "breach" that has opened up "between form and subject-matter" in "the last century" (31). In Burke's view, the "flourishing of science" and the popularity of "scientific criteria" have impinged on what should be "purely aesthetic judgment[s]" (31). This had led to "derangements of taste" (32) in which subject matter has come to be valued over form or technique. Thus, "psychology has become a body of information . . . in art, we tend to look for psychology as the purveying of information" (32). In Burke's view, modernity has brought with it a preoccupation with subject matter or information in art, with a correspondent falling off of interest in form:

> Thus, the great influx of information has led the artist also to lay his emphasis on the giving of information—with the result that art tends more and more to substitute the psychology of the hero (the subject) for the psychology of the audience. Under such an attitude, when form is preserved it is preserved as an annex, a luxury, or, as some feel, a downright affectation. (32–33)

Essentially, Burke wants to reassert the importance of form because he deems it "purely aesthetic." In this respect he is not that far away from the kind of general preoccupation with form we observed in Dewey. Both share the conviction that art's essence inheres in the balance and harmony of purely formal relations, and that those relations are to be measured in terms of classical values of harmony and wholeness. When Burke goes on to insist, for example, that "the distinction between the psychology of information and the psychology of form involves a definition of aesthetic truth" (42), he writes that "truth in art is not the discovery of facts, not an addition to human knowledge," but "the exercise of human propriety, the formulation of symbols which rigidify our sense of poise and rhythm" (42). This last emphasis, of course, recalls the classical elements of Dewey's theory of form.

There is also, however, a pragmatic element in Burke's aesthetic approach to form: its rhetorical orientation. If form is related to the psychology of the audience, then Burke's is an essentially Aristotelian formalism in which the structure of a work is geared to move or affect an audience or reader in certain ways. The rhetorical emphasis here remains latent, but it looks forward to an increasing preoccupation that will culminate in two books on rhetoric, *A Rhetoric of Motives* (1950) and *The Rhetoric of Religion* (1961).

When Burke continues to pursue the question of form in another chapter, however, it is under the influence of Kant, not Aristotle. In "The Poetic Process," Burke argues that forms have an a priori status in relation to art, and he employs Kant's concept of categories of perception in the mind to make his case. Here is how he begins:

> If we wish to indicate a gradual rise to a crisis [in a work of art], and speak of this as a climax, or a crescendo, we are talking in intellectualist terms of a mechanism which can often be highly emotive . . . Over and over again in the history of art, different material has been arranged to embody the principle of the crescendo; and this must be so because we 'think' in a crescendo, because it parallels certain psychic and physical processes which are at the roots of our experience. (45)

From Burke's point of view, formal principles parallel certain a priori processes. This is what makes form "purely aesthetic." "Throughout the permutations of history," he writes, "art has always appealed to . . . certain potentialities of appreciation which would seem to be inherent in the very germ-plasm of man, and which, since they are constant, we might call innate forms of the mind" (46). Here, the aesthete in Burke is thoroughly Kantian (once again, he is not far from Dewey's position in *Art as Experience*): the aesthetic is defined as such by formal relations, and those relations correspond to "innate forms of the mind." When we deal with form in art, following this view, we deal with something that is related to the "universal," not the historical: "So eager were the nominalists to disavow Plato in detail," he writes, "that they failed to discover the justice of his doctrines in essence. For we need but take his universals out of heaven and situate them in the human mind (a process begun by Kant), making them not metaphysical, but psychological" (48). By the logic of this linkage, the rhetorical side of Burke's theory of form is muted, since here the "psychological" is linked explicitly to the realm of essences and universals.

Returning to his theory of form a few years later in the chapter he called "Lexicon Rhetoricae," however, Burke began to modify this Kantian emphasis as he reasserted the importance of rhetorical and historically specific elements in literature. This chapter, along with the "Program" chapter, embodies Burke's shift away from literary criticism rooted in aesthetics toward a form of cultural criticism rooted in a theory of rhetoric and a reading of Marx. This is the moment in Burke's development when what he called the "aesthetic frame" began to give way to the practical, or, to apply the terms of our study, when his metaphysical idealism began to give way to a more pragmatic emphasis.

This shift is signaled by a double impulse in "Lexicon Rhetoricae": the desire to produce what is in effect a structuralist approach to the analysis of form is matched by a desire to find a way to reconcile formalism with a historicist and ideological mode of criticism. Burke begins his chapter by positing "five aspects of form": syllogistic, qualitative, repetitive, conventional, and minor (124). Taken together, these five aspects of form constitute the "nature of form" (124). "Though the five aspects of form can merge into one another," he writes, "or can be present in varying degrees, no other terms should be required in an analysis of formal functionings" (129). In effect, these "aspects" of form correspond to something natural and essential in art, structural elements that seem to transcend history in a way that links them to Kant's categories of the mind and Aristotle's analysis of tragedy. Given this approach to form, the critic's task seems simply a matter of identifying the form—or interplay of forms—in particular works.

Particular forms, however, are not judged correct in terms of their proper correspondence to these a priori "aspects." Rather, "form . . . is 'correct' in so far as it gratifies the needs which it creates. The appeal of the form in this sense is obvious: form *is* the appeal" (138). Here, Burke's structuralist impulse gives way to his commitment to a pragmatic or rhetorical theory of form. Indeed, it turns out that what is important about form in art is less its correspondence to an a priori form than the way in which it *individuates* conventional forms for particular ideological purposes. Burke holds here to the idea that forms of experience are prior to, and determine, the forms we find in works of art, but now he wants to leave to "psychology" and "philosophy" the question of whether or not they are "innate or resultant" (141).[8] Moreover, he plays down the sheerly aesthetic element of form, insisting that "forms of art . . . are not exclusively 'aesthetic' . . . [since] they can be said to have a prior existence in the experiences of the person hearing or reading the work of art" (143).

At this point, Burke mixes formalism and historicism in a way reminiscent of Dewey. He takes two positions at the same time, the one openly Platonic, the other neo-Marxist. On the one hand, he "would restore the Platonic relationship between form and matter," since the subject matter of a "single poem or drama" is "an individuation of formal principles" (143). On the other hand, however, "the images of art change greatly with changes in the environment and the ethical systems out of which they arise" (143). Thus, Burke wants to argue that certain formal "principles of art" (his five aspects of form) "will be found to recur in all art," but that they are "individuated in one subject-matter or another" for specific historical and ideological reasons (143).

Burke devotes two separate sections of "Lexicon Rhetoricae" to discussions of ideology, a topic that doesn't come up in the chapters he wrote in the early '20s. In the first, "Form and Ideology," Burke builds on the theory of form he presented earlier in the book (form as the creation and fulfilling of an appetite) by pointing out the role of ideology in the successful operations of form. "The artist's manipulations of the reader's desires," he writes, "involve his use of what the reader considers desirable" (146). This means that the artist draws on the "vocabulary of belief" operative in his or her culture, that he or she must be "inventive" enough to "find something . . . exploitable in the ideology of his audience" (146). Burke goes so far here as to insist that "the correctness of the form depends upon the ideology" of the audience (147). The metaphysical side of Burke's theory of form seems nearly obliterated here, something he seems to recognize when he writes at the end of this section of the chapter that "shifts in ideology being continuous, not only from age to age but from person to person, the individuation of universal forms through specific subject-matter can bring the formal principles themselves into jeopardy" (147).

The tension in Burke's theory of form between a devotion, on the one hand, to Platonic Universals, and a commitment, on the other, to rhetoric, history, and ideology, represents his version of the tension between forms of transcendentalism and forms of pragmatism we have been charting in American cultural criticism from Emerson through Dewey. The shift in his work from an aesthetic to what he calls a "practical" orientation is completed in his "Program" chapter where, as I have already indicated, Burke turns his attention away from sheerly aesthetic matters toward the demands modernity was making on literary and cultural criticism. He begins his "Program" chapter by insisting that art is not to be defined in terms of some so-called universal set of characteristics having their origin in a consecrated classical ethos, but is always "historical—a particular mode of adjustment to a particular cluster of conditions" (107). He implicitly rejects the idea in both Brooks and Dewey that the artist, faced with a set of social conditions sufficiently new that they suggest something "modern," must turn toward a timeless and universally valid set of premodern aesthetic principles. Rather, he insists that art must actively respond to a particular "cluster of conditions."[9] The "Program" he lays out here attempts to sketch in the mode of adjustment now required for aesthetic practice. His aim, however, is not to "sum up the absolute, unchanging purposes of the aesthetic" (121). In this crucial sense his conception of the aesthetic departs again from Brooks and Dewey, for Burke insists on defining aesthetic practice in historically relative terms. He "would define the function of the aesthetic as effecting an adjustment of one particular cluster of conditions, *at this particular time in history*" (121, emphasis mine). He is not arguing, therefore, that the oppositional nature of aesthetic practice he has endorsed in the chapter represents art's timeless function. His definitions are strategic, not essentialist.

Burke's treatment of art also departs from Brooks and Dewey in that it deals sympathetically with modern and contemporary art. Burke calls attention to the incongruity between both the moral conservatism of the Southern Agrarians and the ethics of the industrial north on the one hand, and the aesthetic experiments of modern artists and writers on the other hand. The modern artist's "sensitiveness to change must place him at odds with the moral conservatism of the agrarians," for they will "prefer" the "unaware artist" who is "free of new emphases" (108–9). At the same time, the "industrialist elements are prepared to meet his innovations with resistance" (109), since they seem, at the very least, to have little to do with perpetuating their own values. The "procedures" of modern artists, then, seem to both conservatives and industrialists simply to represent a "'breakdown'" of old, more understandable procedures (109).[10] Burke, however, wants to articulate an activist role for the contemporary artist whose aesthetic innovations might serve to challenge the monolithic dominance of mechanization, consumption, and industrialization—what Burke calls the "practical."

In characterizing the "practical" and the "aesthetic" as "forces" Burke, like Brooks, sees the "practical" as a "menace" and the "aesthetic" as its "means of reclamation":

> In so far as the conversion of pure science into applied science has made the practical a menace, the aesthetic becomes a means of reclamation. Insofar as mechanization increases the complexity of the social structure . . . the aesthetic must serve as anti-mechanization, the corrective of the practical . . . The present essay asks that the aesthetic ally itself with a Program which might be defined roughly as a modernized version of the earlier bourgeois-Bohemian conflict. (100–11)

Burke's characterization of the "alignment of forces" clustered around the practical presents us with an amusing profile of modernity. The practical is represented by "efficiency, prosperity, material acquisitions, increased consumption, 'new needs,' expansion, higher standards of living, progressive rather than regressive evolution, in short, ubiquitous optimism. Enthusiasm, faith, evangelizing, Christian soldiering, power, energy, sales drives, undeviating certainties, confidence, co-

operation, in short, flags and all the jungle vigor that goes with flags"
(111). The alignment of forces on the side of the aesthetic, on the other
hand, represents values that work wholly to undermine the practical:
"inefficiency, indolence, dissipation, vacillation, mockery, distrust, 'hy-
pochondria,' non-conformity, bad sportsmanship, in short, negativism.
Experimentalism, curiosity, risk, dislike of propaganda, dislike of certainty—tentative attitude towards all manners of thinking which reinforce the natural dogmatism of the body" (111–12). Finally, the "practical" is equated with "patriotism," the aesthetic with "treason" (112).

Thus where the cultural programs of Brooks and Dewey envision art
pulling back from the kind of "practical" engagement Burke envisions
to return to its disinterested roots in self-expression or classical formalism, Burke's "Program" involves contemporary art's interested and
disruptive destabilization of industrial and economic modernity.[11]
Moreover, the disruptive nature of this destabilizing comes from its experimental or avant-garde elements, and from its transgressing the *values* of modernity. "The aesthetic," he insists, "would seek to discourage
the most stimulating values of the practical, would seek—by wit, by
fancy, by anathema, by versatility—to throw into confusion the code
which underlies commercial enterprise, industrial competition . . . would
seek to endanger the basic props of industry" (115).

The position Burke works out here is reemphasized in a later, well-
known essay, "Literature as Equipment for Living" (1938). He begins
the essay by drawing an analogy between literature and proverbs that
helps underscore the "strategic" element he wants to stress in all art.
"Proverbs," he points out, are not "pure literature," for "they are designed for consolation or vengeance, for admonition or exhortation, for
foretelling" (293). Proverbs "name typical, recurrent situations" because
"people find a certain social relationship recurring so frequently that
they must 'have a word for it'" (*Philosophy of Literary Form* 293). If there
is an element of "realism" in proverbs, Burke points out, it is not "realism for its own sake" but "realism for promise, admonition, solace,
vengeance, foretelling, instruction, charting, all for the direct bearing
that such acts have upon matters of welfare" (296).

Burke's simple proposal is that we "extend such analysis of proverbs
to the whole field of literature" (296). To do so, in his view, would allow
for a mode of criticism that would essentially unite its aesthetic and sociological forms. Treating literature as "proverbs writ large" (296) constitutes a turn toward rhetorical analysis that "should help us to discover important facts about literary organization (thus satisfying the
requirements of technical criticism). And the kind of observation from

this perspective should apply beyond literature to life in general (thus helping to take literature out of its separate bin and give it a place in a general 'sociological' picture)" (296). Burke's approach to literature here looks both back to the definition of form in *Counter-Statement* and forward to the kind of rhetorical analysis he proposes in *A Rhetoric of Motives*. For in the view he presents here, literary works "are *strategies* for dealing with *situations*. In so far as situations are typical and recurrent in a given social structure, people develop names for them and strategies for handling them" (296–97).

Burke's propensity for transgressing the categorical norms of critical thought is foregrounded at the end of the essay, where he moves beyond the desire to unite aesthetic and sociological criticism to embrace a violation of critical norms that would consciously "outrage good taste" (302). The outrage he has in mind is twofold. It relates to an approach to art based on principles that tend to disallow the great literature/popular literature dichotomy born of aesthetic criticism, and it leads to a breakdown of disciplinary specializations. Approaching literary works with a view toward analyzing how they "equip us to live" rather than simply judging the aesthetic merits of those works "might occasionally lead us to outrage good taste" because we may sometimes find "exemplified in some great sermon or tragedy or abstruse work of philosophy the same strategy as we found exemplified in a dirty joke" (302). The outrage here, of course, has to do with categorizing the dirty joke with literature, for "at this point, we'd put the sermon and the dirty joke together, thus 'grouping by situation' and showing the range of possible particularizations" (302). This leads Burke to make the oft-quoted response to the following remark by R. P. Blackmur: "I think on the whole his [Burke's] method could be applied with equal fruitfulness to Shakespeare, Dashiell Hammett, or Marie Corelli" (302).[12] Burke not only endorses this idea, but pushes it further: "You can't properly put Marie Corelli and Shakespeare apart until you have first put them together. First genus, then differentia. The strategy in common is the genus. The *range* or *scale* or *spectrum* of particularizations is the differentia" (302). Here, of course, Burke has come to totally reject, in practical terms, the distinction made famous by Brooks and embraced by Dewey between highbrow and lowbrow art. Burke has cut loose completely from a criticism based on the principles of aesthetic formalism. His critical orientation remains strongly formalist, but he has become interested in the strategic elements of form, and in foregrounding the classification of forms with reference to social strategies.

The second outrage to good taste in Burke's proposition is that the method he proposes "automatically breaks down the barriers erected about literature as a specialized pursuit . . . Sociological classification, as herein suggested, would derive its relevance from the fact that it should apply both to works of art and to social situations outside of art" (303). What Burke is acknowledging here is the *institutional* effects of the position he stakes out around the question of grouping Marie Corelli and Shakespeare together. As he moves toward a rhetorical mode of criticism influenced by Marxism, he displaces aesthetic idealism as a principle for grouping works and as a logic upon which to found institutions of education. The problem with "current [critical] pieties," he insists, is that their "categories" have become "inert"; "I think what we need is active categories" (303). Such categories would "lie on the bias across the categories of modern specialization," which too often are taken as "an exact replica of the way in which God himself divided up the universe . . . Among other things, a sociological approach should attempt to provide a reintegrative point of view, a broader empire of investigation" that is crossdisciplinary (303–4).

The "Program" chapter of *Counter-Statement*, anticipating as it does the position he elaborates in "Literature as Equipment for Living," represents an important moment in Burke's development as a cultural critic, one profoundly influenced by aesthetic modernism. During this period Burke emerges from the long shadow cast by nineteenth-century writers like Flaubert, Dostoevski, Pater, and De Gourmont toward an interest in Joyce, the Dadaists, surrealism, and Nietzsche, Marx, and Freud. His intellectual engagement with these figures contributed significantly to his development as a cultural critic who sought to incorporate and synthesize the stylistic experiments and philosophical, psychological, and political thought of modernism in his own work. This synthesis marks the nature of Burke's engagement with the problem of modernity, and underscores what a significant departure it is from the work of critics like Brooks and Dewey who, in many ways, remain tied to the nineteenth century.

Burke's longevity as a critic makes it easy to forget that his intellectual development took place among the New York avant-garde. He was praising (and writing) free verse in 1917, composing experimental fiction in the early twenties, and actively involved as an editor with such avant-garde magazines as *Broom* and *Secession*. Burke makes his interest in avant-garde aesthetics clear in his correspondence during the teens and twenties with Cowley.[13] Though Burke was often critical of the Dadaists—they were, he wrote to Cowley in March of 1923, "too willing to laugh before the joke"[14]—he recognized that "if any of us does anything of lasting import, it will be done with the same equipment which the Dadaists are using."[15]

Burke's conscious incorporation in his literary and cultural criticism of modernist philosophical and political positions was complemented by his attempt to enact a *critical style* consonant with modernist principles like those of Joyce and the Dadaists. That style, which is meant to reinforce in the very language of criticism the kind of subversion of social codes and the disruptive intervention of avant-garde aesthetic practice Burke espoused in his "Program" and in "Literature as Equipment for Living," developed in an approach to critical writing he called "perspective by incongruity."

The concept of "perspective by incongruity" is at the heart of the critical theory he unfolds in *Permanence and Change*. Building on the "Program" and "Lexicon Rhetoricae" chapters of *Counter-Statement*, *Permanence and Change* studies the relationship between interpretive systems (personal, philosophical, political) and social, political, and ideological change. It focuses on the ways in which language and ideology contribute to the formation of our interpretations of the nature of "reality," how those interpretations lead to states of permanence, and how changes in interpretive orientation are necessary for reality to change. The book, then, seems to be a specific response to Dewey's challenge near the end of *Art as Experience*: "there is one problem that artist, philosopher, and critic alike must face: the relation between permanence and change" (322).[16] Since the book marks his break with an earlier formalism, it picks up where Dewey's critical method stalls out. That is, while Dewey's work on art ends with the reassertion of an essentially classical theory of form, Burke moves away from traditional formalism on two fronts: in the metacritical nature of his inquiry into interpretive activity, and in his increasing interest in the relationship between ideology and aesthetic production (and consumption).

The critical style derived from what Burke calls "perspective by incongruity" is directly linked to his critique of philosophical knowledge, and more specifically, to his discussion of the relationship between metaphor and "truth." At the outset of *Permanence and Change* Burke writes that his focus will be on "the criticism of criticism" (6). What he has to say here is, in the light of poststructuralism, rather familiar. In his long opening section, "On Interpretation," Burke insists that our experiences do not have *absolute* meanings, that "any given situation derives its character from the entire framework of interpretation by which we judge it" (35). Moreover, our interpretations are crucially determined by what Burke calls our "orientations," a term he uses in place of ideology. By "orientation" he means "a bundle of judgments as to how things were, how they are, and how they may be" (14). Thus, meanings are not self-evident precisely because we produce them as we interpret events in terms of our presuppositions. For Burke, an "orientation" is, in effect, a "vocabulary" that provides us with a serviceable schema for making sense of the world around us. "Our minds," he writes, "as linguistic products, are composed of concepts (verbally molded) which select certain relationships as meaningful . . . These relationships are not *realities,* they are *interpretations* of reality—hence different frameworks of interpretation will lead to different conclusions as to what reality is" (35). The rest of *Permanence and Change* takes up the implications of this insight, as Burke goes on to examine how interpretive vocabularies both authorize and delimit our views of the Real, and how explanatory accounts of human motivation are themselves motivated by interpretive frameworks.

The question of style comes into play in his ensuing discussion of the "criticism of criticism," since Burke goes on to insist that all truth claims are made by the substitution of a metaphor for a "fact." Burke denies any essential difference between abstract and metaphorical language, and he offers a thoroughgoing deconstruction of the binary oppositions metaphorical/truthful, analogical/logical, poetic/rational. "When we describe in abstract terms," he writes, "we are not sticking to the facts at all, we are substituting something else for them just as much as if we were using an out and out metaphor" (95). As far as Burke is concerned, the poet's metaphors and the philosopher's and scientist's abstractions are both examples of substitution, the discussion of one thing in terms of another. Stressing the "metaphorical nature of all speech," Burke insists on defining words as "symbolizations" rather than as "accurate and total names for specific, unchangeable realities" (110). "Those who have criticized the use of metaphor" as an instrument of analysis, he writes, "have for the most part not realized how little removed such description is from the ordinary intellectual method of analysis" (95).

Burke's critique of the role of metaphor in rationalist, philosophical, and scientific vocabularies of interpretation and explanation constitutes a radical extension of his position in the "Program" chapter of *Counter-Statement.* There, the poetic and metaphoric resources of aesthetic practice are brought critically to bear on the social codes of science and mechanization. Here, the very difference between the two languages or codes is questioned. This move is integral to Burke's own development in *Permanence and Change* of a poetic or dramatistic style of analysis and critical writing. Harold Bloom has written that "the language of American criticism ought to be pragmatic and outrageous" ("Agon" 21)—pragmatic in the sense of accomplishing a specific practical end, and outrageous in the sense of transgressing the codes of critical decorum and "good taste."[17] This transgression is at the heart of Burke's critical style. What Bloom would call his outrageous pragmatism is connected to the "change" side of his focus on "permanence and change." He wants to elaborate what he calls a "corrective philosophy" as against the predominant style of rationalist, scientific thinking, and he wants that philosophy to have poetic "standards" and a poetic style (66). Its "criterion," he continues, should be "based upon pragmatic demands and not offered as revelation." He wants, finally, to make a "direct attempt to *force* the critical structure by shifts of perspective" (169). Here again, we can see the broad outlines of his "Program" being transformed into a *poetics* of cultural criticism. Just as in *Counter-Statement* Burke wanted to be clear that what he was proposing in terms of the aesthetic "menacing" the practical was a historically specific, not an essential, role for the aesthetic, here he puts a "pragmatic" demand on poetry in its service to the language of cultural criticism. The interventionist mode of his "Program"—its desire to use a radical aesthetics to "interfere" with cultural "codes"—is matched by his insistence on forcing shifts in perspective through radical innovations in both the method and the language of criticism.

"By shifts of perspective" turns out to be a crucial term, since in *Permanence and Change* Burke announces and begins to use a style of writing appropriate to a mode of analysis that focuses on the role of metaphor in the production of knowledge, and that seeks to exploit that role in its own elaboration of a "corrective philosophy." It is a critical language meant to offer new *perspectives,* that is, new interpretations, by the *incongruous* juxtaposition of terms from two different, perhaps even contradictory, contexts. He calls this style "perspectives by incongruity," which he defines as "extending the use of a term by taking it from the context in which it was habitually used and applying it to another" (89). If "a word belongs by custom to a certain category," Burke elaborates in *Attitudes toward History,* "by rational planning you wrench it loose and metaphorically apply it to a different category" (308). Based as it is on the power of metaphor to *name* and explain, Burke calls this methodology the "methodology of the pun" (311)—the term itself is a good example of a perspective by incongruity, since we don't usually associate puns with a methodology, or vice versa. Two brief examples from *Permanence and Change* demonstrate what the methodology produces. When Burke uses the phrase "psychoanalytic seer" (125), he creates a perspective by incongruity that amounts to a kind of poetic meditation on psychoanalysis, one that emphasizes the elements of the prophetic and the mystical in what Freud urged was a science. The phrase uses a poetic rather than a rationalist style to generate an interpretation in miniature of psychoanalysis. Likewise, the phrase "terminology of motives" (125) suggests what was then an incongruous linkage between motivation and terminologies. The phrase poetically compresses the notion that motives can have the *logic* of terms in a language, suggesting that there might be such a thing as a grammar of motives. Neither phrase seems to make much sense in rationalist terms, for the style of their coinage is based less on logic than on the surprise inherent in the kind of wordplay we usually associate with poetry.

Burke's critique of the role of metaphor in Western philosophical thought, related as it is to his ideas about the place of style in critical discourse, affects his own writing as it becomes less discursive and more strategically poetic. In "perspective by incongruity" Burke begins to develop an essentially poetic mode of critical writing, for it is designed around a punning strategy meant to constitute both a methodology and an epistemology. It is a nonlinear, pun-based style of writing raised to the instrumental level of method and grounded in a recognition of the inherent metaphoricity of all philosophical and critical discourse.

In *Attitudes toward History* Burke links his critical style with a "dramatistic" critical vocabulary (311), "with weighting and counterweighting" as opposed to the "*neutral* naming" usually associated with what he calls the "liberal ideal." Burke argues here that "terms" are "characters" and the "essay is an attenuated play" (312). The critical style he elaborates here is based on his notion that there is an "element of dramatic *personality* in essayistic *ideas*," and that "names ... are shorthand designations for certain fields and methods of action" (312). Thus he speaks not only of the pragmatic, methodical aims of writers like Henry Adams, Nietzsche, and Blake, but of the "personal moodiness" of their styles, and how they embody certain attitudes (386).[18]

Nietzsche was the key influence for Burke as he thought about critical style, and about the relationship between critical style, interpretation, and the pragmatic *aims* of critical discourse. In fact, his concept of "perspectives by incongruity" developed, as he explains early on in *Permanence and Change*, in his effort to puzzle out the "source" of what he calls Nietzsche's "dartlike" style of writing: "In reading Nietzsche, one must be struck by the pronounced *naming* that marks his page.

Nietzsche's later style is like a sequence of *darts* . . . His sentences are forever striking out at this or that, exactly like a man in the midst of game, or enemies. They leap with a continual abruptness and sharpness of naming, which seems to suggest nothing so much as those saltations by which cruising animals suddenly leap upon their prey . . . He vigorously constructed pages that put the raging of his brain before us" (88).[19] Burke links the sometimes outrageous vocabulary Nietzsche employs—"Nietzsche," he reminds us, "establishes his perspective by a constant juxtaposing of incongruous words, attaching to some name a qualifying epithet which had heretofore gone with a different order of names," using *metaphor* to reveal unsuspected connections (90)—to Nietzsche's theory about the status of truth statements and the pragmatic aims of his "transvaluation of values." Burke noticed that Nietzsche used the words "perspective" and "perspectivism" throughout *The Will to Power* to argue that "facts" are not objective, but subjective. They are interpretations rather than reflections of reality. For example, Nietzsche writes: "Against positivism, which halts at phenomena—'There are only *facts*'—I would say: No, facts is precisely what there is not, only interpretations. We cannot establish any fact 'in itself:' perhaps it is folly to want to do such a thing . . . In so far as the word 'knowledge' has any meaning, the world is knowable: but it is *interpretable* otherwise it has no meaning behind it, but countless meanings.—'Perspectivism'" (267). For Nietzsche—and this is what Burke notes—a perspective gained by the incongruous juxtaposition of "incompatible" terms is knowledge gained by metaphor. Metaphor marks the relationship between knowledge and interpretation, and suggests a style of creating such knowledge in the act of analysis.

In *Permanence and Change* Burke acknowledges that the kind of critical style he elaborates under the rubric of "perspectives by incongruity" violates "good taste," critical decorum, and what he calls the "proprieties of words" (90). But this is precisely why he finds such a style appropriate. It extends into the realm of critical discourse the idea in his "Program" that the aesthetic (or what he is calling here the "poetic") should menace the practical. The violation of cultural codes he advocates for the aesthetic in *Counter-Statement* becomes the very task of the language of cultural criticism he advocates in *Permanence and Change,* since he wants to write in a style that will "force" "critical structures" and enact a "corrective philosophy with poetic standards." Thus, he points out how perspectives by incongruity "appeal by exemplifying relationships between objects which our customary rational vocabulary has ignored" (90). In straining "at the limits of 'good taste,'" his style means to force "analogical extensions, or linguistic inventions, not sanctioned by the previous usages of his group" (103), for, he insists, "one must violate the tenor of one's own culture as the members of his culture know it," if, indeed, one's aim is to overturn conventional structures of thinking, interpretation, and criticism (107). Thus there is something purposefully outrageous and destructive about the kind of style he outlines here: He calls for a "merger of contradictions [and] . . . imperfect matchings, giving scientific terms for words usually treated sentimentally, or poetic terms for the concepts of science, or discussing disease as an accomplishment, or great structures of thought as an oversight" (122). "Planned incongruity," he writes, "should be deliberately cultivated for the purpose of experimentally wrenching apart all those molecular combinations of adjective and noun, substantive and verb, which still remain with us. It should subject language to the same 'cracking' process that chemists now use in their refining of oil" (122). This is a logical extension into the practice of cultural criticism of the position he takes in his "Program" toward aesthetic practice per se.

While Burke in *Permanence and Change* traces the source of his critical style back to Nietzsche, he also links it explicitly to Joyce's punning style and to the styles of symbolism, surrealism, and Dada. In making clear that his writing represents a kind of crossbreeding between the radical philosophical theories and styles of Nietzsche, and the aesthetic styles of the then-contemporary avant-garde, Burke makes the self-consciously modernist nature of his critical project explicit. Burke writes in *Permanence and Change* that "Joyce, blasting apart the verbal atoms of meaning, and out of the ruins making new elements synthetically, has produced our most striking instances" of "perspectives by incongruity" (113). Joyce's "verbal blasting" is akin to the "cracking process" Burke views as central to the play of language at it decomposes and recomposes knowledge. The affinity of Burke's style with other elements of the avant-garde is also emphasized when he links surrealism to "perspectives by incongruity": "The notion of perspective by incongruity has obvious bearing upon . . . the symbolism of both dreams and dream-art," which merges "things which common sense had divided and [divides] things which common sense had merged" (113). He identifies his critical style at work, for example, in the surrealism of Dali, "who may show us a watch, dripping over the table like spilled molasses, not merely as an affront to our everyday experience with watches as rigid, but because a *dripping* watch gives us glimpses into a *different symbolism of time*" (113). And "Dadaism, in many ways the movement out of which [surrealism] grew, revealed an organized hatred of good taste, courted a deliberate flouting of the appropriate, and thus is squarely in the movement toward planned incongruity" (115).

For Burke the style of modernism, from his vantage point in the early thirties, is precisely the style of a planned incongruity that flouts and seeks to undermine "the appropriate." The issue for Burke is *representation*, the representation of the object of critical study in an age when the relation of the critical text to its object shifts from being a mimetic to a constitutive one. The most radical aspect of Burke's evolving theory of language at this time is his recognition that language—inherently metaphorical—constructs rather than reflects knowledge. His development as a modernist critic has its roots in this recognition, and in his understanding that it had to be put into practice—at the stylistic level—in his own work. In Burke we observe a systematic appropriation of Nietzsche's perspectivism grafted to avant-garde aesthetic theories in the attempt to forge a "corrective philosophy with poetic standards." Once the critical issue, for Burke, becomes representation, his own style of representation becomes responsive to that critique.

For all of these reasons Burke's work in the late '20s and early '30s represents a decided break with what Santayana called the "genteel tradition" in American philosophical thought. He shares in good measure Dewey's pragmatist approach to knowledge and truth, and Brooks's response to the rise of science and big business. But at the same time, Burke taps into the "bohemian" side of American thought Santayana associated with Whitman, and merges the pragmatist critique of philosophy with the more radical critique mounted by Nietzsche. Burke's embrace of modernist aesthetic principles, moreover, thoroughly disrupts the more genteel aesthetic of someone like Dewey; the refinement, elegance, and respectability that form the core values of Dewey's view of art give way in Burke to the values of disruption, fragmentation, and opposition in a willful gesture of disrespect. There is, in Burke, over against Dewey, a radical transvaluation of value that marks the end of the genteel tradition. Combining modernist aesthetic principles with a Nietzschean critique of knowledge, Burke breaks with that tradition in a way that looks directly ahead to poststructuralism.[20]

We have seen that the tension between idealism and pragmatism that underlies American cultural criticism from Emerson to Dewey plays itself out quite explicitly in Burke's attempt to shift his work from an "aesthetic" to a "practical" orientation. The "Program" chapter of *Counter-Statement* marks his break with an earlier aestheticism, and by the time he had turned to writing *Permanence and Change,* he was on his way toward producing criticism that drew explicitly on modernist principles and that focused broadly on the relationship between art, criticism, and cultural change, and on the *strategic* elements of form and the social function of ideology and interpretation. Burke's increasing preoccupation with such practical matters came to a head in the theory of rhetoric he laid out in *A Rhetoric of Motives* (1950). It would be inaccurate to argue that Burke simply started out as an aesthete and ended up a rhetorician, that he shifted his work from one fixed and separate category (idealist aesthetics) to another (rhetoric). Burke's project is striking because he consciously blurs these two categories. The transcendentalizing side of his approach to art (the one I have called Kantian) was from the beginning counterbalanced by a desire to deal with art in terms of its historical specificity, to pay attention to its strategic aims, and to insist on its socially disruptive possibilities. A number of Burke's formulations in his early books consciously violate the separate categories of the aesthetic and the practical. His theory of form, in *Counter-Statement,* for example, based as it is on the idea that form is an arousing and fulfilling of desire in the audience, is as rhetorical in its orientation as it is aesthetic, since he defines form in terms of a function that is essentially rhetorical. Likewise, his "principle of individuation" is designed to ground the so-called universal elements of art in historically specific rhetorical contexts. This is the case, as well, with the discussions of ideology we reviewed in *Counter-Statement,* where the form and subject matter of art are understood in terms of an appeal based on a specific set of norms and values. Finally, Burke's approach to critical style collapses the categories of the aesthetic and the practical in its insistence on the instrumental nature of style. These are not moments of contradiction. They represent on Burke's part a methodical attempt to subvert a separation deeply ingrained in Western metaphysical thought since Plato.

Burke desires in *A Rhetoric of Motives* to reclaim rhetoric as an "instrument" (xiii) for literary and cultural criticism. Burke's interest in this regard is twofold: (1) to show "how a rhetorical motive is often present where it is not usually recognized, or thought to belong," and in so doing to "rediscover rhetorical elements that had become obscured when rhetoric as a term fell into disuse, and other specialized disciplines such as esthetics, anthropology, psychoanalysis, and sociology came to the fore" (xiii), and (2) to "develop" rhetoric "beyond the traditional bounds of rhetoric" (xiii), to "systematically extend the range of rhetoric" (35), to "contemplate" its "bearing both on literary criticism in particular and on human relations in general" (169).

A Rhetoric of Motives underscores the extent of Burke's break with the genteel tradition in American philosophy and cultural criticism. Reclaiming rhetoric as an essential tool for literary and cultural analysis, Burke solidifies the shift he began in the early thirties away from the kind of aesthetic orientation we have identified in critics like Brooks and Dewey. Burke's conviction that the value of rhetoric needs to be reclaimed in an era in which specialized disciplines have allowed it to become moribund echoes his remarks about the traditional categories of modern specialization in "Literature as Equipment for Living." There he observed that each of the disciplines had developed "its own peculiar way of life, its own values, even its own special idiom for seeing, thinking, and 'proving'" (303). Developing rhetoric beyond its traditional bounds represents an attempt to use it as a basis for the kind of "reintegrative" approach to knowledge he called "sociological" in the earlier essay. In Burke's view, rhetoric has the potential to methodologically bridge the distances created by disciplinary boundaries, breaking down the kind of discrete specializations Habermas associates with modernity. Moreover, in the context of Burke's approach to rhetoric, the categories of high and low art, which have increasingly driven criticism in the modern period, begin to dissolve. All of this is consistent with the kind of focus on "strategic" rather than purely aesthetic qualities in art we saw in "Literature as Equipment for Living," which led to the position he took on grouping together such disparate writers as Shakespeare and Marie Corelli.

Burke attempts to reclaim rhetoric by extending the range of traditional conceptions of rhetoric associated with Aristotle, Cicero, Quintilian, and Saint Augustine: he claims that the kind of persuasion associated with rhetoric is a persuasion to *attitude* based on a principle of *identification*. Burke begins his discussion of "Traditional Principles of Rhetoric" with Cicero's definition of rhetoric as "Speech designed to persuade" (49), and reminds us that "three hundred years before him, Aristotle's *Art of Rhetoric* had similarly named 'persuasion' as the essence and end of rhetoric" (49). If you add Quintilian's *Institutio oratoria* and Saint Augustine's *De doctrina Christiana* "you have ample material, in these four great peaks stretched across 750 years, to observe the major principles derivable from the notion of rhetoric as persuasion, as inducement to action" (50).

Burke accepts these traditional definitions of rhetoric, but wants to shift the rhetorical analyst's attention away from cataloguing modes of persuasion toward a more subtle focus on how language operates to socialize beliefs and behavior. It would be more accurate, he insists, to "speak of persuasion 'to attitude' rather than persuasion to out-and-out-action . . . Persuasion involves choice, will; it is directed to a man only insofar as he is *free* . . . Insofar as they *must* do something, rhetoric is unnecessary" (50). Since a choice of action resulting from a discursive situation is always restricted in some way, rhetoric has to "seek . . . to have a formative effect upon *attitude*" (50). Thus, any discourse that seeks to have such a formative effect will come under the scrutiny of the rhetorical analyst, and "rhetoric" as a practice will broaden both the forms of representation it deems appropriate for analysis and the forms of attention it will pay to them:

> Thus the notion of persuasion to *attitude* would permit the application of rhetorical terms to purely *poetic* structures; the study of lyrical devices might be classed under the head of rhetoric, when these devices are considered for their power to induce or communicate states of mind to readers, even though the kinds of assent evoked have no overt, practical outcome. (50)

Reclaiming rhetoric in this way for the analysis of poetry, Burke displaces aesthetics (especially the classical kind we observed in Dewey) as the center of the criticism of poetry. Holding aesthetic theory responsible for the very concept of "pure" poetry, Burke applies rhetoric to the study of poetry and does away with the concept of "pure poetic structures" altogether.

Persuasion to attitude, in Burke's view, is related to a second process in discourse: "identification." It is the "key term" in Burke's study (xiii), the "instrument" he uses to "mark off areas of rhetoric" not usually associated with rhetoric (xiii). Communication aimed at persuasion (whether to attitude or action) is communication that somehow identifies the speaker's or writer's language and beliefs with the auditor's. "You persuade a man only insofar as you can talk his language by speech, gesture, tonality, order, image, attitude, idea, *identifying* your ways with his" (55). Identification has the central role it does in Burke's conception of rhetoric because it focuses attention on the socializing function of language and other forms of representation.

Burke insists that a rhetorical form of analysis highlighting the role of identification in discourse develops logically from the fact that societies are structured by "partisan" divisions. "*A Rhetoric [of Motives]*," he writes, "deals with the possibilities of classification in its *partisan* aspects; it considers the ways in which individuals are at odds with one another, or become identified with groups more or less at odds with one another" (22). In Burke's view, "identification is affirmed with ear-

nestness precisely because there is division. Identification is compen-
satory to division. If men were not apart from one another, there would
be no need for the rhetorician to proclaim their unity" (22).

Burke's approach to rhetoric in this regard was influenced in important ways by his reading of Marx, particularly *The German Ideology*. Discussing the book in *A Rhetoric of Motives*, Burke treats it as a contribution to rhetorical theory in a political mode. Indeed, Burke insists on
seeing Marxism itself as a rhetorical system:

> Whatever may be the claims of Marxism as a 'science,' its terminology is
> not a neutral 'preparation for action' but 'inducement to action.' In this
> sense, it is unsleepingly rhetorical, though much of its persuasiveness has
> derived from insistence that it is purely a science, with 'rhetoric' confined
> to the deliberate or unconscious deceptions of non-Marxist apologetics.
> (101)[21]

Sympathetic though he was to many of the tenets of Marxism, Burke
was, by the late '30s, interested less in the "scientific" nature of its insights than in its "inducement to action." He is interested in appropriating Marx's critique of bourgeois ideology as a model of rhetorical demystification.

In his discussion of Marx, Burke focuses on what he calls Marx's "demystification" of the language of both idealism and bourgeois capitalism. In his reading of *The German Ideology*, a kind of strong misreading
in the Bloomian sense, Burke construes the "analysis of 'ideology'" as
a "contribution to rhetoric" (109) by emphasizing the extent to which
Marx's reading of bourgeois capitalism focuses on the economy of the
linguistic transaction whereby historically produced material and social
conditions become the mere embodiment of universal essences (where
"empires . . . striving for *world markets*" become "the ways of 'universal
spirit'" [108]). *The German Ideology* is "a critique of capitalist rhetoric"
because it is "designed to disclose (unmask) sinister *factional* interests
concealed in the bourgeois terms for benign *universal* interests" (102).
Burke is interested less in Marx's critique of factional interests than in
Marx's insight about how language works rhetorically to perform the
kind of masking it does. It is the element of *concealment* in the verbal
economy of bourgeois capitalism Marx isolates that interests Burke, the
economy whereby factional interests are discursively repressed and reproduced as natural, universal ones.

Marxism emerges in this section of Burke's book as a rhetorical mode
of reading that helps extend methods of literary criticism to the criticism of culture. The form of Marxist analysis Burke isolates in *The Ger-*

man Ideology "admonishes us to look for 'mystification' at any point where the social divisiveness caused by property and the division of labor is obscured by unitary terms" (108), that is, at any point where conceptual language presents an interpretation of reality as a *reflection* of reality. Such "mystification" is a function of representation, and is inextricably tied up with the material workings of ideology, so that the kind of reading-as-demystification Burke embraces in Marx is, in his mind, a form of rhetorical criticism that can be applied to the reading of art and culture.

The rhetoric of capitalism's unitary terms is deemed to be a response to real economic and social divisions that become mystified by that rhetoric. Without such division there would be no need for the kind of persuasion through identification Burke is trying to foreground. This seems clearly to apply to political arguments, but Burke wants us to understand its application as well to a form of representation like poetry. The statement about "poetic structures" quoted above is to the point: "the study of lyrical devices might be classed under the head of rhetoric, when these devices are considered for their power to induce or communicate states of mind to readers, even though the kinds of assent evoked have no overt, practical outcome." Such communication, in Burke's view, is always at least implicitly partisan as it moves us to identify with certain experiences, attitudes, and beliefs.

Burke is interested in the process or mechanism he calls identification because it allows for a rhetorical analysis of representation and discourse that can scrutinize how "assent" develops in individuals and groups when there seems to be no "overt, practical outcome" urged by that discourse. Too clean a line between the poetic and the political, Burke suggests, obscures the degree to which poetry and the other arts involve us in a circuit of representation that is both the product of, and productive of, the kinds of norms, standards, and beliefs we associate broadly with the term ideology. This is a point we can trace back to the discussions of ideology in *Counter-Statement*, where we observed Burke writing that "the artist's manipulations of the reader's desires involve his use of what the reader considers desirable" (146). Finding "something exploitable in the ideology of his audience" (146) corresponds to creating an identification between a dramatic situation and the set of values it is dealing with, and the situation and set of values of your audience. Where in *Counter-Statement* Burke is interested in appropriate form ("the correctness of the form depends upon the ideology" the writer must draw on [147]), in *A Rhetoric of Motives* he is interested in appropriate language or rhetoric—the persuasiveness of the discourse depends upon the extent to which it leads the auditor to identify with it.[22]

Focusing on the role of identification in representation is a logical extension of the kind of postfoundationalist orientation Burke developed in *Permanence and Change*. For "the kind of opinion with which rhetoric deals, in its role of inducement to action, is not opinion *as contrasted with truth*. There is the invitation to look at the matter thus antithetically, once we have put the two terms (opinion and truth) together as a dialectical pair. But actually, many of the 'opinions' upon which persuasion relies fall out-side the test of truth in the strictly scientific, T-F, yes-or-no sense . . . 'Opinion' in this ethical sense clearly falls on the bias across the matter of 'truth' in the strictly scientific sense" (54).

Burke's stress on identification also continues the critique of art's autonomy begun in *Counter-Statement*. "Any specialized activity," whether aesthetic or critical, "participates in a larger unit of action. 'Identification' is a word for the autonomous activity's place in this wider context, a place with which the agent may be unconcerned" (27). Thus while we may insist that works of literature or art are autonomous, that they transcend ideological positions or historical moments, that very insistence identifies art with a certain politically charged assertion about art that reveals the impossibility of such autonomy. For example, "with much college education today in literature and the fine arts, the very stress upon the pure autonomy of such activities is a roundabout way of identification with a privileged class, as the doctrine may enroll the student stylistically under the banner of a privileged class" (28).[23] To persuade a student about art's autonomy is less to persuade him or her about some truth than to get the student to identify with a political position toward art (that it should be treated as apolitical). Thus Burke warns that, "in accordance with the rhetorical principle of identification, whenever you find a doctrine of 'nonpolitical' esthetics affirmed with fervor, look for its politics" (28).

Burke's critique of the idea that works of art can in any way be construed as "autonomous" matches his analysis of individual autonomy. He insists on a link between what we think of as "identity" and the process of identification he locates in rhetoric. Individual identity, in Burke's view, is inextricably tied up with processes of socialization that depend heavily on the persuasive powers of identification. "We are clearly in the region of rhetoric," he writes, "when considering the identifications whereby a specialized activity makes one a participant in some social or economic class" (27–28). Our identities develop in response to our sense of "who" we are in relation to groups and their dis-

courses, so that "'belonging'" is itself "rhetorical" (28). Once identification is given a central place in rhetoric, forms of rhetorical analysis
become important in understanding how we come to identify ourselves
by gender, class, political ideology, and so on. Indeed, the ways in
which identification and ideology function in culture turn out to be
quite similar.

Both identification and ideology as Burke uses the terms are related
to the phenomenon we now call, after Gramsci, hegemony. Burke never
uses the word, but Frank Lentricchia has called our attention to how his
interest in "the power of systematic thought to reproduce and extend itself while at the same time engendering internal fissures and conflicts"
suggests Gramsci's concept (75). "Hegemony," in Lentricchia's summary, is a "Marxist account of the decentered subject" that refers "fundamentally [to] a process of education carried on through various institutions of civil society in order to make normative, inevitable, even
'natural' the ruling ideas of ruling interests. The hegemonic process is
a way of gaining 'free' assent" (76). Burke's various discussions of ideology, and his stress in *Permanence and Change* on the role of language
in the construction of subjectivity, effectively decenter the subject in relation to conventional Cartesian notions of identity. This hegemonic approach to the self continues in *A Rhetoric of Motives* in Burke's stress on
how the process of identification becomes internalized. There is, Burke
insists, an "ingredient of rhetoric in all *socialization*, considered as a *moralizing* process. The individual person, striving to form himself in accordance with the communicative norms that match the cooperative
ways of his society, is by the same token concerned with the rhetoric of
identification. To act upon himself persuasively, he must variously re-
sort to images and ideas that are formative. Education ('indoctrina-
tion') exerts such pressure upon him from without; he completes the
process from within" (39). This acting upon oneself is precisely what
Gramsci had in mind in his analysis of hegemony.[24]

We can observe this connection by looking briefly at Burke's treatment of the terms "identity" and "identification" in *Attitudes toward
History*. In a discussion of identity and subjectivity that looks forward
to his comprehensive treatment of identification in *A Rhetoric of Motives*,
Burke begins by questioning the "bourgeois naturalism" of the Cartesian self:

> Bourgeois naturalism in its most naive manifestation made a blunt dis-
> tinction between 'individual' and 'environment,' hence leading automat-
> ically to the notion that an individual's 'identity' is something private,

> peculiar to himself. And when bourgeois psychologists began to discover the falsity of this notion, they still believed in it so thoroughly that they considered all collective aspects of identity under the head of pathology and illusion. That is: they discovered accurately enough that identity is *not* individual, that a man 'identifies himself' with all sorts of manifestations beyond himself, and they set about trying to 'cure' him of this tendency. (263)

Burke's decentering of the Cartesian self here turns on severing the relationships between identity and the individual. Identity is less the reflection of an internal irruption of private, spiritual being (as it was for Emerson) than the effect of a network of identifications resulting from the rhetorical context in which socialization unfolds. The "decentering" in Burke's analysis of identity is rooted in his insistence that no "identity" or ground of being exists outside the social structure of identifications that constitute subjectivity. The tendency of humans to identify themselves with "manifestations" beyond themselves can't be "cured" for "the simple reason that it is *normal*" (263); there can be no cure for such identifications grounded outside the structure of identifications itself. "The psychoanalyst," for example, " 'cures' his patient of a faulty identification only insofar as he smuggles in *an alternative identification*" (264). However, "identification is not in itself abnormal; nor can it be 'scientifically' eradicated. One's participation in a collective, social role cannot be obtained in any other way. In fact, 'identification' is hardly other than a name for the *function of sociality*" (266–67).

For this reason, Burke insists on trading in the metaphor of the self as a singular individual being synonymous with consciousness for one based on a more modern economy. "The so-called 'I,' " he concludes, "is merely a unique combination of partially conflicting 'corporate we's' " (264). There is nothing particularly new about this formulation, coming as it does in the wake—and under the influence of—the critiques of bourgeois subjectivity mounted by Marx and Nietzsche.[25] What is notable about Burke's approach to subjectivity, however, is its explicit connection to a theory of rhetoric. Influenced as it is by the ideological critique of individuality mounted by Marx and by the epistemological one formulated by Nietzsche, it builds on what Burke sees as the implicitly rhetorical orientation of both in its foregrounding of the discursive context in which the social construction of "individuality" takes place. Burke rethinks the relationship between identity and socialization in the process of radically rethinking the very nature of socialization itself from the point of view of rhetorical theory. What is notable about Burke in terms of the critical tradition we have been

exploring is the linguistic turn his criticism takes. In Burke, the engagement with problems specific to modernity (especially the legitimation
crisis and the problem of autonomy) turns into a self-consciously *modernist* one in the sense that he employs the linguistic, stylistic, and
philosophical arsenal of the modernist critique of modernity (from
Nietzsche to Joyce) in his attempt to fashion a language-centered approach to cultural criticism.[26] By this I don't mean that his work becomes "postmodern." Rather, he raises to a new and intensive level the
kind of metacritical self-consciousness we saw Foucault link to modernity in his essay on Kant and the Enlightenment. In Burke, the language of the self, the language of criticism, and the language of culture
become inseparable, so that experience becomes contingent upon language all the way down. Burke advances criticism toward its structuralist and poststructuralist phases (though for the reasons I outlined
earlier, he doesn't have much practical influence in getting it there), emphasizing the kind of linguistic contingency we shall now turn to in the
work of Richard Rorty, Stanley Fish, and Barbara Herrnstein Smith.

Conclusion

Rhetoric, Neopragmatism, Border Studies—
Beyond the Contingency Blues

In the last two chapters we have traced the emergence of two modernist responses to the kind of metaphysical foundationalism associated in America with transcendentalism. Pragmatism and rhetoric emerge in Dewey and Burke in the context of a general recognition among modern philosophers, beginning with Nietzsche, that all philosophical systems, and the truth claims they make, are *contingent* upon the linguistic and representational systems used to articulate them. Pragmatism sets out to redefine the whole notion of truth, replacing the idea that truth is authorized by some transcendental ground with the idea that truth is grounded in a culturally specific consensus about the utility of an idea or assertion when applied toward some specific, agreed-upon end. Both the terms of pragmatism's analyses and its propositions are to be determined with reference to nonfoundational criteria grounded in the material and social worlds. Rhetoric, as reclaimed by Burke, likewise shifts our attention away from a correspondence between language and reality and toward the linguistic and rhetorical systems that enable, and ultimately authorize, assertions about the real. Both pragmatism and rhetoric, in effect, start and stop with the contingency of language and the wholly social construction of value.

I want to conclude my study by examining a little further the *modernist* roots of this turn in philosophy and criticism, and to trace the fortunes of pragmatism and rhetoric in the more recent age of postmodern theory. Throughout this study I have been arguing that cultural criticism in America has unfolded to a significant degree as a response to philosophical, social, and cultural challenges related to the problem of modernity. Here I want to shift the form of this attention just a bit, first

142

by reviewing how Burke's reclamation of rhetoric is a specific example of the resurgence of rhetoric during the period of high modernism, and second by demonstrating how this resurgence intersected in many ways with the philosophical assumptions of pragmatism. Having established how Deweyan pragmatism and Burkean rhetoric emerged in the United States out of a set of modernist philosophical principles that overturned the premises of what Santayana called the genteel tradition in American philosophy, I want to examine how the newer tradition they represent has played itself out in the work of contemporary critics like Richard Rorty, Stanley Fish, and Barbara Herrnstein Smith.

These critics, deeply influenced by poststructuralist theory but committed to a neopragmatist or rhetorical orientation, tend to blur the distinctions between pragmatism and rhetoric in the interests of articulating a postmetaphysical critical discourse based on the contingency of language and committed to a vigilant critique of critical systems claiming some kind of transcendental authority. In doing so, however, each ends up having to face the irony of his or her own position, an irony grounded in their disclaimers about being able to formulate a critical discourse that is not trapped within the very language of metaphysics they are critiquing. Rorty, Fish, and Herrnstein Smith extend the most troubling implications of pragmatism and rhetoric to the point that their systematic claims about the fallacies of absolutism or essentialism cannot be made without absolutizing and essentializing their own claims about the fallacy of absolutism. Since each of these critics recognizes this conundrum, they tend to get caught in a kind of methodological cul-de-sac in which they must foreground their own inability to transcend the language and principles they are critiquing. Ultimately, I will be arguing, the articulation of such a position becomes as counterproductive as the redemptive turn to Emerson, and the canon of American liberalism, that we find in critics like Gunn and Poirier.

Rhetoric and Modernism

Burke's turn to rhetoric is a singular instance of the resurgence of rhetoric in the period of high modernism. In their recent analysis of the return of rhetoric (or "the new rhetoric") in the fields of literary theory, cultural theory, and composition studies, John Bender and David Wellbery suggest that this return is the result of a set of social, philosophical, and epistemological developments related to modernism, developments that overturned premises that kept rhetoric on the margins of literary and cultural criticism since at least the romantic period.

Bender and Wellbery "locate the factors determining rhetoric's demise in a bundle of social and cultural transformations that occurred . . . between the seventeenth and nineteenth centuries." In their view, classical rhetoric fell into disuse during this period for five reasons: (1) the steadily increasing domination of analytical discourse by the concept of scientific objectivity; (2) the conviction that literary creativity was simply an expression of pure subjectivity; (3) the prominence of "liberal political discourse," which came to dominate "communal exchange" (22); (4) the displacement of the spoken by the written word as the dominant mode of communication; and (5) domination of the "linguistic sphere" of cultural communication by standardized national languages, tied to the rise of the nation-state.

Since the concept of rhetoric and the nature of rhetorical power are grounded "in the social structures of the premodern world" of city-state democracies (7), the "demise of rhetoric," in their view, was a logical result of the processes of modernization in the West. The anti-rhetorical effects of modernization at the level of epistemology are represented most clearly by the rise of scientific discourse, which represents "a general movement toward representational neutrality that . . . stresses the . . . transparency of discourse" (13). The influence of such a discourse, which assumes a point of view with access to the "naturally" and empirically given, undermines the need for persuasion grounded in rhetoric. A new subject emerges in the modernization of discourse: the "neutral or abstracted subject" (8) as formulated by Descartes and Kant. Kant's subject is "arhetorical" in the double sense of being a unique, self-expressive individual personality, and being supposedly capable of taking a position of neutral disinterest. As Bender and Wellbery point out, Kant's "foundational subjectivity—be it the subject as . . . unique individual personality or as disinterested free agent within the political sphere—erodes the ideological premises of rhetoric" (12). Since in Kant's view Enlightenment is founded in a kind of communication "that unfolds within a free public sphere . . . separated from particularist interests . . . the subject speaks . . . as a . . . free inquirer whose only guide is the light of impartial reason" (14).

Such a conception of cultural discourse carried over into the domain of aesthetics as well. Romanticism, they argue, in its privileging of "imaginative expression" over the calculated and strategic deployment of language associated with rhetoric, represents a "second death of rhetoric" (15). A new creative subject and a new conception of litera-

ture emerged out of romanticism, both of which fed on and perpetuated the demise of rhetoric begun by a modernizing Enlightenment.
That is, the insistence in an aesthetican like Kant on the "originating
power of subjectivity" seems to render the strategic development of
rhetorical power irrelevant (19). With the romantic commitment to aesthetic creativity as inspiration or genius came a new conception of
"originality" that led to a narrowing of the "literary," so that the "spontaneous overflow of powerful feelings" and not the strategic deployment of rhetorical forms produced poetic persuasion. "Prior to the last
decades of the eighteenth century," note Bender and Wellbery, "the concept of literature covered virtually all of writing; the breadth of its application was made possible by the overriding unity of rhetorical doctrine, which governed all of verbal production" (15). However, with
romanticism emerged the concept of literature as "imaginative writing," an "autonomous field of discourse endowed with its unique inner
laws and history" (15). From this perspective, it is possible to trace the
rise of such "postrhetorical" paradigms of cultural analysis as interpretation, historiography, and philology to the demise of rhetoric, since
the "emergence of Romanticism" coincides with the "replacing [of] rememorative conservation (*traditio*) with an insistence on originality"
(15–16).

    In effect, Bender and Wellbery trace what they call "the logical im-
possibility" of rhetoric to two very different, but converging sources:
the rise of science and romantic transcendentalism. This means that the
hegemony of rhetoric fell victim to a split in the modern world between
positivist and idealist orientations toward knowledge. As long as these
two orientations remained separate, there was little use for rhetoric as
a mode of literary or cultural analysis. From the point of view of the
positivist, rhetoric was superfluous, since language could transpar-
ently render the nature of things. From the point of view of the romantic or metaphysical idealist, rhetoric was superfluous because moving
and persuasive discourse had its origins in individual genius or the
kind of transcendental force Emerson associated with poetic creativity.
In either case, the classical resources of rhetoric had become superfluous; as long as the two poles of American thought were positivist
and transcendentalist, this very structure of division made rhetoric an
anachronism.

    The "modernist return of rhetoric" identified by Bender and Well-
bery is not, of course, a return to classical rhetoric and rememorative
conservation. The Enlightenment and romanticism made classical rhetoric permanently "anachronistic" by estranging it "from cultural pro-

duction and the most advanced forms of inquiry" (23). What they call "the new rhetoric," while it emerged out of a *reversal* of the five conditions enumerated above, breaks with classical rhetoric in being a "transdisciplinary field of practice and intellectual concern" that does "not assume the stable shape of a system or method of education" (25). *"Modernism,"* they write, *"is an age not of rhetoric, but of rhetoricality,* the age, that is, of a generalized rhetoric that penetrates to the deepest levels of human experience":

> The classical rhetorical tradition rarified speech and fixed it within a gridwork of limitations: it was a rule-governed domain whose procedures themselves were delimited by the institutions that organized interaction and domination in traditional European society. Rhetoricality, by contrast, is bound to no specific set of institutions. It manifests the groundless, infinitely ramifying character of discourse in the modern world. For this reason, it allows for no explanatory metadiscourse that is not already itself rhetorical. (25)

Modernist rhetoricality thus emerges from the reversal of the *"conditions of impossibility* of rhetoric" associated with modernization. This reversal involved a collapse of the kind of "representational transparency" associated with the language of scientific objectivity (23); an erosion or decentering of the romantic (originary, disinterested) subject; a crisis in the centrality of reason as the ordering principle of society brought on by the work of philosophers like Nietzsche; the "dethroning" of print by film, television, and video (which led to the rise of a verbal medium in which rhetoric became, once again, an important instrument of entertainment and persuasion); and the collapse of separated national languages in the emergence of a polyglot and multicultural discourse that shattered "the idea of national uniqueness and of an individual national history" (24–25).[1]

When Bender and Wellbery insist that the twentieth century is an age of *"rhetoricality"* they mean to call our attention to how it has altered the very "conditions of discourse" inherited from the eighteenth and nineteenth centuries (25). "Rhetoricality" is meant to suggest a cultural condition rather than a system of analysis, one in which communication is marked by contingencies that are both linguistic and institutional. On the one hand, modernist theories of knowledge develop a critique of foundationalism that sees all written and verbal expression as contingent upon the resources and possibilities of culturally specific languages. On the other hand, recent forms of cultural analysis from Adorno and Horkheimer to Foucault have increasingly stressed the role of institutions in determining contexts that make certain forms of meaning possible and others impossible or suspect.

In Bender and Wellbery's view, the modernist return to rhetoric represents the reemergence of rhetoric as an "explanatory" discourse that is not a "metadiscourse" and that is "itself rhetorical." It is in this sense that the "rhetoricality" they describe seems not only to question both the positivist grounds of science and the metaphysical grounds of transcendentalism, but to deconstruct the very opposition that structures their difference. The claim that "rhetoricality" is not a metadiscourse and is itself rhetorical is based on the insistence that no explanatory discourse is really a metadiscourse, because no explanatory discourse can escape its own rhetoricality. This goes also for the "new rhetoric" they espouse: "We are dealing no longer with a specialized technique of instrumental communication . . . there can be no single contemporary rhetorical theory: rhetoricality cannot be the object of a homogeneous discipline . . . [O]ne cannot study rhetoric *tout court,* but only linguistic, sociological, psychoanalytic, cognitive, communicational, medial, or literary rhetorics" (38). Moreover, they insist that rhetoricality is not a mode of analysis but "a general condition of human experience and action" (38). Rhetoricality is meant to signify "the groundless, infinitely ramifying character of discourse in the modern world" (25). They see rhetoricality not as "the title of a doctrine and a practice," but, instead, as "something like the condition of our existence" (25).[2] It is worth emphasizing how different the conceptualization of "experience" here is from what we saw in Gunn. Where Bender and Wellbery's postmodern rhetorician wants to understand "experience" in its highly contingent relationship to language, ideology, and institutionally specific forms of discourse, Gunn wants to isolate a form of experience ("experience itself") that somehow is able to stand outside—and escape the mediations—of these contingencies.

"Rhetoricality," then, marks a break with the kind of pragmatism espoused by Gunn and Poirier; indeed, it sketches out a history of discourses linking their version of pragmatism to an essentially romantic moment that helped suppress rhetoric. Gunn in particular attempts to articulate a pragmatist position in direct response to a moral and critical crisis brought on by just the kind of radical contingency rhetoricality stands for. In this context his turn, along with Poirier, to a "redemptive" pragmatism grafted with hindsight onto Emerson's transcendentalism is telling, since it underscores the latent idealism informing their version of pragmatism.

So far in this chapter, and in my previous discussion of Burke's turn to rhetoric, I have been making a distinction between pragmatism and rhetoric. I have been arguing that while there is a loosely pragmatic orientation in all of Burke's work, it gets channeled into the articulation of a rhetorical approach to literary and cultural criticism that is hard to reconcile with the kind of pragmatism articulated by Gunn and Poirier. Indeed, both these critics want pragmatism to help redeem us from just the kind of crisis Bender and Wellbery's rhetoricality has helped usher in. Burke, far from assisting in their redemptive project, actually helps inaugurate the kind of rhetoricality they deplore (I will have more to say about this in a moment). Having insisted on making this distinction between pragmatism and rhetoric, however, I now want to begin to examine their recent convergence in the work of critics like Richard Rorty, Barbara Herrnstein Smith, and Stanley Fish. The striking departure *rhetoricality* marks from traditional rhetoric (or even the "new rhetoric" articulated by Perelman) is that it is meant to signify a general cultural condition in the West, a cross-disciplinary range of intellectual concerns and practices responding to that condition that expands the concept of "rhetoric" beyond its older associations with argumentation per se, or with a system or method of education. As such, it participates in a generalized postmodern epistemological condition that links it (sometimes loosely, sometimes quite specifically) to the poststructuralist discourses of deconstruction, the New Historicism, and the kind of pragmatism articulated by Rorty and Herrnstein Smith. The "altered conditions of discourse" (25) Bender and Wellbery link to the condition of rhetoricality, that is, are grounded in the same fundamental ontological and epistemological changes that ground postmodern theory in general.[3]

In this regard, all roads lead back (perhaps a little too predictably) to Nietzsche. In Bender and Wellbery's genealogy Nietzsche stands as the progenitor of rhetoricality, since his attention to the constitutive and contingent nature of language laid the groundwork for those coming after him in the fields of philosophy, linguistics, communication, and literary criticism. For "nowhere," write Bender and Wellbery, "is the modernist shift in the meaning of rhetoric—the shift from rhetoric to what we are calling rhetoricality—more forcefully evident than in Nietzsche," who "set the agenda for the modernist reconceptualization of rhetoric" (26). He does so by recognizing "the human 'drive to form metaphors' as the basis of our rendering of the world" and by insisting on "the essential rhetoricity of our rendering of the world" (26). Figures of speech move, in Nietzsche's thought, from being vehicles or devices "of an *elocutio* that adorns and presents the invented thoughts of the speaker" to constituting the very possibility of what is called "truth" (26). Nietzsche in this way inaugurates the set of reversals that led to the reemergence of rhetoric, since "this conceptual move tears the underpinnings from the notion of an arhetorical language of observation: the truth claims of science, in Nietzsche's reading, are themselves merely one rhetoric among others" (26).

What Bender and Wellbery see as the modernist return to (and remaking of) rhetoric is, then, part of a much more general response to late-nineteenth- and twentieth-century insights, following on Nietzsche's, that knowledge and truth are contingent on a set of human assumptions and practices fundamentally embedded in language and language systems. This insight formed the foundation for a renewed interest in rhetoric,[4] but it also ushered in an avalanche of work in anthropology, linguistics, philosophy, and literary criticism that shared with rhetoric its attention to the discursive constitution of knowledge and truth. The figures Bender and Wellbery invoke for purposes of illustration are familiar ones—Barthes, Kuhn, Jakobson, Geertz, Chomsky, Lacan, Kristeva, Bakhtin, de Man, and Derrida. Of course, these critics, invoked in a positive way by Bender and Wellbery, represent the kind of poststructuralism critics like Gunn and Poirier blame for the crisis of belief they insist is currently undermining American cultural criticism. Where Gunn and Poirier want to counter poststructuralism with Emersonian pragmatism, however, another group of neopragmatist critics—Rorty, Fish, and Herrnstein Smith—have tried to develop a theoretically sound, antifoundationalist epistemology grounded in poststructuralist principles. Rather than try to read Dewey backward into Emerson, these critics extend pragmatism's critique of metaphysics forward in order to examine its logical relationship to contemporary theory, and they have done this in a way that links it to what Bender and Wellbery have called rhetoricality.

The New Pragmatism and American Studies

Rorty's attempt to reconcile Deweyan pragmatism to poststructuralist theory began to take shape in *Philosophy and the Mirror of Nature* and was worked out in more detail in the essays collected in *Consequences of Pragmatism*. In the latter book, Rorty defines pragmatism in a way that suggests how closely it intersects the basic assumptions of rhetoricality: (1) "It is . . . anti-essentialism applied to notions like 'truth,' 'knowledge,' 'language,' 'morality,' and similar objects of philosophical theorizing"; (2) it asserts that "there is no epistemological difference between truth about what ought to be and truth about what is, nor any metaphysical difference between facts and values" (163); and (3) it represents "the doctrine that there are no constraints on inquiry save conversational ones—no wholesale constraints derived from the nature of the objects, or of the mind, or of language, but only those retail constraints provided by the remarks of our fellow-inquirers" (165). Rorty's neopragmatism is thus reconciled to the same "groundless, infinitely ramifying character of discourse" that characterizes the condition of rhetoricality (Bender and Wellbery 25), and it is linked in a number of essays in the volume to poststructuralist theory (particularly in the essay on Heidegger and Dewey, "Philosophy as a Kind of Writing," and in "Pragmatism, Relativism, and Irrationalism").

Rorty reinforces and expands on the link between Deweyan pragmatism and postmodern theory in *Contingency, Irony, and Solidarity*, and he does so in a way that consistently draws a connection between his brand of neopragmatism and what Bender and Wellbery treat as rhetoricality. Here, Rorty insists that the challenges of contingency and solidarity, and the necessity of irony, must be understood historically as legacies of post-Enlightenment modernity. For Rorty, the key historical moments in the development of modernity were the Enlightenment, the French Revolution, and the advent of romanticism, the Enlightenment because it ushered in the age of reason, instrumental thinking, and the slow but steady displacement of religion by science, the French Revolution because it showed that "the whole vocabulary of social relations, and the whole spectrum of social institutions, could be replaced almost overnight," and romanticism because it showed "what happens when art is thought of no longer as imitation but, rather, as the artist's self-creation" (3). In Rorty's view, the history of modernity is launched first in the Enlightenment shift from the idea that truth resides "out there" in some spiritual or transcendental realm to the idea that it exists "out there" in a natural world that can be measured and quantified by the sciences. This history is later made even more complicated by philosophers like Nietzsche who insisted on the contingency and constructedness of all discourses about "reality," scientific or otherwise, so that the whole idea of some verifiable "out there"— spiritual or material—had to be questioned. Thus the early split between religious belief and Enlightenment rationality was replaced in the nineteenth century by a more general split—Rorty calls it an "old tension" (xiii)—between a metaphysical and a historicist turn in philosophy and social thought. Where the idealist looks to some form of theology or metaphysics for "an escape from time and chance," the "historicist" insists that "socialization, and thus historical circumstance, goes all the way down—that there is nothing 'beneath' socialization or prior to history which is definatory of the human" (xiii).

The convergence between Rorty's pragmatism and rhetoricality is most clear in his chapter "The Contingency of Language." The contingency of language is Rorty's point of departure because he argues that the world is made meaningful not through the accurate identification of meanings intrinsic to nature, but through the instrumental deployment of figures and tropes in the interests of presenting a persuasive account, or redescription, of things.[5] This stress on forms and systems of philosophical, social, or cultural explanations as *vocabularies* and *redescriptions* underscores the essentially rhetorical nature of those explanations. Like Burke, Rorty sees things like "the correspondence theory of truth" or "the idea of the 'intrinsic nature of reality'" as "vocabularies," ways of talking about phenomena grounded in the metaphoric resources of language (8). Drawing a distinction between thinking of language as a *medium* and thinking of it as an *instrument*, he underscores the rhetorical nature of such vocabularies by stressing the fact that they are "tools" (11). In a sentence Bender and Wellbery could have written, Rorty insists that philosophical, social, or cultural explanations of phenomena "are not discoveries of a reality behind the appearances, of an undistorted view of the whole picture with which to replace myopic views of its parts," but "the invention of new tools to take the place of old tools" (12).

The historical side of Rorty's discussion also replicates Bender and Wellbery's, since the pragmatist position he outlines shares the modernist genealogy of rhetoricality.

> Insofar as one can attribute philosophical views to Freud, one can say that he is as much a pragmatist as James and as much a perspectivalist as Nietzsche—or, one might also say, as much a modernist as Proust. For it somehow became possible, toward the end of the nineteenth century . . . to see redescription as a tool rather than a claim to have discovered essence. It thereby became possible to see a new vocabulary not as something which was supposed to replace all other vocabularies, something which claimed to represent reality, but simply as one more vocabulary, one more human project, one person's chosen metaphoric . . . [Nietzsche, James, Wittgenstein, Freud, Proust, Heidegger—] all the figures of this period play into each other's hands. (39)

The link Rorty forges here between pragmatism, perspectivism, modernism, and a general point of view that all discourses are grounded in metaphor, turns out to be strategically crucial, since he ultimately wants to articulate a "poeticized . . . redescription of liberalism" grounded in the literary trope of irony (53), a redescription in which philosophy has systematically given way since Hegel and Nietzsche to literature. His first step, following Davidson, is akin to one we have already seen in Burke: to reject altogether the distinction between "literal" and "metaphoric" expressions (18). Rorty insists that to create meaning either through conventionally literal or metaphoric expressions is to participate in a "language game," one that involves us less in "conveying meanings" than in the rhetorical act of "producing effects" (18). For this reason, Rorty groups together Nietzsche, Proust, James, and Yeats in a single historical continuum. Discovering the contingency of language is for him discovering the complicity between philosophical, analytical, or critical discourse and the discourse of literature.

In Rorty's view, there is an almost necessary connection between the irreducibly rhetorical status of critical discourse and the condition of irony. The way to irony is through literature and literary criticism, a path I would argue parallels Dewey's reinvestment of metaphysical idealism in a privileged realm of art: both locate in literature what philosophy will no longer sustain. Where Dewey, that is, tends to turn to art and literature as an ideal realm beyond the limits of philosophy, Rorty turns to literature because it is the most contingent of discourses. Rorty sees the "quarrel between poetry and philosophy" as one between "an effort to achieve self-creation" and the effort to "achieve universality by the transcendence of contingency" (25). Post-Nietzschean philosophy in particular, beginning with Wittgenstein and Heidegger, has sought to "work out honorable terms on which philosophy might surrender to poetry" (25). Rorty joins the forces of surrender by linking himself to the Nietzschean recognition that "only poets . . . can truly appreciate contingency. The rest of us are doomed to remain philosophers, to insist that there is really only one true lading-list, one true description of the human situation, one universal context of our lives. We are doomed to spend our conscious lives trying to escape from contingency rather than, like the strong poet, acknowledging and appropriating contingency" (28). The poet, for Rorty, is "paradigmatic" (34) because the language of poetry is the contingent language of redescription par excellence.

There is a key moment in Rorty's discussion of contingency and community where the terms of opposition he has been invoking (between the idealist and the pragmatist or the metaphysican and the historicist) get reduced to the opposition between "logic" and "rhetoric," with rhetoric marking the position of the historicist or ironist Rorty himself wants to claim. It is a passage that highlights the link I have been tracing between Rorty's pragmatic ironist and Bender and Wellbery's rhetoricality. Discussing the standoff between the "traditional view that it is always in point to ask 'How do you know?' and the view that sometimes all we can ask is 'Why do you talk that way?' " Rorty observes that

> we would only have a real and practical standoff, as opposed to an artificial and theoretical one, if certain topics and certain language games were taboo—if there were general agreement within a society that certain questions were *always* in point, that certain questions were prior to certain others, that there was a fixed order of discussion . . . This would be just the sort of society which liberals are trying to avoid—one in which "logic" ruled and "rhetoric" was outlawed. (51)

It turns out that the kind of culture Rorty has been trying to evoke is a *rhetorical* culture, a community of social discourse ordered and empowered by the figurative and persuasive possibilities of language rather than by the privileged "logic" of a set of transcendental rules. Rorty's liberalism is committed to the notion that knowledge and truth claims continually evolve within systems of representation. He refers here (and elsewhere) to "language *games*" in order to acknowledge the irony of his position, a position that, after all, must ground the political, moral, and ethical value of its views in the representational terrain of a closed and arbitrary system. His language game, as this passage makes clear, is played by the rules of rhetoric (which determine the possibilities and limits of both figuration and persuasion), and therefore participates in the kind of cultural condition Bender and Wellbery call rhetoricality.

The whole point of Rorty's neopragmatist position is to formulate an approach to cultural and social criticism that, having given up the illusion of the transparency of language, can assess culturally specific "realities" and "truths" in a way that not only recognizes but in fact *exploits* the contingencies of language. Toward this aim, Rorty insists on the link between a rhetorical and a *poeticized* culture. He does this by relegating logic to science, which (like Horkheimer and Adorno before him) he sees as the legacy of a debilitating Enlightenment commitment to rationality. Then, he insists that we need to look to literature and politics for a redescription of culture that would liberate it from the fetters of logic and objectified reason. "Unfortunately," he writes,

> the Enlightenment wove much of its political rhetoric around a picture of the scientist as a sort of priest, someone who achieved contact with non-

human truth by being "logical," "methodical," and "objective" . . . We
need a redescription of liberalism as the hope that culture as a whole can
be "poeticized" rather than as the Enlightenment hope that it can be "rationalized" or "scientized." (52–53)

Rorty loosely links the contingency of language with rhetoric, the poetic, literature, and the faculty of the imagination in order to make the
same move we saw Dewey make in *Art as Experience*, reinvesting in art
and imaginative thinking the social and cultural work formerly ceded
to philosophy.

The narrative that takes Rorty from the inadequacies of science to the
demise of philosophy and the ascendancy of literature runs from Hegel
to literary critics like Leavis, Wilson, Trilling, and Harold Bloom. Where
Hegel, in Rorty's view, reoriented philosophy toward the poetic and the
rhetorical by turning it into a "literary genre" (79), the modern liberal
critics Rorty cites ended up displacing the philosopher altogether, since,
in his view, "literary criticism does for ironists what the search for universal moral principles is supposed to do for metaphysicians" (80).
Rorty in effect takes what he deems to be the primacy of literature and
reads it back into the history of philosophy, so that Hegel's dialectic becomes "not an argumentative procedure or a way of unifying subject
and object, but simply a literary skill" (78). Hegel's literary skill translates for Rorty into an ironist position in philosophy continued after
Hegel by Nietzsche, Heidegger, and Derrida, extended by Rorty himself, and taken up in the end by literary criticism ("a more up-to-date
word for what I have been calling 'dialectic,'" he writes, "would be 'literary criticism'") (79).

As elegant as this genealogy is, it has a number of elements that
ought to give us pause. In the first place, Rorty views cultural and social criticism as an elite, priestly activity open only to a class of male
Brahmins sufficiently removed from ordinary life to be able to focus
their attention on the complex of epistemological contingencies underlying it. Progress or change in social and cultural criticism seems for
Rorty limited to the question of who will get to play the role of priest.
During the Enlightenment it was the scientist, in the nineteenth century it was the philosopher, and since the rise of liberal criticism in the
1930s it has been the literary critic. Barbara Herrnstein Smith has quite
correctly taken Rorty to task for his ethnocentrism, but we ought to
note as well the astonishingly limited nature of his priestly class of critics.[6] Since in Rorty's view all vocabularies are simply redescriptions of
other vocabularies, the privileged moral advisor is someone who has

read a lot of these redescriptions. Thus, Rorty elevates the literary critic to a kind of supreme position, explaining that "ironists read literary critics, and take them as moral advisers, simply because such critics have an exceptionally large range of acquaintance. They are moral advisers not because they have special access to moral truth but because they have been around. They have read more books and are thus in a better position not to get trapped in the vocabulary of any single book" (80–81). Rorty asserts that his own priestly pantheon of voracious readers (Blake, Arnold, Nietzsche, Mill, Marx, Baudelaire, Trotsky, Eliot, Nabokov, and Orwell) form a "beautiful mosaic" who, if they are in turn redescribed by others, will "enlarge the canon" (81). It is of course hard to see what kind of "mosaic" this relatively homogeneous group of canonical writers composes, or why we ought to read Rorty's defense of poetic thinking about moral and social ideas as anything more than an updated version—redescription, to use Rorty's term for it—of Shelley's defense of poetry. It is hard to escape the conclusion that Rorty's irony is necessitated by the fact that his position is, in the final analysis, a blend of Shelley and Harold Bloom, souped up by a poststructural rhetoric and suffused with postmodernist paradox.[7]

As I pursue the question of neopragmatist irony a bit further, I want to draw the link between Rorty's poststructural pragmatism and rhetoricality a little closer by comparing Rorty's characterization of pragmatism with Stanley Fish's conception of rhetoric. Where Rorty argues, in effect, that there is no critical position beyond the merely contingent or pragmatic one, Fish argues that there is no critical position that is not "merely rhetorical." From the contemporary rhetorican's point of view, Fish insists, the world is "teeming with roles, situations, strategies, interventions, but containing no master role, no situation of situations, no strategy for outflanking all strategies . . . no neutral point of rationality from the vantage point of which the 'merely rhetorical' can be identified and held in check" (215). For this reason, Fish's rhetorician is Rorty's ironist. For Fish, as for Rorty, everything comes down to the contingency of language, or to an opposition between "two kinds of language . . . language that faithfully reflects or reports on matters of fact uncolored by any personal or partisan agenda or desire" and "language that is infected by partisan agendas and desires, and therefore colors and distorts the facts which it purports to reflect. It is use of the second kind of language that makes one a rhetorician, while adherence to the first kind makes one a seeker after truth and an objective observer of the way things are" (205). Fish's distinction between the rhetorician and the "seeker after truth" mirrors the distinction Rorty makes between the ironist and the historicist. Like Rorty, Fish insists that "one does not escape the rhetorical by fleeing to the protected area of basic communication and common sense because common sense in whatever form it happens to take is always a rhetorical—partial, partisan, interested—construction" (214). Fish's "Rhetorical Man" is caught up in the same kind of language game as Rorty's neopragmatist.

For this reason, Rhetorical Man confronts the same kind of irony Rorty's neopragmatist cheerfully embraces. Fish's rhetorician has the specifically deconstructive task of continually uncovering "the truth of rhetorical operations, the truth that all operations, including the operation of deconstruction itself, are rhetorical" (215). Fish links Rhetorical Man to deconstruction in the same move and for the same reasons Rorty links his ironist to the procedures and practices of literary criticism. Fish cites Derrida's critique of J. L. Austin in order to connect Derrida's insistence on the inescapably rhetorical nature of all philosophical discourse—its *contingency*—to his own account of the contemporary resurgence of rhetoric. Fish sees what Bender and Wellbery call rhetorically as a general characteristic of deconstructive or poststructuralist thought, since it "systematically asserts and demonstrates the mediated, constructed, partial, socially constituted nature of all realities" (215). Traditional philosophical positions (like those of Rorty's historicist or Fish's seeker after truth) rest "on a contradiction [they] cannot acknowledge, [rest] on the suppression of the challengeable rhetoricity of [their] own standpoint" (215). A deconstructive reading is an ironist reading in the Rortean sense, because, according to Fish, "it will surface those contradictions and expose those suppressions and thus 'trouble' a unity that is achieved only by covering over all the excluded emphases and interests that might threaten it" (215). Fish's Rhetorical Man, working in a deconstructive mode, runs up against the same limitations Rorty's ironist does, since his or her "act [is not] performed in the service of something beyond rhetoric. Derridean deconstruction does not uncover the operations of rhetoric in order to reach the Truth; rather it continually uncovers the truth of rhetorical operations, the truth that all operations, including the operations of deconstruction itself, are rhetorical" (215). In this sense, the discursive logic of the new rhetoric and the discursive logic of the new pragmatism end up amounting to the same thing. The irony of the position Fish articulates for Rhetorical Man, who is always unable to escape the rhetorical by fleeing to some other kind of discourse which is not rhetorical, matches precisely the irony of Rorty's Pragmatist Man, the critic who has no final or absolute vocabulary that is not just another vocabulary, no description that is not a redescription. Irony for both means being positioned within contingent discourses about reality or truth that acknowledge, police, accept, and even celebrate contingency.[8]

I began this chapter by noting that critics like Rorty, Fish, and Herrnstein Smith pursue theoretical and methodological issues related to the philosophical problem of modernity in a way that extends the work of Dewey and Burke and recalls a set of critical problems that date back in the United States to Emerson. Deconstruction, rhetoricality, and Rorty's kind of poststructuralist pragmatism all try to resolve the tension or contradiction we have been tracing in this study between metaphysical idealism and traditional forms of pragmatism. But the question remains as to whether or not they are able to resolve this tension in a satisfactory way.

I don't think that they do. All three develop similar critiques of metaphysical foundationalism in the interests of producing an epistemology or critical system based on the contingency of language and devoted to a vigilant critique of all systematic forms of analysis or revelation that claim an absolute or transcendental authority. However, the strength of this position is also its weakness, since in all three instances critical attention gets continually caught up with policing the grounds of discourse. Deconstruction, rhetoricality, and Rortean pragmatism, that is, necessarily become metadiscourses about the grounds of discourse, redescriptions of how descriptions are always only redescriptions. This is precisely the reason why both Fish and Rorty end up underscoring the irony of their positions, and why Derrida resorts to what he calls the "double gesture," the need to continually foreground the fact that one must use the language of metaphysics or the processes of "end oriented reason" to *critique* metaphysics and the fetishizing of end-oriented reason.[9] Rorty's ironist can't produce a vocabulary grounded in anything other than redescriptions of previous vocabularies, and Fish's Rhetorical Man is rhetorical because he must continually and systematically assert and demonstrate the mediated, constructed, partial, socially constituted nature of all realities, including the one he represents under the rubric of rhetoricality. The deconstructionist, likewise, must produce a critique of the grounds of other discourses while using those grounds in the interest, not so much of producing a postmetaphysical or nonfoundational critical methodology, as of demonstrating continually the inability of other discourses to do so. The irony invoked by Rorty and Fish marks a paradoxical doubling in their positions, while the double gesture invoked by Derrida marks an irony in his position that mirrors those of Fish and Rorty.

For all of these reasons, Rorty's neopragmatism and the kind of rhetoricality articulated by Fish and Bender and Wellbery end up producing a kind of theoretical and methodological cul-de-sac. The road seems philosophically sound—indeed, unavoidable—but the only way out seems to be the way that got them in in the first place. It is hard to see anywhere, practically, to go. There is certainly, as Barbara Herrnstein Smith argues, no road that will lead back to a vocabulary that will take us to the underlying nature of things. At the conclusion of *Contingencies of Value*, in her own neopragmatist attempt to work through the problem of relativism Rorty confronts, she defines "relativism" as a "conception of the world as continuously changing, irreducibly various, and multiply configurable," beyond any "logical deduction," "scientific experiment," or "insight into the underlying nature of things" (179). In her view, every philosophical, scientific, or critical discourse that seeks to explain what *is* cannot do so without simply replicating the terms and concepts that allow for its particular explanation in the first place. There is, in this respect, no getting out of or beyond the system-bound nature of one's explanation. A "conception of the world" that seeks to get at the underlying nature of things "requires that there be 'something' other than itself, other than the process of conceiving-the-world; but it cannot conceive of a single other thing to say, or way to think, about that 'something'—not a single feature to predicate of it, or any way to describe, analyze, or manipulate any of its properties—that would be *independent* of that process" (183, emphasis mine). The truth for Herrnstein Smith (and for Fish, Rorty, and Derrida) is that all epistemological, analytical, and evaluative systems are contingent, and each is willing to purchase that truth at the expense of both moral and methodological certainty. The key value for them is contingency itself because each is convinced in his or her own way that contingency is an absolute fact of human experience. It is because they have deduced something like an absolute fact from a critique of absolutism that they must make the Derridean double gesture, embracing some form of methodological or systematic irony (if not the in-your-face irony Rorty espouses). Less (an accurate theory of contingency that disallows certainty) is more (than an inaccurate essentialism that falsifies it).

At this point we have come full circle back to Gunn and Poirier's complaint about the crisis in American criticism ostensibly brought on by the influence of French poststructuralism in America. However, we have seen that *pragmatism itself*, along with the growing popularity of contemporary American rhetorical theory, is as much to blame for this crisis as are the French. Barthes, Derrida, and Foucault undeniably gave shape, focus, and continental cachet to postfoundationalist forms of cultural critique, but those forms of critique were already rooted in U.S. critical thought.[10] Moreover, if the ironic and nonfoundational elements of deconstruction, rhetoricality, and Rortean pragmatism are problematic, so too is the humanist assurance and essentialism of the loosely "Emersonian" pragmatism espoused by Gunn and Poirier. In their view, pragmatism is based on a broadly liberal and pluralist dedication to "experience," the "actual," and the "practical." It conceives of cultural criticism in an intuitive Emersonian mode, a criticism wary of methodology, and interested in the political mainly through an investigation of the moral imagination. According to Gunn, liberal critics writing in this broadly pragmatic Emersonian and Jamesian tradition, like Trilling and Wilson, "show us that culture should be studied and judged 'as life's continuous evaluation of itself'; therefore its service is in behalf of those *irreducible*—or, better, indispensable—elements of the self, of the human, that resist complete conditioning by all that culture does to shape the experience of the self and to stabilize and control that experience in socially approved ways" (40).

With its focus on what might "lie beyond mental frames," and its interest in the supposedly "irreducible" elements of subjectivity that resist social "conditioning," this form of pragmatist cultural criticism is grounded in a transcendental form of essentialism that rejects the antifoundationalist orientations of Fish, Rorty, and Derrida. Indeed, it aims to ground itself in just the kind of insight into the "underlying nature of things" Herrnstein Smith insists is beyond our reach. It wants to return to a system of thought in which knowledge and truth can be grounded in and authorized by something outside the contingencies of language and the shaping experience of culturally and socially specific rules, norms, and beliefs. It wants, in effect, to ground belief in something transcultural and essential, based on a form of pragmatism untainted by Rorty's poststructuralism.[11]

We are now in a position to see that while critics like Gunn and Poirier are ostensibly responding to a *postmodern* crisis of belief, they are in fact dealing with a much older problem endemic to *modernity* itself. As Pippin in particular has noted, modernity is characterized through and through with the philosophical problem of autonomy.[12] We saw that for critics like Habermas, Foucault, and Pippin the Enlightenment ushered in the concept of subjectivity as rational and autonomous, characterized in theory by a self-legislating reason that could be independent and self-sufficient. The problem with instrumental reason, however, freed as it is from dependence on knowledge based on belief in a metaphysical or transcendental ground, is that it denies us access to the nature of things in themselves. Instead, it provides the principles and rules by which empirical judgments are made. Thus, the kind of autonomy associated with instrumental reason is purchased at a steep price: humanity loses the concept of metaphysical certainty about the nature of things in themselves. Everything becomes, in a word, contingent. As Pippin rightly points out, the central problem of modernity emerges in the *aporia* that emerges from the tension between the disappearance of a metaphysical ground for epistemological and ethical judgments and the seemingly empirical objectivity of instrumental reason.[13] The ambivalence we saw in Emerson about the value of reason and belief in a transcendental agency, and the tension between metaphysics and pragmatism that persisted into the twentieth century in American cultural criticism, underscore how the "crisis" of belief Gunn and Poirier are concerned with is not specific to postmodernity, but is a central characteristic of modernity itself. Now that we have traced these problems in their perpetual treatment from Emerson and Dewey to Fish, Rorty, and Herrnstein Smith, it is hard to avoid the conclusion that this line of American cultural criticism is going in circles, or that it has simply produced increasingly subtle, nuanced, and philosophically sophisticated redescriptions of the same basic epistemological and theoretical quandary. We seem to have no choice left but Gunn and Poirier's nostalgia for an anachronistic version of transcendentalized pragmatism, or the hall-of-mirrors kind of irony embraced by Fish and Rorty.

How are we to avoid such a dissatisfying choice? Quite simply, by refusing to make it. There is no reason why American literary and cultural criticism ought to follow Gunn and Poirier in renouncing the unavoidable and often sound implications of antifoundationalist theory, whether it be traced back through Foucault and Derrida to Nietzsche, or back through Herrnstein Smith and Rorty to Dewey and James. What is the point of trying to save criticism from irony by regrounding it in a completely discredited foundationalism? Likewise, we can acknowledge the force and import of Rortean irony, Derrida's double gesture, or Herrnstein Smith's stress on the contingency of both values and critical systems, without orienting our criticism toward a reiteration or redescription of their arguments. What is the point of trying to save American criticism from error by continually writing about how criticism cannot, epistemologically speaking, be saved from error? Emersonianism married to a '90s version of '50s liberalism reinvestigating transcendentalist themes in canonical American writers won't do, but neither will essays perpetually working through the theoretical and philosophical necessity of irony and contingency.

Peter Carafiol suggests one way out of the dilemma of having to choose between these positions in his book *The American Ideal* (1991), a study of American literary and cultural studies that attempts to blend the antifoundationalism of Rorty and Fish with a form of American pragmatism derived from Emerson and Thoreau. Carafiol's work is more specifically engaged than are Rorty, Fish, and Herrnstein Smith's with American literary and cultural criticism, and it is decidedly more sympathetic than are Gunn and Poirier to the implications of poststructuralist theory. Arguing that American criticism remains trapped in an essentialist, idealizing discourse about "America" and the "American self" it inherited from Emersonian transcendentalism, Carafiol insists that antifoundationalist theory must be the point of departure for any radical revision of our criticism. Rejecting Gunn and Poirier's assertion that poststructuralist theory has created a "crisis of belief" in American criticism, Carafiol insists that American criticism needs to develop a *historicist* methodology based on a pragmatist version of poststructuralism. "Poststructuralist discourse," writes Carafiol—especially in the work of Fish and Rorty—has "taken up the question of how to connect text and context" in a particularly forceful way, moving "literary and cultural practice off the ideal high ground" and placing "all interpretation, all human activity, in human history" (15).

Carafiol's critique of this "ideal high ground" unfolds as a contemporary version of Santayana's attempt to purge the genteel tradition at the beginning of the century, since its central argument is that American criticism remains hobbled by its commitment to a set of outmoded transcendentalist ideals first fashioned by Emerson, and later codified by O. B. Frothingham, H. C. Goddard, and F. O. Matthiessen.[14] Carafiol is less interested in criticizing transcendentalist thought as Santayana did, than in tracing its "invention" by critics in the nineteenth and twentieth centuries (and the cultural uses to which it has been put). Transcendentalism, he insists, is not a "natural fact" but an *obsolete* critical invention" (93), one whose basic assumptions have for too long provided a false or misleading coherence for American literature. The invention of transcendentalism from Emerson to Matthiessen involved subordinating the complex material and social history of the United States to an idealized vision of the "American self" and "American experience" grounded in German idealism.[15] The coherence of American literature came to depend on thematic and formalist readings of a narrow set of New England writers, readings that insisted on establishing a link between American literary form and an amorphous American national character. Carafiol caps off his critical analysis of this project with a discussion of how Matthiessen's epic treatment of Emerson, Thoreau, Whitman, Hawthorne, and Melville in *The American Renaissance* "set the modern agenda for critical practice in American literary studies by recasting the spiritual idealism of earlier scholarship into a powerful amalgam of aesthetic and political idealisms" (86). Whereas Goddard's efforts were aimed at completing Frothingham's reinvention of transcendentalism as an "American" system of thought at the beginning of the twentieth century, and whereas Brooks sought to appropriate transcendentalist ideals for a critique of the hegemony of pragmatism and capitalism during and after the Great War, Matthiessen in one epic textual move reasserted the dominance and originary character of transcendentalism for American literature and grounded its value in the contemporary standards of the New Criticism.

Carafiol proposes his pragmatist historicism both as an antidote to this traditional project and as an alternative to current forms of revisionist American literary scholarship, which in his view do not follow up forcefully enough on the antifoundationalist critique of essentialism found in neopragmatist critics like Rorty and Fish. He insists that too many contemporary revisionists are driven by an old desire to present a coherent picture of "America," "American experience," "American identity," and "American literature" that remains essentialist at its core. He understands the logic of contemporary revisionism, but he doesn't think it goes far enough in incorporating the antifoundationalist logic of theorists like Rorty and Fish. He praises critics like Annette Kolodny, Jane Tompkins, Laurence Buell, Sacvan Bercovitch, and Walter Benn Michaels for, collectively, trying to redefine and reinterpret American literature in "a larger social matrix," and for broadening "the notion of the literary into textuality so as to encompass not only nonliterary texts but nonlinguistic cultural acts" (18). Such recontextualizations, he acknowledges, have been based on more soundly historical approaches to the study of literature than were previous criticism, and they have redefined and diversified the canon and curriculum in ways that more accurately reflect the nature and history of American populations and cultures. However, if these revisions are simply aimed at more nuanced and complicated historical contextualizations of "American" literature, concerned simply with "diversifying" the texts and authors of a newly expanded canon, Carafiol questions how far they really move American literary scholarship from its traditional preoccupation with creating a coherent and idealized myth about America and American identity. In his view, there is nothing very radical about diversity and inclusiveness if all the old idealist paradigms still hold sway, and he sees our complacency as something like complicity with dominant strategies of containment.

Carafiol's antidote to this problem, as I suggested earlier, is neither the irony of Rorty nor the nostalgic, moralizing pragmatism of Gunn and Poirier, but a "thoroughgoing and reconceptualized historicism" based on a neopragmatist critique of "idealist categories" that have underwritten previous attempts to tell a "coherent story" about American writing, a story that has belied "the convictions of a posttheological age" (148). The pragmatic historicism he sketches out in his study is potentially preferable to both versions of neopragmatism I have been discussing in this chapter. However, there are a number of problems with the historicism he proposes, which is rather oddly derived from the poststructuralist discourse of Fish and Rorty, and in the final analysis is not able to shake the traditional paradigms it sets out to critique. "Poststructuralist discourse" makes an abrupt appearance in his first chapter, where a loosely described antifoundationalism associated with Rorty and Fish gets quickly translated into a form of *historicism* the "general aim" of which is "explaining the relationship of texts to their historical contexts" (15). This is an awfully informal way to characterize the complex theoretical poststructuralism of Rorty and Fish, critics who in any case are not readily associated with historical (or new historicist) criticism. Tracing the genealogy of American New Historicism back through Rorty and Fish (with nary a mention of Foucault) is odd, and he makes no attempt to connect feminist American criticism to a critical tradition outside Rorty and Fish.

More important, despite the rhetoric in his book about decentering and displacing dominant critical paradigms, his own proposals remain grounded in them. His pragmatic historicism aims to read "historical texts as voices in contemporary conversations" (122) rather than trying to recuperate what they meant in their own time:

> If Americanists want to reclaim the cultural authority that the work of their professional predecessors derived from their nationalist focus, then they need to account not so much for the place of individual texts in the circumstances of their production as for their continuing interest (or lack of interest) over time for both professional and lay readers . . . to explain better, to themselves as well as to nonspecialists, why they are reading books, especially old books. (34–35)

Carafiol, quite simply, wants to shift historical criticism from using old texts to tell essentializing stories about the past to using old texts to tell useful stories about the *present*. Pragmatist historicism of the kind he proposes opts out of what he views as the impossible task of recapturing historical meaning and instead focuses critical attention on how to use historical texts in order to intervene in contemporary cultural debates, a historicism that, in his words, "will confront us with the problems of our own time rather than of the nineteenth century" (45).

This project has a number of virtues, chief of which is that it avoids the nostalgic idealism of Gunn and Poirier's version of American pragmatism. However, while it does not indulge in the kind of ironic posturing we often find in Rorty, Carafiol's pragmatist method turns out, like Rorty's, to produce readings of canonical writers that simply redescribe their ideas in contemporary terms. For this reason, he is not able to do what he sets out to do: to "decenter" the dominant paradigms of American criticism. There isn't anything particularly wrong with Carafiol's desire to find in older texts answers to problems in our own time, but there isn't anything terribly *radical* about it either, since wanting to read older texts in ways that make them comment on contemporary cultural problems with a point of view you endorse has been the backbone of modern British and American criticism since Arnold. There is no paradigm shift here. Moreover, since Carafiol concludes his book with new readings of Emerson and Thoreau, New England (and its canonical writers) remain at the center of Carafiol's project (like all of the criticism he complains about, his extrapolates from Emerson and Thoreau a set of ideals that supposedly cast another light on American experience).[16] What we get here is something rather like Rorty's idea of a redescription. Carafiol does not really opt out of the game of describing America through a reading of our principal transcendentalists. Instead, he redescribes selections of their writing that accord with his own critical project. While this offers a different, and potentially more useful, pragmatist intervention than the ones we get from the other critics I have been discussing, it too quickly dismisses the work of feminists and minority scholars, and it leaves patriarchal New England at the geographical and intellectual center of American literature.

The problem with all of these neopragmatist choices is that none of them recognizes, or responds very effectively to, the challenges of an American culture that has become increasingly preoccupied with its own hybridity. Rorty, for example, shares with Gunn and Poirier the paradoxical belief that American criticism can create a "beautiful mosaic" that will "expand the canon" if it simply redescribes the work of a narrow and familiar group of Anglocentric writers (among them Blake, Arnold, Nietzsche, Marx, Baudelaire, Eliot, and Orwell). This genealogy is as inbred and familiar as the one we get in Carafiol (Emerson and Thoreau), the one Poirier offers in *The Renewal of Literature* (Emerson, Thoreau, Whitman, William James, Frost, and Stevens), and is not that far removed in spirit from Gunn's American "pragmatists" (Emerson, Dewey, Henry Adams, Howells, Wilson, and Trilling). It is not just that the fabric of American intellectual life for these critics is not threaded with the voices of women, or Americans of African, Hispanic, Asian, or Native descent. It is that the very history (intellectual and social) of America's development and the heterogeneity of experience it has contained get shrunken and distorted by these critics. For all of the differences I have been stressing between Rorty's pragmatism, on the one hand, and that of Carafiol, Gunn, and Poirier on the other, in the final analysis they are all committed to the enterprise of redescribing for its contemporary redemptive value the critical discourse of a familiar group of Anglocentric critics who collectively reinforce in an American critical context a very narrow vision of "experience." There is nothing wrong with Rorty's wanting to make us face the consequences of linguistic contingency, nor would we want to lament his desire to increase our sense of solidarity with others and therefore reduce instances of cruelty in our world. Likewise, it is tempting to applaud Gunn's desire to tackle the problem of "disbelief," to try to "reconstitute the relationship between literature and values, between art and morality" (*Culture of Criticism* 22), to affirm Poirier's desire to explore the relationship between what he calls "aboriginal" and "inherited" power (*Renewal* 142), and to appreciate Carafiol's call for a more rigorous and politically engaged historicism.[17] However, as long as these issues are pursued within the neatly circumscribed context of an Anglocentric liberal discourse about abstract ways of conceiving value, the self, truth, and community—which I am arguing is what we ultimately get in each of these critics—critical discourse is doomed to the mode of redescription Rorty insists we can't escape.

It is important to recognize that Rorty's inability to escape redescription is not a given. It is not something he is locked into for ontological or epistemological reasons; it is a choice he himself has decided to make for moral and political reasons. No one has coerced Rorty to work out and defend the position that "there is nothing to be said about either truth or rationality apart from redescriptions of *the familiar procedures of justification which a given society—ours—uses in one or another area of inquiry*" ("Solidarity" 6, emphasis mine). When he endorses Hillary Putnam's claim that "we can only hope to produce a more rational *conception* of rationality or a better *conception* of morality if we operate from *within* our tradition" (9, my emphasis), he does not do so because language itself or some unbending system of signification leaves him no other choice. He does so because he wants to discuss concepts and issues in a way that remains within, and is specific to, a certain philosophical and critical "tradition" he has been expertly trained to discuss and critique. As long as Rorty chooses to follow the familiar procedures of justification that operate within a tradition of critical discourse demarcated by his liberal ironist line of writers, it will hardly be surprising that all he can produce are redescriptions of what he thinks is significant in that tradition.

However, as I have already insisted, this is a choice he has made himself. When he draws his distinction between the "objectivism" of metaphysical idealists and the "ethnocentrism" of pragmatists, it is not to draw a distinction between critics hobbled by traditional "habits of intellectual, social, and political life" (11) and critics who aren't. It is toward the end of demonstrating that "these same habits" can be "justified . . . by a pragmatist conception of truth" (11). The only real difference between the two is that the pragmatist is willing to admit that he "cannot justify these habits without circularity" (11), whereas the objectivist is not. But both the objectivist and the ethnocentric pragmatist represent, endorse, perpetuate, and privilege a familiar and circumscribed kind of philosophical, literary, and cultural discourse bounded by a set of presumptions that emerged between the lives of Kant and Nietzsche. Rorty's dilemma produces a kind of postmodern tragic irony that has its corollary in Harold Bloom's theory of poetic belatedness. In Bloom's view the modern poet can only struggle hopelessly to avoid rewriting other poems, while in Rorty's view the philosopher/critic can only struggle hopelessly to avoid rewriting other criticism.

In a sense, Rorty's decision to label his position "ethnocentric" is inspired, since it has the kind of paradoxical shock value that helps sell philosophy near the end of the twentieth century. However, the choice also starkly foregrounds the weakness of his position. Herrnstein Smith, as we have already noted, has pointed out that "Rorty's resolution of the pragmatist's dilemma [over the accusation of relativism] in favor of ethnocentrism is altogether dubious" (172). His working sense of "community" or "ethnos," she points out (166–73), is remarkably circumscribed ("the liberal intellectuals of the secular modern West"), and his whole discussion of community in terms of tolerance and inclusion is organized within an us-versus-them framework in which primitive people, if they knew better, would embrace the ways of the secular

West. I would add to Herrnstein Smith's general point the more specific observation that Rorty's ethnocentrism reinforces (or redescribes) an extremely traditional conception of "America," as both a geographical place and a community of people. Committed as it is to procedures that have historically justified the dominant intellectual tradition in America, it is positioned to redescribe the terms of that dominance rather than to critique them. Rorty's ethnocentrism is necessitated by what he calls "the lonely provincialism" of the modern secular Western intellectual (the term is meant to elicit our sympathy). Where in Rorty's view the "realist thinks that the whole point of philosophical thought is to detach oneself from any particular community and look down at it from a more universal standpoint," the pragmatist insists that his desire for solidarity simply makes him take "his own community *too* seriously" for that (13). In an almost instinctive or reflexive reaction to the accusation of relativism, Rorty falls back on a narrowly circumscribed *ethnos*, defending not only its habits of justification but the necessity of having to make that defense in the first place. Having methodically rejected the whole conception of essences, foundations, and "metaphysical comforts" (13), Rorty turns right around, when push comes to shove, and embraces a foundational or essential "ethnos" as the "centrism" for his own position. The fact that this term is not metaphysical in the classic sense of the word matters little, for "ethnos" has the same reductive, centralizing, essentializing function such terms have always had in Western philosophy. At once narrow and vague, Rorty's ahistorical and purified "ethnos" is fundamentally idealist in terms of both its definition and its rhetorical deployment as a centering term.

As I have already suggested, Rorty's position doesn't leave room for critical inquiry that interrogates the premises of its own discourse. It doesn't allow, that is, for an examination of the "familiar procedures of justification" he is using, or for a careful look at what it means to stay "within our tradition." I don't mean this in the sense of an inquiry at an abstract level. That would simply lead to an epistemologically circular redescription of the kind Rorty calls ironist. I mean a concrete historical inquiry into the construction of "America" as a place, a nation, and a fluid community of people (something Carafiol at least begins to do). Such an inquiry simply falls outside the terms of redescription Rorty is willing to invoke. He wants to "attach a special privilege to our own community" (12), defined as "those who share enough of one's beliefs to make fruitful conversation possible" (13). However, the real "special privilege" here is the privilege he gives to an intellectual tradition that is at once familiar and ill-defined, and in terms of American cultural criticism, decidedly out of touch with the nation's complex social, intellectual, cultural, and creative history. It is hard to see how Rorty's ethnocentric response to difference, his falling back on a familiar set of secular humanist Western writers in the face of our increasing recognition of how difference and hybridity have structured what he calls our "ethnos," can be construed as constructive. Though it is informed by elements of poststructuralist theory rejected by critics like Gunn and Poirier, it is ultimately not much more satisfying than their Emersonian prescription for cultural renewal.

Border Studies: From Ethnocentrism to Ethnocriticism

Earlier I suggested that we do not need to choose between neopragmatist ethnocentrism and the redemptive Emersonianism we get in Gunn, Poirier, and Carafiol. A much more promising path for American literary and cultural criticism is offered by a different group of revisionary critics whose work systematically critiques the kind of ehtnocentric habits of intellectual justification Rorty is unwilling to question. I have in mind here critics influenced by work on African, Hispanic, Asian, and Native American literatures, and by those seeking to reformulate our conception of, and approach to, American literature and culture within a multiculturalist, postcolonial, border studies context. These critics share Carafiol's desire to release American criticism from its ongoing obsession with a narrow nationalist ideal, but instead of doing so by redescribing the ideals of canonical transcendentalists in a way that leaves American literature's traditional geographical and intellectual borders in place, they put the *politics of location* at the very center of their enterprise. Where Carafiol wants to question the primacy of idealized conceptions of "America" and its national and cultural identity, other critics of American literature are attempting to complicate how we think about American literature by *retheorizing the space(s) in which it has emerged,* attempting to dislocate American literature by directing critical attention to the liminal margins and permeable border zones out of which cultures in the Americas have emerged. Attention here turns away from creating narratives about the coherence of cultures *within* national borders to an analysis of what Carolyn Porter has called "cultural force fields" (468), border zones in which individual and national identities migrate, merge, and hybridize.[18]

Carolyn Porter discusses some of the representative texts of American "border zone" criticism in "What We Know That We Don't Know: Remapping American Literary History." Her focus is on a body of criticism that both constructs a rhetorically persuasive redescription of "American" geography and culture and explores the contingency of American values, while challenging the kind of ethnocentrism endorsed by Rorty in his writings on "solidarity." Recent American cultural studies has attempted to reground American literary and cultural criticism in the politics of location through analyses of the historical and geographical displacements that have configured both the Americas and our conception of "American" identity and culture. In doing so this criticism has fashioned a whole set of poststructuralist insights into subjectivity, historiography, gender, race, ideology, and nationhood into a critical enterprise intent on reconfiguring our geographic and historical senses of the term "America," and therefore, the kind of criticism we accept as "American" cultural criticism. Without minimizing the theoretical complications of its work, it has pushed beyond both the fetishizing of irony and double gestures and the awkward fashioning of a neopragmatic Emersonianism in the interests of historical and literary scholarship undertaken in areas formerly considered either off limits or inconsequential by critics interested in American literature and culture.

This criticism offers a striking alternative to the conversation Rorty wants to have about culture, tradition, belief, community, solidarity, and cruelty. In the first place, it deals in a concrete, historical way with these issues, eschewing Rorty's abstract metropolitanism. In this context, it moves to challenge the fundamentally Arnoldian sense of culture we get in Rorty, pursuing instead a wide-ranging historical analysis of how ethnocentric conceptions of culture, tradition, and community such as Rorty's have been constructed and deployed in the interests (sometimes conscious, sometimes unconscious) of shoring up the hegemony of modern liberalism in the West. Texts like Gloria Anzaldúa's *Borderlands/La Frontera*, José David Saldívar's *The Dialectics of Our America*, Lewis Owens's "The Song Is Very Short": Native American Literature and Literary Theory," Arnold Krupat's *Ethnocriticism*, and the essays collected by Hortense Spillers in *Comparative American Identities: Race, Sex, and Nationality in the Modern Text* have developed an altogether different conversation about American culture and criticism from the ones neopragmatists like Rorty, Gunn, Carafiol, and Poirier have generated.[19]

Where Rorty limits his conversation to ironized redescriptions resigned to the ethnocentric limitations of a humanist discourse about how best to justify and perpetuate "European . . . habits of intellectual, social, and political life," Saldívar, for example, wants to get beyond the "naiveté" of an "old historicism" based on these habits in order to redirect its "Eurocentric focus" toward the identification of "a distinctive postcolonial, pan-American consciousness" in the Americas (xi). Where Rorty's "mosaic" of critical and creative writers actually redescribes a very traditional canon, Saldívar's attention to José Marti, Ntozake Shange, Rolando Hinojosa, Americo Paredes, Arturo Islas, and Gloria Anzaldúa is in the interests of both an expanded American canon and "the notion of America itself" (xii). The ethnocentric critic wants to rely on writers who have read a lot. Saldívar, by contrast, wants to rely on writers the ethnocentric critic has read around, or ignored. Where Rorty's legitimate wariness about epistemological or truth claims based on some "transcultural" concept of human nature drives him into an ethnocentric corner, that same wariness on Saldívar's part stimulates an examination of the dynamically *intercultural* context in which not only epistemologies and truth claims, but selves, communities, and nations unfold. Rorty wants to avoid the charge of relativism a pluralist position on culture creates, so he falls back on the interests of "our" group, but one very narrowly defined in terms of class, educational background, and, one presumes, ethnicity. Saldívar, on the other hand, does not envision culture in America as the product of ever subtle, careful, nuanced redescriptions of an essentially European set of social habits. He envisions "our America" as the product of a dialectic in which both the "our" and the "America" evolve in a much more complicated, hybrid fashion.

Saldívar insists that since cultures evolve dialectically—in the sense that any particular culture is ultimately a hybrid of other, prior ones—criticism has to inhabit and attend to the liminal, marginal, border spaces and states *between* cultures. "Ethnos" here is "our group" construed not as those who share our beliefs (as Rorty would have it), but as those whose beliefs have evolved and shifted in contact and conflict with one another. This in-between space is different from the *center* that grounds Rorty's ethno*centrism*. It is an off-center or decentered space figured in material terms by border regions like the Southwest, Louisiana, or Florida, but also, in methodological terms, by a critical position that moves back and forth between opposed epistemologies, value systems, political economies, and so on.

Saldívar's interest in theorizing the spaces between national borders in the Americas is symptomatic of a larger preoccupation among revisionist American critics with what I earlier referred to as the "politics of location." Saldívar is only one of a growing number of American critics working to theorize and practice a form of criticism that, while it may share something of Carafiol's pragmatic aims, is based on careful attention to the inherently transcultural nature of writing in the Americas.[20] This project has been pursued in the context of attempts by a range of critics to theorize the space between cultural and national borders. In her study of the nature and role of "transculturation" in travel writing, for example, Mary Louise Pratt coined the term "contact zone." "Contact zone," she writes, "refer[s] to the space of colonial encounters, the space in which peoples geographically and historically separated come into contact with each other and establish ongoing relations, usually involving conditions of coercion, radical inequality, and intractable conflict . . . By using the term 'contact,' I aim to foreground the interactive, improvisational dimensions of colonial encounters [which] . . . emphasizes how subjects are constituted in and by their relations to each other" (6–7). The key terms here, it seems to me, are "colonial" and "improvisational." Pratt borrows the term "contact" from linguistics where, she reminds us, "the term contact language refers to improvised languages that develop among speakers of different native languages who need to communicate with each other" (6). Pratt equates the creole or pidgin *languages* resulting from this improvisational interaction with the creole or hybrid *cultures* that also result from prolonged contact.[21] Although the relations of power in contact zones are "radically asymmetrical," Pratt rightly starts with the premise that something like a third culture evolves syncretically within them, since they are characterized by "copresence, interaction, interlocking understandings and practices" (7). Contact zones—and the literature that comes out of them—provide a context for studying the production of subjectivity (in both senses of the word) and culture in a historical and geographical space that foregrounds the sometimes arbitrary, syncretic, improvised, and hybrid nature of personal and social forms of expression.

Pratt's contact zones cover the globe. She writes about imperial travel writing in Africa, Latin America, and Central America. American critics, like the Native American writer Louis Owens, have drawn on Pratt's term to help reconceptualize the improvisation of individual subjectivity and hybrid cultures characteristic of the "American" frontier. Owens borrows Pratt's term to help reconceptualize the "colonized space" of European/Native contact in the United States as a "transcultural frontier" (51), which in James Clifton's words is "a culturally defined place where peoples with different culturally expressed identities meet and deal with each other" (5). Owens, of course, is concerned less with theorizing a context for reading travel writing on a global scale than with theorizing a context for reading Native American literature.

Pratt's "contact zone" is useful to him in trying "to achieve a theoretical discourse that might help to illuminate the complexities of multicultural literature," which, along with Bakhtin, he sees as unfolding in
a "dialogically agitated space" where "discourse is multidirectional and
hybridized" (58). The multidirectional and hybrid quality of experience
on the transcultural frontier, characterized as Owens sees it by instabil-
ity, "heteroglossia," and indeterminacy (59), gives it the improvisational character Pratt ascribes to contact zones. As such, it contrasts
markedly with the historical term "territory," a "space which is mapped,
fully imagined as a place of containment, invented to control and subdue the wild imaginations of imagined Native peoples" (59). On the
transcultural frontier, neither the colonized nor the colonizing cultures
last very long, for the kinds of improvisation such zones necessitate
quickly produce through a process of syncretization what we have
somewhat problematically come to call "hybrid" cultures. Owens, in
adapting Pratt's term, wants to avoid fetishizing Native American literature for its pure, indigenous, native qualities. Acknowledging that to
Native Americans critical theory can simply represent "little more than
a new form of colonial enterprise" ("why," he writes, "should people
who have borne the brunt of authoritative discourse for five hundred
years participate in a theoretical discourse that originates from the very
center of colonial authority?" [56]), Owens nevertheless wants to avoid
"opting out" or inhabiting a "separatist intellectual" position (57). What
is attractive for Owens about working in and with Pratt's contact zone
is precisely that it gets beyond the kind of essentialist theories of identity and culture that can lead to separation and paralysis.[22]

Both of the terms for liminal spaces Owens invokes, of course, are
predated by the Chicana critic Gloria Anzaldúa's groundbreaking attempt to theorize what she calls "borderlands" (la frontera). Anzaldúa's
conception of borderlands grows out of her own experience growing up
in South Texas, and from her study of the radically unstable, migrating
cultures of the mestiza/o diaspora in what is now Mexico and the Southwest United States. She writes that "borders are set up to define the
places that are safe and unsafe, to distinguish us from them. A border is
a dividing line, a narrow strip along a steep edge. A borderland is a
vague and undetermined place created by the emotional residue of an
unnatural boundary. It is in a constant state of transition" (5). Literal
borders are a postcontact phenomenon, of course, and so need to be distinguished from "contact zones." However, the quality of experience in
border zones essentially reflects the quality of experience in contact
zones. Border zones, as articulated by Anzaldúa, simultaneously orga-

nize and disorganize space, identities, and cultures. Borders draw violent dividing lines between the "safe and unsafe," between "us" and "them," but at the same time border*lands* are "vague and undetermined," in a "constant state of transition." Like Pratt's "contact zone," Anzaldúa's "borderland" is a fluid and improvisational space in which languages and identities hybridize and evolve. As such, her concept of the "borderland" is inextricably tied to the production of a "mestiza/o" identity: the borderland is a place whose "inhabitants are the prohibited and forbidden . . . the squint-eyed, the perverse, the queer, the troublesome, the mongrel, the mulatto, the half-breed . . . in short, those who cross over, pass over, or go through the confines of the 'normal' " (5).

Porter, as I have noted, is also interested in this kind of conceptual framework for rethinking national and cultural spaces in her speculations about how to "remap" American literary and cultural studies. She wants to fuse Saldívar's transcultural perspective with Anzaldúa's interest in the creation of hybrid identities and cultures, to get criticism in and of the Americas to reorganize itself around "tracking the *histories* of creolization that generated the cultural formations in which they are produced" (471). She believes that such histories would more effectively than what Carafiol proposes "force a reconstellation of the field of 'American' studies along lines that rupture the nationalist myths" of traditional American literary criticism (471). This desire to track a complex network of transcultural formations leads her to propose for study an even more ambitiously conceptualized border zone (or what she calls "cultural force fields" [468]) than the one we get in Anzaldúa, a hemispheric zone like the one theorized first by José Marti, and later by Roberto Retamar and Saldívar. The "America" that emerges in their work, she points out, is "plural and contestatory in its reference: because of their permeability as national boundaries, geopolitical borders are foregrounded [by these critics] as regions, borderlands that in turn reveal and renew cultural networks linking the Caribbean and Latin America to the North" (468). Porter is interested not in discarding a New England vantage point toward American literature, but in complicating it with a Latin American one. "A Latin American vantage point," she writes, "might serve to fracture and destabilize the normative assumptions of an American studies whose clean focus has traditionally been achieved at the considerable cost of its nearsightedness" (509). The value of this Latin American vantage point, she notes, is that "it brings into view . . . more complex geopolitical relations between Europe and both Americas" than we get from the more traditional, Anglocentric one. It gets beyond "the traditional US/British or North America/Europe binary" that has centered American studies, complicating it with "a quadruple set of relations between (1) Europe and Latin America; (2) Latin America and North America; (3) North America and Europe; and (4) Africa and both Americas" (510). Redrawing the map of American studies in this way would, she insists, allow us to "grasp how the cultural, political, and economic relations between and within the Americas might work to reconstellate the field" of American studies (510). "Theoretically speaking, 'America,' both geopolitically and historically, would become at once internally fissured and externally relativized" (510).[23]

As I noted earlier, attempts by American critics to theorize the space between cultural and geographic borders has been accompanied by the attempt to find a methodological or critical space between conventional discursive borders like "essentialist/anti-essentialist," "objectivist/relativist," or "centralist/pluralist." This kind of methodological imperative can be observed in Arnold Krupat's attempt to theorize what he calls "Ethnocriticism." Krupat (writing about the study of Native American literature) commits his analysis to the "shifting space in which two *cultures* encounter one another," not a "fixed or mappable," space, but, rather, a culturally defined place that usually cuts across mapped national borders (5). Grounding his own critical position in anthropological modes of description, Krupat defines ethnocriticism as a practice "founded upon ethnohistorical descriptions of the frontier," which "must involve a recognition that the topics it takes up from an anthropological, historical, or literary perspective all must be set against the backdrop of a pervasive Western imperialism" (5). Krupat rightly worries, however, that ethnocriticism can seem to be just another form of Western imperialism, "inasmuch as the conceptual categories necessary to Ethnocriticism—culture, history, imperialism, anthropology, literature, interdisciplinarity, even the frontier—are Western categories" (5). Other critics, he acknowledges, have urged a *nativist* approach to the criticism of Tribal literatures, one that has recourse to specifically "Indian" modes of thinking and analysis (6). However, Krupat rejects the idea (along with Owens) that either Western or Native forms of cultural expression and analysis can be purely and absolutely indigenous in the first place, since both have long ago been influenced and transformed by the other in a syncretic process.[24] "An ethnocritical frontier orientation," he writes, "soon shows that one of the things that occurs on the borders is that oppositional sets like West/Rest, Us/Them, anthropological/biological, historical/mythical, and so on, often tend to break down" (15).[25] The space between, for Krupat, is thus a *method-*

ological as well as a geographic one. Like Owens (but unlike Rorty), he sees no choice but to move within and between "Native" and "Western" theories and practices; the transcultural frontier he traverses takes him back and forth across critical and discursive borders. "Ethnocritical discourse," Krupat writes, "in its self-positioning at the frontier, seeks to traverse rather than occupy a great variety of 'middle grounds,' both at home and abroad" (25–26). It will try to move between "humanist" and "antihumanist" positions, between what he calls postmodern "fragmentariness" and "social scientific aspirations to cognitive adequacy" (26). The border Krupat and Owens want to inhabit, then, is a double one: the border zone between Native and Western culture, and the border zone between what Krupat calls "objectivism" and "relativism" (27).

Like Rorty's "ethnocentrism," then, Krupat's "Ethnocriticism" is a response to the problem of relativism. We have already seen how Rorty's ethnocentrism is an attempt to redescribe relativism in a way that makes it more palatable by stressing the interested commitment of a group to a certain set of "habits," even if those habits cannot be underwritten with some kind of transcendental claim. In Rorty, the emphasis is on an "ethnos" narrowly constituted, and on a position that is *centered* within a certain set of familiar beliefs, values, and forms of justification. Krupat's ethnocriticism, on the other hand, stresses critical inquiry into contested, fluid, border spaces. His conception of "ethnos" is meant to foreground the element of anthropological description in any cultural criticism rather than, as in Rorty, the singular and self-sustaining nature of a group held together by shared beliefs. Moreover, *ethnocriticism,* unlike ethno*centrism*, is interested in positioning itself not at the center of something, but in critical relation to it. Ethnocriticism inhabits the interactive space between cultures in order to understand the hybrid processes of cultural formation, deformation, and reformation that take place there, while Rorty's ethnocentric pragmatism positions itself in the metropolitan center of a small discursive community in order to redescribe its habits of justification.

Both Rorty and Krupat, as I have already noted, are trying to formulate a position for cultural criticism that is tolerant of a range of cultures and views, but that nevertheless avoids the charge of relativism. Krupat wants to formulate an "Ethnocriticism" that seeks to achieve a certain level or kind of empirical accuracy about cultures, yet at the same time recognize how that accuracy will be embodied in a culturally specific discourse that is other than its subjects. That is, "given its frontier condition of liminality or betweenness, Ethnocriticism by its very nature must test any appeals to 'reason,' 'science,' 'knowledge,' or 'truth' it would make in relation to Other or non-Western constructions of these categories, or, for that matter, to any alternative categories Others may propose" (27). Rorty, on the other hand, having taken the position that there can be no "ahistorical standpoint" ("Solidarity" 12) from which one culture can be privileged over another, wants to avoid the charge of relativism (an "impossible tolerance for every other group" [12]) by privileging his own group or community over others. The "pragmatist," he writes, "should grasp the ethnocentric horn of this dilemma. We should say that we must, in practice, privilege our own group, even though there can be no noncircular justification for doing so" (12).

In my view, Rorty's ethnocentrism is a retreat backward in the face of relativism, while the kind of ethnocriticism critics like Saldívar, Porter, Anzaldúa and Krupat are struggling to work out is a step forward, since it refuses to get caught up in having to make a choice between objectivism and relativism. Rorty's response to the cry of relativism is to give in, to say, in effect, I don't believe in the relative value of all cultures, really. I privilege my own. Saldívar and Krupat, on the other hand, want to insist that cultures themselves evolve relative to other cultures, so that "relativism" is not the name for an embarrassing epistemological or philosophical position we must shun, but something nearer a description of the hybrid nature of all cultures. They want a criticism that inhabits and interrogates the dynamic space between cultures because they understand that all cultures unfold *relative to each other in that space*. Ethnocriticism, inhabiting a space between objectivism and relativism, takes up a position at the very site of the production of cultures, so that its "inbetweenness" stands in metonymic relation to what it studies. "Ethnocritical discourse," Krupat writes, "regards border and boundary crossings, with their openness to and recognition of the inevitability of interactive relations, as perhaps the best means to some broadly descriptive account of the way things 'really' work in the material and historical world" (26).

Of course, when Krupat puts "really" in quotation marks he is signaling something like the same kind of irony we find more enthusiastically foregrounded in Rorty. Krupat's ethnocriticism aims to be more materially, ideologically, and historically embedded than Rorty's, but at the same time it is wary about making claims regarding the ultimate accuracy of its descriptions.[26] This wariness has to do less with the relativism of ethnocriticism than with its potential *imperialism*. Since ethnocriticism's "conceptual categories . . . culture, history, imperialism, anthropology, literature, interdisciplinarity, even the frontier—are Western categories, the objection may be raised that Ethnocriticism is itself no more than yet another form of imperialism" (5). Krupat sees this objection arising on two fronts. The first is a nativist front, in which writers like Leslie Marmon Silko and Gerald Vizenor insist that we ought to abandon these Western terms of analysis in favor of more appropriately "'Indian' modes of thinking" (6). The second front is postmodernist, represented by Lyotard, Baudrillard, the anthropologist Stephen Tyler, and Rorty himself. All of these critics, Krupat writes, want to abandon "overarching explanatory narratives of historicism, philosophy, and science as no more than discourses of legitimation" (7).[27] The "between" space Krupat wants to articulate is partly defined in terms of ethnocriticism's desire to chart a way between these two fronts, to avoid the charge of imperialism on the one hand and a discredited empiricism or historicism on the other.

Rorty's desire to avoid the kind of explanatory narratives associated with old historicisms, we have seen, drives him toward a form of ethnocentrism open to the very charge of imperialism Krupat wants to avoid. Krupat's dilemma is something like the reverse of Rorty's: having staked his claim against ethnocentrism and imperialism, how is he to avoid the kind of naive "objectivism" or historicism associated with the master narratives so effectively discredited by critics like Lyotard and Rorty? Krupat's strategy, essentially, is not to let himself get forced into making the kind of choice Rorty makes (rejecting objectivism and embracing ethnocentrism), choosing, rather, to move back and forth between de-essentialized realms of Western and Native forms of experience and conceptualizations. "To move back and forth across border lines," he writes, seems "far richer in [its] potential for criticism, pedagogy, and politics than any turn to an exclusively defined, monolithically 'Indian' or 'Western' way" (17). I am arguing that Rorty makes just this kind of choice in his ethnocentric embrace of a monolithically intellectual, secular Western *ethnos*.

In the final analysis, Krupat's choice may not seem to be any more defensible, from a *theoretical* point of view, than Rorty's. That is, if one wants to take the side of (some version of) Rorty's ethnocentric pragmatism, the theoretical arguments in support of that position can seem to be quite compelling. If, on the other hand, one wants to take the side of (some version of) Krupat's ethnocriticism, the theoretical arguments in support of that position can seem equally compelling. Ultimately, of course, while theory is important, it is not going to make the difference. Those who choose Rortean solidarity with liberal irony will do so out of a sense of solidarity with the habits and justifications of the essentially European, Western humanist tradition he embraces. The theoretical justifications for this position will help explain that choice, but they won't necessarily convince someone else to make it. Likewise, those who choose the kind of ethnocritical approach to social and cultural criticism Krupat articulates will do so out of a sense of solidarity with the aims and justifications of the hybrid mix of traditions he tries to bring together. Again, the theoretical justifications will help explain one's choice, but they probably won't be sufficient to convince someone else to make it. In both cases, the choice will be an ethical one, not a theoretical one.

I have concluded with Rorty and Krupat because they dramatize in a clear way some of the choices facing American cultural criticism as we near the end of the twentieth century. Rorty's ethnocentric position represents a relatively extreme articulation of the ironist impulse in contemporary cultural criticism. That impulse does not necessarily require an embrace of ethnocentrism, but in making that choice, Rorty underscores how short a distance the ironist has to travel to get to a position that conserves an insular sameness in the face of complexity and difference. The ultimate irony of Rorty's ironist position is how it turns a poststructuralist critique of metaphysics into a critical position that ends up idealizing and reinforcing the status quo. Krupat's ethnocriticism (and the work of border studies critics in general), on the other hand, offers a way out of the philosophical morass of contingency theories, a way that endorses a more complex, heterogeneous "ethnos" rooted in material and social culture. Krupat, as we have seen, is the first to acknowledge the difficulties and paradoxes confronting any version of ethnocriticism, but what he proposes is an approach to cultural criticism much better equipped to deal with the social, cultural, and political realities of the twenty-first century than is Rorty's genteel, backward-looking liberal ironist.

It would be nice to end this study by arguing that the tension between ethnocentrism and ethnocriticism I have been discussing represents our own contemporary version of the tension between metaphysical idealism and the loosely pragmatist or materialist position I have been tracing in this study. There *is* a way, I would argue, in which Rorty's pragmatism, paradoxically, modulates into a kind of idealist position, while Krupat's ethnocriticism basically represents a pragmatic choice about the practice of cultural criticism. In his attempt to assimilate philosophy to literary criticism, Rorty follows Dewey in banishing idealism from philosophy only to relocate it in literary discourse. Krupat, on the other hand, eschews the ironist position, in theory and in practice, and instead turns to the ostensibly more materialist practice of anthropology.[28] It is more than ironic to observe the philosopher abandoning philosophy for literary criticism at the very moment when the literary critic is busy transforming literary criticism into ethnography. In making these choices Rorty and Krupat together dramatize a certain inexorable trajectory in recent criticism, which has gone from a poststructuralist critique of foundationalist criticism to a focus on the potentially circular systematicity of all representational systems to a renewed interest in generating a materialist and historical form of criticism, one that is aware more than ever of the contingencies of language and ideology, but is nevertheless committed to what Krupat would call the ethnographic element in cultural criticism. While it would be too reductive to say that this recent history simply plays out the tension we have been tracing in this study between metaphysical idealism and pragmatism in American criticism, the idealist dimension in Rorty's position and the materialist commitment in Krupat's suggest the degree to which their positions evolve out of that tension. In part it dramatizes a certain kind of theoretical or methodological dilemma that cuts across history and cultural contingencies. But the tension between ethnocentrism and ethnocriticism is ultimately particular to our own time and place, for it represents a clash of contemporary values and commitments no one can avoid.

Notes

Works Cited

Index

Notes

Introduction

1. There are of course important differences between each of these critics that I will sort out in the Conclusion. Carafiol's pragmatism, for example, is substantially different from the more nostalgic pragmatism of Gunn and Poirier.

2. As Pippin notes, "modernism" has always been a fairly ambiguous term, but it has usually carried these two contradictory senses, one denoting "a heightened and affirmative modern self-consciousness (a final attempt to be 'truly' modern, to create in a radical and unprecedented way a form of life, indeed a sensibility, finally consistent with the full implications of the modern revolution), as well as an intense dissatisfaction with the sterile, exploitative, commercialized, or simply ugly forms of life apparently characteristic of social modernization (or 'bourgeois' forms of modernization)" (29). Also, see T. Jackson Lears's discussion of "antimodernism."

3. For another approach to the relationship between modernity, modernism, and the literature of the American "renaissance," see Pease 7–10 and passim.

4. I don't mean to downplay, of course, the importance of relating the work of these critics to the material and social conditions of modernity. I am, rather, simply trying to be clear about the aims and limits of this study. For an excellent example of analyses of this sort, see Posnock's treatment of the complex response to modernity we find in Henry and William James. By dealing with Henry as a cultural critic influenced by his brother William's pragmatist outlook, Posnock is able to helpfully complicate our received view of Henry as a genteel aesthete. His book also contains a fascinating discussion of the relationship between Frankfurt School critical theory and Deweyan pragmatism (particularly the relationship between the thought of Dewey and Adorno). See chapter 5.

5. I don't mean to deny here that there is such a "thing" as postmodernism, and that it can be distinguished from modernism, though this topic has been a major source of debate. My main point will be that it is a mistake to construe the poststructuralist pragmatism of Rorty, Fish, and Herrnstein Smith as postmodern, since in my view they continue to struggle with modernist philosophical and epistemological problems, and in fairly conventional ways. To consider the relationship between modernism and postmodernism at length

here, however, would divert me from the project at hand. For excellent discussions of this topic, see Connor, Huyssen, McGowan, and Waugh.

6. I discuss some of the problems with the term "border" in my Conclusion. Here I am merely using "border studies" as a convenient and familiar umbrella for a group of critics influenced by border criticism and postcolonial studies.

7. In addition to Habermas, Foucault, and Pippin, my approach to the philosophical problem of modernity has been informed by the following works: *Modernity and the Holocaust*, by Zygmunt Bauman; *All That Is Solid Melts into Air*, by Marshall Berman; Paul de Man's "Literary History and Literary Modernity"; *Dialectic of Enlightenment* by Max Horkheimer and Theodor Adorno; *Modern and Modernism*, by Frederick Karl; *Postmodernism and Its Critics*, by John McGowan; *Poets, Prophets, and Revolutionaries*, by Charles Russell; and *The Matrix of Modernism*, by Sanford Schwartz. Pippin's bibliography provides a comprehensive overview of modernity studies. For a cogent critique of this tradition of modernity studies, see Gilroy.

8. See especially Pippin 61–64 and 116–21.

9. I use the term "modernity" in this study 'principally to denote a set of philosophical, social, political, and cultural conditions related specifically to the influence of Enlightenment rationality and dating, therefore, from the latter part of the eighteenth century. "Modernity" ought always to be distinguished from "modernism," which I assume for the purposes of this study to be the collective reaction against Enlightenment values emerging during the romantic period and achieving its apotheosis in Dada, cubism, surrealism, and the literary movements they helped spawn. For a thorough treatment of modernity and modernism in this context, see Berman, Habermas, Pippin, and Russell.

10. For helpful discussions of American criticism in the 1930s and its relation to these different camps, see Vincent Leitch's *American Literary Criticism from the Thirties to the Eighties* and Gerald Graff's *Professing Literature*.

11. For an extended discussion of Burke's modernist critical style, see my "Modernism, Postmodernism, and Critical Style: The Cases of Burke and Derrida."

Chapter 1. Modernity and Nature in Emerson

1. Chai underscores the centrality of Emerson's metaphysical idealism, and stresses the extent to which Emerson stood at the end of Neoplatonism rather than at the beginning of pragmatism. Emerson follows Schleiermacher, Chai points out, in seeking an accommodation with Enlightenment secularism by linking romantic subjectivity to the "divinization of thought" (193–94). Chai thus draws a line back from Emerson's transcendentalism to Renaissance Neoplatonism, rather than forward to James and Dewey. Moreover, Chai demonstrates that many of the concepts Emerson's pragmatist advocates focus on— his linguistic skepticism, his approach to the self, to reason, and to nature—can easily be understood in relation to his transcendentalism, not his pragmatism.

For example, Chai shows how what Poirier calls Emerson's linguistic skepticism does not approximate a pragmatist epistemology at all, but rather language's inability to name the divine (69–70). He also reminds us that reason in Emerson is less a pragmatic instrument rooted in experience than an attribute of divinity (286). Chai's conclusion—that Emerson's pantheistic concept of consciousness, finally and "above all," is a "renunciation of rationalism in favor of a more immanent and immediate mode of being" (341)—helpfully complicates the too-easy assimilation of Emerson to a pragmatist tradition. For Bloom, Emerson is essentially a religious writer whose *Nature* shares an affinity with Blake's *The Marriage of Heaven and Hell* ("Emerson" 106). Bloom traces Emerson's mystic genealogy from the Orphic Mysteries and Hellenistic Neoplatonism in general through the Italian Platonism of Marsilio Ficino and seventeenth-century Cambridge Neoplatonists like Ralph Cudworth (108). Bloom assimilates virtually all of Emerson's major ideas about the mind, the self, and the universe to an Orphic mystical tradition so that, in the end, Emerson becomes an "Orphic Shaman" (113). This Emerson contrasts radically with both the one we get in the pragmatist treatments of Poirier, McDermott, and West, and the transcendentalist Emerson Chai discusses, owing to Bloom's stress on Emerson's mysticism and his insistence that what he calls Emerson's "optics of transparency" (113) actually fathered the "pragmatic strain" in American thought represented by James, Peirce, and Dewey (113).

2. Poirier's eloquent, representative assertion of this position is worth quoting at length:

> Emerson's contribution to American philosophy, much less to poetry and to literary and linguistic theory, has been scandalously neglected . . . I continue to marvel at his genius. He is the inspiration for the kind of criticism practiced in these lectures and that will, I hope, come to be practiced beyond them with some frequency, a kind of criticism that might show literary and cultural studies how it is possible to move ahead of their current tedium, rancor, confusion, and professionalist overdetermination. (*Poetry and Pragmatism* 6)

Integral to this project is Poirier's insistence on reading Emerson as an Emersonian. This necessity is echoed by Bloom in passing when he writes that "a discourse upon Emerson's Gnosis, to be Emersonian rather than literary historical, itself must be Gnosis, or part of a Gnosis" ("Emerson" 115). This distinction between a "literary historical" reading of Emerson and an "Emersonian" reading of Emerson is implicit in much of the recent work on Emerson. It is based on two questionable assumptions. The first is that there is in fact some such thing called "Emersonian" that we can be when we read and write about Emerson that somehow stands outside and before our reading of him. The second is that criticism of real value on Emerson can come only from "Emersonian" readings. I would reject the first assertion as an ontological fallacy, which means the second simply does not hold water.

3. West relates Emerson's "relative inaction" and "minimal active opposition to American capitalist society" to a form of "mysticism that extols receptivity,

detachment, praise and worship" (23–24). Michael T. Gilmore makes the same point in a more lengthy discussion of the "anti-market" side of Emerson, what he calls his "revulsion from commodity" (26). This side of Emerson, Gilmore points out, is most prominent in his writings during the period 1837–43. In general Emerson urges that Americans "resist the dangers of commerce," which he links negatively to the violation of nature by commerce. Gilmore insists in his reading of *Nature* that its transcendentalist epistemology is a pointed counter to the negative effects of materialism and commerce, an assertion that the only thing that is permanent and reliable is the Soul. This is a specific instance of the phenomenon I will be tracing in Emerson, his tendency to respond to modernity and modernization with the reassertion of a pre-Enlightenment form of metaphysical idealism.

4. Another problem with Gunn's general treatment of cultural criticism is his failure to note the constitutive role that structuralist and poststructuralist theory has played in American cultural studies. This failure underscores the highly provincial nature of Gunn's conception of "American" cultural criticism. Committed as his historical analysis is to tracing a redemptive American tradition of criticism, and holding fast to the belief that continental theory has undermined that tradition in contemporary culture, Gunn is unable to find much room for continental theory in his conception of cultural studies. The rhetorical and strategic reason for this is clear enough, but it commits him to an unnecessarily limited and misleading conception of cultural studies. To deal adequately with this issue would take us off in another direction. I would simply point out here that the most cursory review of recent work in cultural studies (Nelson et al.), or of introductory overviews of its development (Brantlinger, Easthope) will demonstrate that cultural studies, whether of the Birmingham School or as practiced in a more eclectic way by a range of feminist, materialist, postcolonial, or African American critics, is deeply indebted to forms of continental theory. Gunn's commitment to an American pragmatic tradition for cultural studies forces him to underplay the role of poststructuralist theory in American cultural studies.

5. For Emerson, the problem of modernity is related to the familiar argument about imitation in the eighteenth-century "querelle des anciens et des modernes." This is, of course, one of the central contexts in which the concept "modern" evolved. The moderns' break with the principle of imitation during the Enlightenment, their turn to what Habermas calls "the criteria of a relative or time-conditioned beauty" (8), plays itself out in early-nineteenth-century American thought in the context of thoroughly nationalist needs, for the development of specifically American cultural forms depended, ostensibly, on rejecting the strategy of imitating European art. The "querelle" becomes a backdrop for a specifically American effort to define a modern national culture.

6. Foucault's assertion, in a way, begs the question of whether or not "modernity" denotes a historical period. For if it is marked by the emergence of a certain kind of metacritical attitude he associates with Kant, then modernity, mea-

sured from the point of that attitude's emergence, seems indeed to be related to a specific historical period.

7. As David Held has observed: "On Horkheimer's and Adorno's account, the Enlightenment's fundamental character is contained in the concept of nature to which most of the Enlightenment thinkers adhered. The concept suggests a "radical disjuncture between subjectivity and nature." In contradistinction to the Greek concept of nature which did not sharply distinguish mind or subjectivity and the world of objects, the Enlightenment concept refers to nature as essentially pure matter, structured according to laws and capable of being known through a mathematically formulated universal science" (152).

8. Gunn is correct in noting that "the Enlightenment has become the absent, or at least the forgotten, integer in the American equation of the relationship between faith and knowledge" (*American Grain* 131). However, where he insists on a continuity between romanticism, pragmatism, and modernity, I am suggesting that Emerson's transcendentalism is a form of romanticism that is more Neoplatonic than modern. In his treatment of the relationship between the Enlightenment, romanticism, and pragmatism in *The Culture of Criticism and the Criticism of Culture*, Gunn (following his own reading of Rorty) insists that we not "reunite Romanticism with its spiritual roots" in "metaphysical idealism," but that we understand romanticism as having "inaugurated the revolution that pragmatism, according to Rorty, has now completed" (70). This view places romanticism or transcendentalism at the *beginning of the end* of metaphysics as an agent in its demise, whereas I am insisting that forms of transcendentalism like Emerson's represent a *pre-Enlightenment* struggle against its principles of rationality, materialism, and the primacy of instrumental reason. In my view, transcendentalism stands at the end of an epistemological era, not at the beginning of one. It is less a mark of modernity's emergence than a resistance to its emphasis on the rational and instrumental. Moreover, Gunn turns to the Enlightenment in the belief that it represents a positive legacy for American cultural criticism. It has the same kind of redemptive function he attributes to pragmatism, whose legacy he wants to extend into the present (*Culture of Criticism* xiii). What is missing from this relatively enthusiastic treatment of the Enlightenment is any indication that Enlightenment principles and values have had negative as well as positive effects, and that much modernist art and philosophy have developed in reaction against them. There is simply no recognition in Gunn's discussion of the Enlightenment that it has been complicit in some of the worst barbarities of the eighteenth, nineteenth, and twentieth centuries (see Gilroy's attempt to revise this approach to modernity studies). What one misses is not some kind of wholesale condemnation of the Enlightenment, but more subtlety in Gunn's discussion of its legacy.

9. Where I deal with Emerson in an attempt to understand more precisely his historical relationship to modernity (and, to a lesser degree, modernism), Poirier invokes Emerson in *The Renewal of Literature* to dehistoricize and aestheticize the concept of the modern:

Feelings associated with modernism—a mosaic compounded of nostalgia, belatedness, cultural burden, and a distrust of language—are, from an Emersonian perspective, part of the human condition itself, so that what has gotten arrogated to
recent times can be said to belong to any period. (96)

The emphasis here is on defining modernism as a vague set of "feelings" and
then flattening out whatever historical significance they might have by assim-
ilating them to "the human condition itself." Poirier does go on to remark that
even if one is persuaded by Emerson's position, the argument that "modernism
is a literary phenomenon of fairly recent date" still makes sense (96). However,
while this qualification begins to solve one problem, it reveals another, even
larger one. On the one hand the decidedly unhistorical conception of "modernism" Poirier attributes (after the fact, of course) to Emerson is qualified here,
but on the other hand, he makes no distinction whatsoever between modernism as a literary phenomenon and the social, cultural, and political epoch
we call modernity. As I've already indicated, such a distinction is crucial to any
discussion of modernism, "aesthetic" or otherwise. Poirier, however, wants to
separate the phenomenon of aesthetic modernism from the "social condition"
we have seen Habermas, Pippin, and a host of other critics associate with
modernity:

Modernism is only incidentally an idea or a social condition and more particularly
an experience of reading, an experience of *how* certain ideas, which are not in
themselves peculiar to any historical period, have recently been apprehended.
(101)

10. For the most recent book-length treatment of this topic, see David Jacobson's *Emerson's Pragmatic Vision: The Dance of the Eye.* This book will probably
disappoint those who assume from its title that it will discuss Emerson's thought
in relation to the philosophical pragmatism developed later in the century by
James, Dewey, and Peirce. It turns out that Jacobson uses the term "pragmatic"
in the loosest of senses, and he makes virtually no attempt to articulate a relationship between Emerson and American pragmatism. In fact, Jacobson devotes the bulk of his energies to producing a Heideggerian reading of Emerson.

11. Van Leer has a helpful discussion of the structure of *Nature* in chapter 2
of *Emerson's Epistemology.* He argues, I think correctly, that the book's structure
is determined by the logic of Emerson's metaphysical idealism. "The ends of
commodity, beauty, language, and discipline," he writes, "need not appear in
that order, nor need they even be the sole ends of nature. Any number of any
kind in any order will suffice if the final step is merely to compress all particu-
lars into an ineffable unity, which can in turn be swallowed by the noble doubt
of a voracious ego" (39).

12. In his discussion of *Nature* Evan Carton begins by pointing out that Emerson's discussion of nature is often obscure and contradictory. Unlike Poirier, he
does not attribute this to Emerson's linguistic skepticism, nor does he attempt
to identify two parallel arguments in the collection of essays, as Van Leer does
(his "high" and "low" arguments). Rather, Carton insists that Emerson is en-

gaging in a conscious bit of "self-parody." "Self-parody," he writes, "is the way in which Emerson's fundamentally ambivalent, or 'inwardly disrupted,' enterprise sustains and regulates its animating tension (and thus preserves itself) against both the impulse to eliminate that tension and the danger of being overwhelmed by it" (26). While I find the argument about Emerson's conscious self-parody finally not very plausible (at its worst, it strikes me as an anachronistic gesture linking Emerson to postmodernist strategies), Carton's discussion of how Emerson's "ambivalence" about how to characterize nature carries over into his ambivalence about both art and the self is illuminating. See in particular chapter 2, "Originality and the Self."

13. See, for example, the final paragraph:

> [W]ill you not tolerate one or two solitary voices in the land, speaking for thoughts and principles not marketable or perishable? Soon these improvements and mechanical inventions will be superseded . . . cities rotted, ruined by war, by new inventions, by new seats of trade, or the geologic changes:—all gone, like the shells which sprinkle the beach . . . But the thoughts which these few hermits move to proclaim by silence, as well as by speech, not only by what they did, but by what they forbore to do, shall abide in beauty and strength, to reorganize themselves in nature, to invest themselves anew in other, perhaps higher endowed and happier mixed clay than ours, in fuller union with the surrounding system. (208–9)

14. On the contradictions inherent in such a project, see Carafiol 39–70.

Chapter 2. Emerson, Whitman, and the Problem of Culture

1. That position is articulated in the following passage from "The Painter of Modern Life": "By 'modernity' I mean the ephemeral, the fugitive, the contingent, the half of art whose other half is the eternal and the immutable" (Baudelaire 13). Later we will see in Emerson's insistence that an American art taking its subjects from everyday life must nevertheless be infused by a transcendental and timeless power something like the same position toward art and modernity.

2. For another valuable discussion of Baudelaire and his critical relationship to modernity, see chapter 3 of Marshall Berman's *All That Is Solid Melts into Air* (131–71).

3. For an important historical analysis along these lines, see Reynolds, *Beneath the American Renaissance*.

4. Emerson's critics are often at odds over the extent to which his thinking is historical. At one end of the spectrum are critics like Bloom, who claim that Emerson's aim is in part "to deny that human existence is a historical existence" ("Emerson" 120), and on the other critics like West, who insists that Emerson's "perspective is infused with historical consciousness" (11). For Chai, on the other hand, the problem with Emerson's approach to history is precisely that it locates history in consciousness. "Precisely because of his reduction (of knowledge to self-knowledge), there can be for Emerson no fundamental problem of historicity and historical knowing . . . If knowledge is equated with self-

knowledge, knowledge itself is nothing more than consciousness" (255–56). Chai goes on to quote from Emerson's essay "History" to underscore his point: "Truly speaking, all history exists for the Individual. Each of us stands absolutely alone in nature, and the great events of history only colossally represent the tendencies, the emotions, and the faculties of one man . . . He takes them all up in his progress into himself" (quoted in Chai 256). Bloom's position is contradicted by West, who reminds us of the extent to which Emerson *was* a historical thinker (we need recall only "Representative Men," for example, to see his point), but West's point is qualified by Chai's reminder that historical knowing in Emerson is suffused by his romantic subjectivity. Olaf Hansen makes essentially the same point, i.e., that Emerson wants us to see history "in a metaphysical light, by which he means that somehow the series of events that constitute history according to our common-sense understanding of it must have a relationship to an unchanging truth" (89).

5. See Emerson's neglected essay "Quotation and Originality," where he explores this topic.

6. To reiterate a point I made at the outset of this chapter, pragmatist Emersonians like McDermott tend to stop their analyses just at the point where Emerson's privileging of the everyday and the practical starts to get qualified by his transcendentalism in just the ways I have been discussing.

7. Emerson here seems to direct criticism toward the material and social dimensions of art and poetic creativity. However, Emerson's metaphysical idealism tends to cancel out the potential for steering criticism toward an ideological critique of poetry. While his pragmatist side might have developed such a critique, the metaphysician in him directs his attention toward "aboriginal Power": "The reference of all [artistic] production at last to an aboriginal Power explains the traits common to all works of the highest art,—that they are universally intelligible; that they restore to us the simplest states of mind; and are religious" (434). Emerson values universal intelligibility over historically specific features of a work of art because his idealism insists he locate value in the transcendentally constant. "Local and special culture" is finally relegated to the category of the "accident"; the "best critic" is able to focus his attention on "the great human influences" that transcend culture (435).

8. In what follows I will be drawing on Lawrence Levine's study of nineteenth- and early-twentieth-century American culture in *Highbrow/Lowbrow*. Levine demonstrates that the now conventional distinction between high and popular culture is in fact a relatively recent invention. This means that Emerson's desire to conceptualize culture in relation to the working class, while breaking with a conception of culture rooted in European forms of high culture, was the dominant way of conceptualizing culture until elitist reactions against it began later in the century. See in particular Levine's third chapter, "Order, Hierarchy, and Culture."

9. Whitman, in fact, condemns "business" ("this all-devouring modern word" [461]) both for its "depravity" and for its inability to foster in America a "moral

consciousness" (461). "The depravity of the business classes of our country," he writes, "is not less than has been supposed, but infinitely greater. The official services of American, national, state, and municipal, in all their branches and departments, except the judiciary, are saturated in corruption, bribery, falsehood, maladministration" (461).

10. Whitman's remarks about the need for American writers to break with European traditions is a direct echo of Emerson: "What has fill'd, and fills today our intellect, our fancy, furnishing the standards therein," he writes, "is yet foreign" (474). Moreover, "the great poems, Shakspere included, are poisonous to the idea of the pride and dignity of the common people, the lifeblood of democracy" (474). He points out that "the models of our literature . . . have had their birth in courts, and bask'd and grown in castle sunshine," and that American writers who have written "after their kind" have not "touch'd . . . the standards of democratic personality," and so they "wither to ashes" (474).

11. Raymond Williams observes that the word *cultural* does not emerge until the 1870s, which means that Whitman's particular interest in redefining "culture" and "cultural" is related to a historically specific rethinking of the whole concept of culture (92). Levine locates the development of an increasingly hierarchal approach to the idea of culture in America in the last decades of the nineteenth century and attributes it specifically to the influence of Matthew Arnold's theory of culture. "Arnold," writes Levine, "was perhaps the single most significant disseminator" of a hierarchal concept of culture in America. According to Levine, Whitman dismissed Arnold as "one of the dudes of literature" (223).

12. See Levine's discussion of the idea of "trickle down" culture (226–27). The result of this process, by the end of the nineteenth century, was that "the taste that now prevailed was that of one segment of the social and economic spectrum which convinced itself and the nation at large that its way of seeing, understanding, and appreciating music, theater, and art was the only legitimate one; that *this* was the way Shakespeare, Beethoven, and Greek sculpture were meant to be experienced and in fact *had* been experienced always by those of culture and discernment" (231).

13. Levine makes this point in passing (225). My own discussion of *Democratic Vistas*, while taking Levine's observation as its starting point, will focus on ways in which Whitman's position was more complicated and conflicted than Levine suggests.

14. As Betsy Erkkila points out, Whitman's position had a symmetrical relation to Arnold's, the difference being that Whitman's sympathies were the reverse of Arnold's. "In presenting the poet as a cultural authority and bridler of leviathan," she writes, "he was saying nothing new. In *Culture and Anarchy* (1869), Matthew Arnold had also found in culture 'a principle of authority, to counteract the tendency to anarchy.' What made Whitman's 'culture theory' different was that he challenged the hegemonic dominance of an elite class" (252). Where "Arnold located culture in the best that had been thought and said,"

Whitman "located the sources of culture in the common life of the masses" (252).

15. See chapter 1, "William Shakespeare in American," in Levine.

16. "The great poems," writes Whitman, "Shakspere included, are poisonous to the idea of the pride and dignity of the common people, the lifeblood of democracy" (474).

17. Erkkila points out that "a good part of Whitman's *Vistas* is taken up with the question of how and in what degree to democratize," and that he "struggled with the conflict at the foundation of the American republic: how to reconcile the desire for personal liberty with the demands of social union" (254). She locates in Whitman a "pragmatic and Madisonian" side and a "utopian and visionary" side (254–55). Erkkila sees Whitman as trying to strike a balance or synthesis between "the individualistic ethos of Emerson and Thoreau" and Hegel's subordination of "the interests of the individual to those of an ethical state" (255). My point is that, philosophically, Whitman's system was in fact weighted toward the kind of transcendentalism Erkkila associates with Whitman's Hegelian side.

18. This privileging of the metaphysical or transcendental as ground in *Democratic Vistas* is mirrored and reinforced, as Erkkila has noted, by the essentially Hegelian structure of the essay. Remarking on Whitman's general interest in Hegel, she writes that "the structure of *Democratic Vistas* is itself Hegelian, working through oppositions and contradictions toward some higher synthesis" (248). The Hegelian, that is to say, dialectical nature of his vision is clear from the outset: "We shall . . . continually find the origin-idea of the singleness of man, individualism, asserting itself, and cropping forth, even from the *opposite ideas*. But the mass, or lump character, for imperative reasons, is to be ever carefully weigh'd, borne in mind, and provided for. Only from it, and from its proper regulation and potency, comes the other, comes the chance of individualism. The two are *contradictory, but our task is to reconcile them*" (463, emphasis mine).

Chapter 3. George Santayana and Van Wyck Brooks: Pragmatism and the Genteel Tradition

1. See Posnock's treatment of the "genteel tradition" (passim) and his discussion of Santayana in chapter 8.

2. In his brief critique of Calvinism, Santayana paves the way for the kind of strong reaction against Puritanism and its legacy produced by writers like Brooks and Randolph Bourne. See in particular Bourne's "The Puritan's Will to Power" in *The Radical Will: Selected Writings, 1911–1918*.

3. James wrote with a sense of affinity for and deep interest in Hawthorne, but insisted that he labored under severe limitations, since he worked in a country with no history (which for James included ruined abbeys and ivy-covered cathedrals). James thus drew much the same conclusion as Brooks about Haw-

thorne's being driven within in a necessary attempt to mine his own limited resources as an artist.

4. Santayana's insistence on linking Whitman to "bohemia" is prescient, for it establishes what would soon become a familiar genealogy in which Whitman came to stand as the father of modern poetry. If we recall Malcolm Cowley's treatment of the Village in the teens and twenties as a "bohemia" consciously evoking the Parisian bohemia made famous by Henry Mürger, we can see that Santayana is already envisioning the extent to which 1920s modernism, and the cultural criticism about America it developed, looks back to a kind of possibility latent in Whitman. See *Exile's Return* 55–63.

5. Santayana is not wholly at ease with pragmatism. His praise for James is tempered by his recognition that pragmatism "may seem a very utilitarian view of the mind; and I confess I think it a partial one" (50). The problem with pragmatism, in his view, is that "it is an external view only, which marks the place and condition of the mind in nature, but neglects its specific essence" (50). On the other hand, pragmatism's approach to nature undoes the transcendentalist one we observed in Emerson. For James, "nature must be conceived anthropomorphically and in psychological terms. Its purposes are not to be static harmonies, self-unfolding destinies, the logic of spirit, the spirit of logic, or any other formal method and abstract law; its purposes are to be concrete endeavours" (51).

6. While Santayana is basically resigned to the necessity of this relationship to nature, his language here is tinged with regret about the transgressing of nature's "forces" by "industrial agents." However, he is more intent on facing the reality, and drawing out the implications, of this relationship than on nostalgically recalling a more "harmonious" one it has displaced.

7. This kind of response, of course, became a fairly typical one among modernist writers who appeared after Santayana. Hart Crane, for example, wrote in an essay on modern poetry that "the function of poetry in a Machine Age" is in part to "absorb the machine, i.e, *acclimatize* it as naturally and casually as trees, cattle, galleons, castles and all other human associations of the past" (261–62). Crane was not urging mere "romantic speculation on the power and beauty of machinery," but a rendering of the "unconscious nervous responses of our bodies" to the machinery of modern life, and the development of a "terminology of poetic reference" for such experiences (262).

8. On Brook's influence during this period, see Raymond Nelson's biography of Brooks, *Van Wyck Brooks: A Writer's Life* (91–172).

9. In Brooks's view, the piety of Puritanism modulates into Emerson's metaphysical idealism, while the practical orientation of Franklin is an early precursor of the pragmatist sensibility. The first tradition is an agonized reaction against modernity, the second an embrace of modernity meant to accelerate it.

10. I agree with the broad outlines of Brooks's critique, that is, the idea that Emerson's metaphysics served to obscure the potentially more productive materialist element in his thought. For another point of view on Brooks's critique

of Emerson, see David Bromwich, who believes Brooks wrong in his reading of Emerson. Where Brooks sees "the personal culture that Emerson invented" foreclosing "the possibility of a common culture," Bromwich counters (writing about Brooks's stress on how Emerson was appropriated by business interests) that "Emerson is so expansive a friend of revolt as to be favorable to no particular party" (153–54). While the last point is no doubt true, Bromwich's criticisms of Brooks remain undocumented. He does not say *why* Brooks is wrong, nor does he go into much detail in discussing Brooks's argument in *America's Coming-of-Age*.

11. For a more detailed discussion of these and other related terms, see Bloom, *Anxiety of Influence*.

12. See, for example, the chapter entitled "Our Critics," where Brooks insists that what American critics need is to follow Arnold's injunction to "see the object as in itself it really is" (126). In Brooks's view, the "object" of criticism in America should be *America*. "If any of our critics," he writes, "had been able to act upon [Arnold's] principle, if they had been able to put aside their prepossessions and merely open their minds to the facts of American life . . . I think the predicament of the younger generation would be far less grave than it is" (126). One of the models he cites in this regard is Irving Babbitt. Brooks's genealogy as a critic clearly runs back through Babbitt's new humanism to Arnold.

13. Of course while Arnold's point is ostensibly that criticism should proceed above and outside social and cultural politics, his whole program for criticism is aimed at producing a specific kind of moral and cultural sensibility, and so is interested and political through and through.

14. Carafiol comes to a similar conclusion in his discussion of Brooks, observing that he ends up identifying "American cultural coherence with a principle of aesthetic coherence, reconceiving American culture as a work of art" (67).

15. In this regard he qualifies as one of Lears's "antimodernists." There is an excellent discussion of Brooks along these lines in Posnock 59–64.

16. Such a point of view can be traced at least back to German aesthetic theorists like Schiller, who insisted on the ultimate integrative primacy of the aesthetic imagination. See *Letters on the Aesthetic Education of Man*, especially numbers 12 through 15.

17. Brooks writes in this regard that the only hope of improving the lot of modern society, especially the new "immigrant population," is through the civilizing processes of art. "The only way in which we can absorb their life," he writes, is not by "improving their environment, in offering them comfort, in minimizing fatigue and shortening hours of work . . . but in quickening our own consciousness . . . This a pragmatic sociology cannot accomplish; nor can it be accomplished except through an appeal from sociology to the higher court of literature," to the "poetic view of life" (149–50). "When we have poets to formulate" our "feelings and desires," he continues, "our social problems . . . will begin to solve themselves." In this view Brooks was heavily influenced by William Morris. See Brooks 152.

Chapter 4. John Dewey: Pragmatism, Modernism, and Aesthetic Criticism

1. On the relationship of Dewey's thought to democracy, the standard work is now Robert B. Westbrook's *John Dewey and American Democracy*. Westbrook's is an indispensable work that examines Dewey's career as a philosopher in terms of his advocacy of democracy, and it seeks throughout to make connections between his philosophical writings and his political activism. Westbrook puts "the development of [Dewey's] democratic theory within the context of the stresses and strains of his own experience and of American culture generally in the last century . . . [treating] Dewey's philosophy as one that developed in the face of the intellectual, social, and political problems he confronted as an engaged intellectual" (xi).

2. Dewey's conception of philosophy, it should be pointed out, has an insistently *rhetorical* orientation. Or rather, Dewey's pragmatism leads him to define philosophical discourse as fundamentally rhetorical. Whereas metaphysics constitutes itself as a discourse grounded in absolute, transcendental "realities," Dewey insists that philosophy in fact always "exhibits itself as a reasonable persuasion" (847). Both Dewey's insistence that "philosophy is an . . . excursion of the imagination" (*Philosophy and Civilization*, 177) that is intimately linked to literature and the plastic arts, and his insistence that it is "a form of desire, of effort at action" ("Philosophy and Democracy" 843), suggest how deeply he conceives philosophy to have a rhetorical function. Dewey understands philosophical discourse to be rhetorical in two senses of the word: its language is based on figuration (rhetorical tropes), and it means to intervene persuasively at certain historical moments on behalf of identifiable values and beliefs. Dewey's critique of metaphysics is based, in large measure, on his foregrounding of this rhetorical orientation. (In this respect Dewey's critique of metaphysics anticipates Derrida's, and we will see that it also has its parallel in Kenneth Burke's approach to rhetoric in *A Rhetoric of Motives*.)

3. West recalls here his earlier emphasis on what separates Emerson from Dewey: "Emerson's ambivalence toward the common folk and their experiences . . . the contemplative and mystical aspects of Emerson, reminiscent more of Plato's Seventh Letter and Plotinus than of Dewey and the pragmatists" (74–75).

4. The question of Dewey's idealism or organicism in *Art as Experience* has been debated for decades, spurred by the publication of two essays in the early 1950s by Benedetto Croce and Stephen Pepper, both of which argue that the idealism in Dewey's book contradicted pragmatist principles. Pepper in particular complained that the book's organicist aesthetics cannot "be harmonized with a pragmatic esthetics" (372), that "the organicist embeds his work of art in the absolute structure of the world, whereas the pragmatist finds the esthetic experience in historical processes as they come, and considers nothing more real or ultimate than an actually had experience" (377). For a thorough discussion of this debate and a detailed discussion of Dewey's aesthetic theories, see Thomas

M. Alexander's *John Dewey's Theory of Art, Experience, and Nature; The Horizons of Feeling.*

Recent critics often echo Pepper's criticism. West, for example, cites Pepper in making the remark that Dewey's book is "shot through with an organic idealism unbecoming a card-carrying pragmatist" (95). Gunn and Westbrook, as we shall see later, are less willing to accept the kind of criticism Pepper makes.

5. Dewey's image of "the fire-engine rushing by" seems to be a direct allusion to William Carlos Williams's poem "The Great Figure." Other references (such as the one to "the human-fly climbing the steeple-side") recall the photographs of Bernice Abbott.

6. Recall, for example, this passage from "The American Scholar":

Instead of the sublime and beautiful; the near, the low, the common . . . The literature of the poor, the feelings of the child, the philosophy of the street, the meaning of household life, are the topics of the time . . . I ask not for the great, the remote, the romantic . . . I embrace the common, I explore and sit at the feet of the familiar, the low (Emerson 68–69).

7. This focus on the museum as an institution, and its concrete relation to aesthetic experience and our conception of "art," has been taken up repeatedly in recent cultural criticism. See Hal Foster's *Recordings: Art, Spectacle, Cultural Politics* (1985), and *Exhibiting Cultures: The Poetics and Politics of Museum Display*, ed. Ivan Karp and Steven Lavine (1991).

8. See, for example, where Dewey writes about how the "growth of capitalism has been a powerful influence in the development of the museum as the proper home for works of art, and in the promotion of the idea that they are apart from the common life" (*Art as Experience* 8).

9. A bit later in the book, writing about self-expression and the aesthetic object, Dewey insists that while "a poem and picture present material passed through the alembic of personal experience . . . nonetheless, their material came from the public world and so has qualities in common with the material of other experiences" (82). He wants not to abandon the idea of art as self-expression, but to incorporate social experience and the realm of concrete, material reality in the expressing subject. However, we will see that later in the study aesthetic production tends to get retheorized in a way that cuts self-expression off from these social and material conditions, as Dewey lapses back into the very position he criticizes in the early portions of the book.

10. In noting the chasm between ordinary and aesthetic experience, and how art has become systematically relegated to a rarefied realm, Dewey is tracing the hierarchizing of culture Levine analyzes in *Highbrow/Lowbrow*. Dewey's observations underscore the extent to which the process Levine found accelerating at the end of the nineteenth century continued well into the twentieth.

11. Shusterman's is by far the most ambitious and successful attempt to reassert the meaning and value of Dewey's project in *Art as Experience*. Shusterman begins by showing how Dewey's aesthetic theory was eclipsed in America by a "mainstream tradition in Anglo-American aesthetics" grounded in ana-

lytic philosophy (3). He argues, quite correctly, that "while analytic aesthetics followed the romantic and modernist tradition of defending art's value and autonomy by identifying the concept of art with the concept of . . . 'high' or fine art" (18), Dewey wanted to shift attention away from the formal aesthetic object toward aesthetic experience itself, thus undermining an elitist conception of art that kept it holed up in museums. I don't have an argument with Shusterman's characterization of Dewey's *aims*. Indeed, I think he offers an excellent analysis and explication of what Dewey set out to do. What I want to do is to read against the grain of Dewey's intention by examining key points in his text (which Shusterman and others tend to ignore) where Dewey seems to me to reintroduce the very categories and principles he wants to be rid of. In short, I find Dewey's text to be much more at odds with itself than does Shusterman. For another treatment of these issues, see Levin's "The Esthetics of Pragmatism."

12. By "esthetic criticism," as will be clear shortly, Dewey does not mean just that branch of literary criticism that deals specifically with aesthetic questions. Rather, he uses the term more broadly to designate the activity of literary criticism in general.

13. Westbrook, Bernstein, Gouinlock, and Alexander all discuss the concept of "experience" in Dewey in very helpful ways. Alexander's brief summary of the issue is worth quoting at length:

> Ever since Locke, the term [experience] had come to mean a subjective event, a constellection [*sic*] of "ideas" lodged inside a "mind" brought about by the operation of certain physical powers upon us. From the start, Dewey's philosophy was opposed to such a theory. "Experience" for him meant a process situated in a natural environment, mediated by a socially shared symbolic system, actively exploring and responding to the ambiguities of the world by seeking to render the most problematic of them determinate. The persistent failure of his critics to adapt themselves to these new meanings had Dewey so frustrated by his eighties, that he toyed with dropping the term "experience" altogether, along with several others. *Experience and Nature*, his major work, was to be retitled *Nature and Culture*. (xiii)

14. As Richard Bernstein points out, Dewey wanted, in his approach to experience, to "show the limitations of these two positions" in the context of developing his own conception of experience. See Bernstein 60–74 for a review of Dewey's critique of traditional conceptions of experience.

15. See Westbrook 128–30 for a discussion of how Dewey's theory of experience was developed in relation to idealist and realist approaches.

16. For a helpful review of Dewey's concept of "primary experience," see Alexander, chapters 1 and 4. Alexander stresses the link between knowledge gained from primary experience and knowledge produced by scientific observation and inquiry.

17. Of course this is the conception of "experience" we earlier observed Giles Gunn endorsing in his call for a pragmatist orientation for cultural criticism.

18. "An experience," Dewey writes, "has a unity that gives it its name, *that* meal, that storm, that rupture of friendship. The existence of this unity is con-

stituted by a single *quality* that pervades the entire experience in spite of the variation of its constituent parts" (*Art as Experience* 37).

19. "The enemies of the esthetic" also include "the humdrum; slackness of loose ends; submission to convention in practice and intellectual procedure . . . Rigid abstinence, coerced submission, tightness on one side and dissipation, incoherence and aimless indulgence on the other, are deviations in opposite directions from the unity of an experience" (*Art as Experience* 40). The extent to which Dewey's allegiance to classicism qualifies or cancels out the pragmatist and materialist impulses of his study suggests a "submission to convention in practice and intellectual procedure" that would, ironically, make his own study an enemy of the aesthetic in the sense he means here.

20. See Shusterman (20–21, 51) for a somewhat different approach to the question of the relationship of Dewey's position on art and popular culture to Adorno and Horkheimer's. Where Shusterman insists that Dewey does not take their view toward the "culture industry," I will be arguing that in a number of ways their positions are actually not that far apart. Also, see Posnock, especially chapter 5, for a discussion of Dewey and the Frankfurt School.

21. This is something critics tend to miss in focusing their criticism of the book on the question of its idealism or organicism. Westbrook, for example, while he acknowledges that *Art as Experience* reveals remnants of Dewey's early Hegelianism (397), does not pursue the implications of Dewey's classical organicism for the critique of the museum culture of art that the first chapter of the book articulates (and that Westbrook so strongly stresses). It is important to recognize that a classical aesthetic and a museum conception of art *function together*. Since classical aesthetic theory sets out the criteria by which art is housed in museums, a critique of the museum conception of art ought to be accompanied by a critique of the classical aesthetic theory that forms its very foundation. There is, then, a real contradiction between Dewey's critique of the museum concept of art at the beginning of his book, and his adherence to a classical formalism in the later parts of the book. One cannot, in these discussions, separate the cultural role of art from aesthetic theory, as Westbrook does. This is something the avant-garde understood in its combined attacks on the museum culture *and* classical aesthetics.

22. This is a point that simply does not get mentioned in discussions of the Pepper-Croce debate about idealism in *Art as Experience*. The issues in this debate, as we have seen, remain restricted largely to aesthetic, philosophic, and formal questions. There is virtually no attention paid to Dewey's attitudes toward contemporary cultural forms in the book, and the extent to which these, as well as his formalism, tend to qualify the book's progressive tendencies. Shusterman, on the other hand, takes up these questions at length. However, I think he fails to acknowledge the extent to which Dewey takes at the least an equivocal position on popular art. He does not catch, for example, that the references to "cheap and vulgar" aesthetic forms in the passage I just quoted seem to refer to jazz, cinema, and the comic strip. See Shusterman 19.

Chapter 5. Kenneth Burke: Modernism and the Motives of Rhetoric

1. See for example Boris Eichenbaum's "The Theory of the 'Formal Method'" and Paul de Man's "Literary History and Literary Modernity."

2. I refer here to Richard Rorty's *Philosophy and the Mirror of Nature*, a study of philosophy's claim that it can represent "the truth," that its language has a more privileged access to "reality" than does so-called literary language.

3. For a discussion of the relationship between modern philosophy and high modernism, see Sanford Schwartz, *The Matrix of Modernism*. His discussion of the relationship between modernist poetics and modern philosophy focuses on Eliot and Pound, but the "matrix" of influences he traces clearly applies to Stein (and others) as well.

4. Gunn's reading relies heavily on Lentricchia's. The idea that Burke's work is fundamentally aimed at "social change" comes from Lentricchia and is appropriated by Gunn in order to define Burke's pragmatism. However, in doing so Gunn not only overstates Burke's pragmatism. He overstates the extent to which Lentricchia is dealing with Burke as a pragmatist. Though Lentricchia's book begins with some criticisms of (early) Rorty and the new pragmatism, he is much more interested in treating Burke as a social and political critic, and in contrasting his work with the deconstructive thought of de Man. Here Lentricchia has made a major contribution to Burke studies, which too often deal narrowly with his relationship to philosophy and language theory (see the excellent studies by Henderson and Southwell, for example). Lentricchia's focus on Burke's early cultural criticism, and the relationship of Burke's work to contemporary criticism grounded in social and political theory, helped pave the way for studies like my own.

5. On Burke's work as a rhetorician, see the essays collected by Herbert Simons and Trevor Melia in *The Legacy of Kenneth Burke*. The interest in his pragmatism is relatively new. The interest among rhetoricians, communication theorists, and composition teachers in Burke's work predates the interest in his pragmatism by many years.

6. This letter is in the collection of Burke's papers at the Pennsylvania State University Rare Books Library.

7. Interview with the author. The way his predicament figured into his writing of *Permanence and Change* is made clear in the following passage from the book's prologue:

> This book . . . was written in the early days of the Great Depression, at a time when there was a general feeling that our traditional ways were headed for a tremendous change, maybe even a permanent collapse. It is such a book as authors in those days sometimes put together, to keep themselves from falling apart. Not knowing quite where he was, this particular author took notes on "orientation." Not being sure how to read the signs, he took notes on "interpretation." Finding himself divided, he took notes on division . . . In sum, being in a motivational quandary, he wrote on "motivation." The result is a kind of transformation-at-one-remove, got by inquiry into the process of transformation itself. (xlvii)

8. He would soon come down on the side of "resultant," a point he fore-grounds in the 1952 preface to his reissued (and somewhat revised) book: "Any reduction of *social* motives to terms of sheer 'nature' would now seem to me a major error. Naturalism has served as deceptively in the modern world as su-pernaturalism ever did in the past, to misrepresent motives that are intrinsic to *the social order*" (xv, latter emphasis mine).

9. One might argue that in both Brooks and Dewey we *have* a mode of adjust-ment, their adjustment being the reassertion of art's timeless function. But I have been arguing that this is less an adjustment than a nostalgic retreat.

10. Burke writes that by these "procedures" or "innovations" he does not mean "something new under the sun. By innovation is meant simply an emphasis to which the contemporary public is not accustomed" (*Counter-Statement* 110).

11. For an illuminating discussion of Burke's *Counter-Statement* and the po-litical program it contains, see Lentricchia, part 3. Lentricchia's stress here on the literary/political dimension of Burke's early work, and how it modulated into a rhetorical theory, has been particularly helpful to me in thinking through Burke's relationship to modernism.

12. For Burke's later, more extended treatment of Blackmur's criticisms, see "Formalist Criticism: Its Principles and Limits," in *Language as Symbolic Action*.

13. See part 1 of *The Selected Correspondence of Kenneth Burke and Malcolm Cowley: 1915–1981*.

14. Kenneth Burke to Malcolm Cowley, 4 March 1923. Pennsylvania State University Rare Book Library, Pennsylvania State University.

15. Kenneth Burke to Malcolm Cowley, 18 January 1923. Pennsylvania State University Rare Book Library, Pennsylvania State University.

16. It is impossible to conceive that Burke had not read this passage in Dew-ey's book. He regularly reviewed Dewey's books during this time for the *New Republic*, and *Art as Experience* was published while Burke was in the midst of writing the book he would call *Permanence and Change*. It seems likely that the title came from Dewey's passage.

17. Bloom's remark is meant, of course, to be both critical and prescriptive. "Most of what the Academy considers acceptable critical style is of course merely a worn-out neoclassical diction," he insists, "garlanded with ibids and civilly purged of all enthusiasm" (19–20). American criticism, on the other hand, "ought to be pragmatic and outrageous." It should always ask of a text: "what is it good for, what can I do with it, what can it do for me, what can I make it mean?" ("Agon" 21). It is precisely this kind of outrageous pragmatism in Burke that Bloom finds himself attracted to.

18. It is helpful in understanding the relationship between Burke's analytical procedures and his critical style to see perspectives by incongruity as the styl-istic equivalent of his interdisciplinary mode of analysis. That is, his conflation of philosophical, literary, poetic, sociological, and psychological material and topics in any given book is the *methodological* equivalent of that same kind of conflating at the level of his terminology. In this regard, there is little difference

in Burke between the style of his writing and the style of his analyses. His books are organized as well as written by the principle of gaining new perspectives by incongruous juxtapositions.

19. Jacques Derrida's metaphor for Nietzsche's styles, of course, is similar: "spurs." See in particular Derrida, *Spurs* 39. It is interesting to compare Burke's use of "darts" to characterize Nietzsche's style with Derrida's reminder in his discussion of Nietzsche's styles that "style" is related to "stylus," a pointed object: "In the question of style there is always the weight or *examen* of some pointed object. At times this object might be only a quill or a stylus. But it could just as easily be a stiletto, or even a rapier" (*Spurs* 37). Or a dart.

20. In stressing here the ways in which Burke began to resolve some of the tensions I reviewed earlier by developing a rhetorical approach to cultural study within what he called a "practical frame," I don't mean to suggest that his work was without problems. What is remarkable about Burke, looking back, is the self-consciously modernist orientation of his critical project. However, the efficacy of that project was often blunted by the opaque nature of his writing, and by the fact that his books often seemed to lurch from one topic or avenue of inquiry to another. One of the reasons that Burke's impact on American criticism has been so late in coming is that his work never seemed to cohere in a clear and understandable way. It was often simply unclear just where he was headed, or what the applicability of his work was. His greatest strength as a critic—his ability to write with such brilliance and originality about a host of topics—was also his greatest weakness, since it often left his books seeming unfocused.

21. Burke makes somewhat the same point about psychoanalysis when he writes, in *Permanence and Change*, that "Freudians" call their terms "analysis," while they call the analyses of others "rationalization[s]" (17).

22. Burke elaborates on his point a bit later in *Counter-Statement*: "Expanding our earlier discussion of ideology: If people believe something, the poet can use this belief to get an effect. If they despise treachery, for instance, he can awaken their detestation by the portrait of a traitor. If they admire self-sacrifice, he can set them to admiring by a tragedy of self-sacrifice" (161). Though written to explain a certain concept of literary *form*, this passage serves as a concise characterization of what Burke means by "identification" in *A Rhetoric of Motives*. For a recent extended treatment of the relationship between rhetoric and ideology in Burke, see Bygrave.

23. Burke here clearly has in mind the kind of autonomy associated with the New Critics. But his argument here also holds for a critic like Matthew Arnold, who insisted on the autonomous nature of great art at the same time that he enlisted it in his drive to make proper citizens of the working class. Poetry, for Arnold, was at the same time transcendental and instrumental.

24. Hegemony, according to Gramsci, is in part "the 'spontaneous' consent given by the great masses of the population to the general direction imposed on social life by the dominant fundamental group" (12). This consent is "sponta-

neous" in the sense that it seems freely chosen, but in fact results from the internalization of dominant ideological formations.

25. Burke's critique of the subject here is close to that of contemporary poststructuralists influenced by Derrida, Foucault, and Lacan. See, for example, Kaja Silverman's discussion of the subject in *The Subject of Semiotics*. She begins by drawing a distinction between the "subject" and the "individual": "The concept of subjectivity . . . marks a radical departure from [the] philosophical tradition by giving a more central place to the unconscious and to cultural overdetermination than it does to consciousness" (126). Both ethnology and psychoanalysis, she points out, locate "the production of human reality beyond the boundaries of consciousness, they dismantle concepts like 'individual' and 'man,' deny the possibility of a timeless human essence" (129). She insists, drawing on Foucault, that neither culture nor the unconscious can be approached apart from a theory of signification" (129). Her gloss of the "subject," while using a different terminology, is quite congruent with Burke's ideas about the relationship between identity and symbols of authority:

> The term "subject" . . . helps us to conceive of human reality as a construction, as the product of signifying activities which are both culturally specific and generally unconscious. The category of the subject thus calls into question the notions both of the private, and of a self synonymous with consciousness. It suggests that even desire is culturally instigated, and hence collective; and it de-centers consciousness . . . by drawing attention to the divisions which separate one area of psychic activity from another, the term "subject" challenges the value of stability attributed to the individual. (*The Subject of Semiotics* 130).

26. It would be helpful at this point to recall Pippin's distinction between "modernity" and "modernism," along with the two senses he notes are usually associated with the latter. Modernism, he writes, is "a heightened and affirmative modern self-consciousness (a final attempt to be 'truly' modern, to create in a radical and unprecedented way a form of life, indeed a sensibility, finally consistent with the full implications of the modern revolution), as well as an intense dissatisfaction with the sterile, exploitative, commercialized, or simply ugly forms of life apparently characteristic of social modernization (or 'bourgeois' forms of modernization)" (29). Burke's modernism is a blend of the two, for his criticism is born of the intense dissatisfaction with modernity Pippin describes, but it is *enacted* in a style that tries to be consistent with the full implications of the "modern revolution" in art and philosophy.

Conclusion: Rhetoric, Neopragmatism, Border Studies— Beyond the Contingency Blues

1. One problem with their analysis ought to be noted here: the failure to distinguish between modernism and postmodernism. Bender and Wellbery use "modernism" as a kind of catchall term to cover literature from Baudelaire to Beckett and Blanchot. Moreover, they use the term "modernist" to denote the

culture and economy of high capitalism, with its informational technologies (advertising, the computer, television, video, etc.) and forms of mass production. Since writers like Blanchot and the culture of mass reproduction are usually associated with a postmodern condition, their blanket use of the term "modernism" can be confusing. I would insist that what they call "rhetoricality" would have to be seen as developing out of a set of reversals grounded in modernism, and accelerated by a set of postmodern conditions they fail to discuss in their essay.

2. The problem is that the authors come close to replicating here the very foundationalism the condition of rhetoricality is supposed to get beyond, for what can the word "condition" mean in this sentence but a kind of essence or foundation in experience? While rhetoricality insists on its own rhetorical status, it sets itself up as something near a metadiscourse or master narrative about metadiscourses and master narratives. The force of its explanatory power is precisely lodged in its realization that all explanatory discourses are, literally, groundless. Grounded in this realization, rhetoricality claims a kind of transcendental status among analytic or explanatory systems. Moreover, their rigorously historical analysis of the demise and reemergence of rhetoric cannot help but reproduce a vaguely Hegelian structure in which the logic of history seems to produce rhetoricality in the operations of a necessary dialectic. Thus, the deconstructive turn rhetoricality seems to represent is itself caught up in the very structure it seeks to undermine. For an alternative historical discussion of the history of rhetoric, see Barilli.

3. See the essays in Mailloux's collection *Rhetoric, Sophistry, Pragmatism* for an excellent overview of the convergence of rhetoric and pragmatism in contemporary theory. They pay particular attention to pragmatism's relationship to other forms of antifoundationalism, including rhetoric, and deal with the question of whether or not a neopragmatist position leads, inexorably, to political quietism. See Mailloux's Introduction for an excellent discussion of these issues.

4. The centrality of Nietzsche to Burke's reclamation of rhetoric suggests how closely Burke's work on rhetoric is related to Bender and Wellbery's thesis about the link between "modernism" and rhetoricality (see *Permanence and Change* 87–96). Burke's deconstruction of the conventional relationship between scientific and poetic language, which leads him to insist that "when we describe in abstract terms we are not sticking to the facts at all, we are substituting something else for them just as much as if we were using an out and out metaphor" (95) draws on Nietzsche to make the same point Bender and Wellbery do about modernism's undoing of the transparency and neutrality of language. Burke's attempt to develop rhetoric beyond its traditional bounds and to "systematically extend the range of rhetoric" across the traditional specializations of academic discourse constitutes the replacing of "rhetoric" with something like what Bender and Wellbery call "rhetoricality." Burke's recognition that the very forces of socialization operate rhetorically led him to the kind of modernist re-

turn to rhetoric they outline, where rhetoric was reconceived not as a mode of classification and analysis, but as a sign of the very condition of being.

5. "Truth cannot be out there," Rorty insists, it "cannot exist independently of the human mind—because sentences cannot so exist, or be out there. The world is out there, but descriptions of the world are not. Only descriptions of the world can be true or false. The world on its own—unaided by the describing activities of human beings—cannot" (*Contingency, Irony, and Solidarity* 5).

6. See Herrnstein Smith 168–70. I will take up the issue of Rorty's ethnocentrism a bit later in this chapter.

7. Rorty's neopragmatist irony surfaces in Bender and Wellbery's characterization of rhetoricality as well. Recall that for Bender and Wellbery "rhetoricality . . . manifests the groundless, infinitely ramifying character of discourse in the modern world. For this reason, it allows for no explanatory metadiscourse that is not already itself rhetorical" (25). Rorty's ironist position is articulated in almost identical terms. "For us ironists," he writes, "nothing can serve as a criticism of a final vocabulary save another such vocabulary; there is no answer to a redescription save a re-re-description" (*Contingency, Irony, and Solidarity* 80). Where in the first instance the irony is that all discourse is rhetorical, therefore no discourse can be a metadiscourse, in the second instance the irony is that all vocabularies are redescriptions of other vocabularies, therefore no vocabulary can be a final (or meta) vocabulary. On this point Bender and Wellbery converge absolutely with Rorty. Their rhetoricality is an ironist position through and through, for in their view rhetoricality is a position in which "irony is no longer a figure of speech or an educated habit of mind; it is the fundamental condition of language production" (36). Indeed, Rorty could have written their conclusion: "Since there is no such thing as a first, original, or direct statement," every "utterance" is "intrinsically figural, unstable," so much so that "poetry is no longer a privileged kind of discourse but a specific case illustrating the general instance of language itself" (36).

8. For further discussion of the relationship between rhetoric and contemporary cultural criticism, see Kirwin, Farrell, Fuller, and Wihl.

9. For an extended analysis of this problem in Derrida's work, see my essay "Bridging the Gap: The Position of Politics in Deconstruction," particularly 63–71.

10. See John Patrick Diggins's discussion of some of the parallels he sees between poststructuralism and American intellectual thought in the conclusion to *The Promise of Pragmatism* (427–94). On the one hand, Diggins suggests that "when one studies the problems of postmodernism from the perspective of American intellectual history, the theoretical crises of our times seem less urgent," since we will see that "some American thinkers lived with the postmodern condition in premodern times" (427–28). On the other hand, he argues that Rorty exaggerates the parallels between Dewey's thought and French poststructuralism (450–62). While there is not room here for a full discussion of Diggins's position, I would argue that Rorty's exaggeration of the parallels

between Dewey and poststructuralism is more than matched by Diggins in his attempt to draw analogies between poststructuralism and early American intellectual thought. For another discussion of the relationship between pragmatism and contemporary theory, see Wheeler.

11. Diggins attempts this same kind of move in his section on Reinhold Niebuhr (434–43). He sees in Niebuhr's Christian existentialism, committed as it is to showing "us how to put the pessimistic wisdom of tragedy and irony to positive use" (434), an antidote both to poststructuralist pessimism and to the kind of endless conversations endorsed by Rorty and Habermas. It is hard to criticize the values he wants to recall from Niebuhr—"our Moral truth need not have access to metaphysical truth," a "morality that arises out of guilt to reach the state of grace can take place within the fragmentary nature of human existence" (439)—values not that far removed from the ones Gunn invokes in his discussion of how to deal with our current "crisis of disbelief." However, it is hard to take anything substantive away from Diggins's invocation of Niebuhr. Like Gunn and Poirier on Emerson, he seems to want to hark back to a religious discourse he finds comforting in the face of complicated contemporary philosophical and social problems. When Diggins quotes Niebuhr on the need for "hope," "faith," "love," and "forgiveness" (439–40), it is a little like the end of Eliot's *Waste Land*, moving enough, but not much to really grab onto.

12. Pippin calls "autonomy" the "great, single modernity problem in the German tradition" (12). "Most generally construed," he writes, the ideal of autonomy "simply expresses the oldest classical philosophical ideal: the possibility that human beings can regulate and evaluate their beliefs by rational self-reflection, that they can free themselves from interest, passion, tradition, prejudice and autonomously 'rule' their own thoughts" (12–13). See also 116–21.

13. Pippin, it ought to be noted, sees no way out of the philosophical problems ushered in by modernity. In his final chapter, "Unending Modernity," he writes that "once the great uneasiness and uncertainty provoked by [Enlightenment self-consciousness] originates . . . it cannot be forgotten or ended . . . the very notion of epochality or the closure and determining force implied by some epochal view of history, is foreclosed and 'modernity' is indeed (ironically and paradoxically) the 'last' epoch, because [it is] the end of epochality itself" (166). For this reason, he sees "postmodernity" as an increasingly radical extension of modernity, rather than as an epoch in itself.

14. See Chapter 2, "Reading the Tradition." Carafiol's basic point is that once American literary scholarship got fixated on transcendentalism it never let go. What started out in the early nineteenth century as the attempt to import European philosophical idealism as the ground for American culture ended up in the twentieth century defining the history, canon, and curriculum driving American literary studies. Beginning with a discussion of Frothingham's 1876 study *Transcendentalism in New England*, and dealing in turn with Goddard's *Studies in New England Transcendentalism* (1908), Brooks's *America's Coming-of-Age*, V. L. Parrington's *Main Currents in American Thought* (1927), and Matthiessen's *Amer-*

ican Renaissance (1941), Carafiol demonstrates how, from Emerson and Whitman on, American literature was defined in terms of its ability to dramatize a coherent national myth of American exceptionalism based on an ideology of manifest destiny and individual self-reliance. He demonstrates how the *idea* of American literature has always been determined by the needs of a thoroughly idealist nationalism, one that charged American literature from the beginning with the job of articulating a coherent and cohesive vision of America and American identity, one that would distinguish it from Britain in the nation's early years, and later, help establish an autonomous, specifically "American" social and political culture.

15. Carafiol points out how this project was fraught with paradox. On the one hand, the value and authority of transcendentalism were undeniably connected to its origins in European high culture, yet it had to be reinvented in America as something nearly indigenous to the New World. Furthermore, its tendency toward airy metaphysics and spiritual essences jarred with the development of an American commitment to the practical and the pragmatic.

16. Carafiol's reading of Thoreau, for example, is unabashedly pitched as a contemporary lesson: Thoreau, he insists, can be read analogically to reflect on "current critical debates" (138). He "offers a model of experience that depends on descriptions, on accounts, on language as a representation of empirical fact" (139). Thoreau, it turns out, does in Carafiol's account just what he thinks *we* should be doing: "Thoreau . . . [tries] to explain the continuing uses of the past without ignoring either historical fact or contemporary interests," and therefore in an exemplary way "abandons the debate between real and ideal that shaped scholarly study of American literature and Thoreau's own first narrative intentions" (145). What Thoreau has to teach us, finally, is that "there is no escaping the constraints of the socially conditioned relations among the terms we use and criticize" (146). After twenty years of learning this in our graduate school educations, how can it possibly be news, and why do we have to discover it—or why does it need the authority it gets—in Thoreau?

17. Poirier takes from Emerson the conviction that power involves a kind of dialectical process, a struggle between inherited and aboriginal power that can produce real, creative power only as a synthesis between the two. In Poirier's view, Emerson is superior to critics he calls modernist because Emerson believes in "animal nature" and aboriginal power (166). Like Gunn, Poirier endorses the Emersonian conviction that "cultural formations, no matter how imposing, can be manipulated or transformed" by an individual in touch with his aboriginal nature, so that there is "no need for any radical social or cultural upheaval in order to liberate the self from inherited ideas that contain him" (185). This formulation is not that far from Rorty's conviction that the discourse of the creative self can remain aloof from the discourse of justice. In their view, the self can liberate itself from whatever oppresses it through the sheer act of recreation, empowered by a force prior to and free from social conditioning.

18. Nearly all of these terms have become quite problematic. "Hybridity," for

example, worked effectively for some years to draw critical attention to how colonized and border cultures developed by synthesizing themselves out of elements of multiple cultures. This called attention to what seemed their special or distinguished status vis-à-vis supposedly monocultural colonial societies, especially to the extent that colonial cultures relied on purist notions of identity and belonging. However, the metaphor of hybridity as an explanation of cultural origins turned out to be so powerful that it very rapidly seemed to deconstruct any kind of purist notion of cultural origins. As Renato Rosaldo has explained:

> On the one hand, hybridity can imply a space betwixt and between two zones of purity in a manner that follows biological usage that distinguishes two discrete species and the hybrid pseudospecies that results from their combinations . . . On the other hand, hybridity can be understood as the ongoing condition of all human cultures, which contain no zones of purity because they undergo continuous processes of transculturation (two-way borrowing and lending between cultures). Instead of hybridity versus purity, this view suggests that it is hybridity all the way down . . . (xv)

Once we realize the more general truth about hybridity as an explanation of cultural origins and a map of how identity evolves (that it is "hybridity all the way down"), the term loses its specific applicability to border or contact zones. If all cultures and identities are at their core hybrid, then two things happen: hybridity loses its value as an explanatory term specific to border cultures, and the term itself becomes essentialized and foundational, since it comes to stand for a general truth about the ontological nature of all forms of subjectivity and identity.

19. Other texts Porter discusses at length include Gregory Jay's *America the Scrivener: Deconstruction and the Subject of Literary History; The New American Studies,* ed. Philip Fisher; and *The American Ideal: Literary History as a Worldly Activity,* by Peter Carafiol. See also *Reinventing the Americas: Comparative Studies of Literature of the United States and Spanish America,* ed. Bell Gale Chevigny and Carl Laguardia; and *Do the Americas Have a Common Literature?* ed. Gustavo Perez Firmat.

20. See, for example, the emphasis Gregory Jay gives to location in "The End of 'American' Literature." Jay invokes Adrienne Rich to insist on the critical importance of reading, thinking, and feeling "the differences that our bodily locations—in history, in geography, in ethnicity, in gender, in sexual orientation—can make" (264). Attention to what Rich calls "the politics of location," Jay insists, has the best potential to resist "the abstract liberal humanism" that has driven American criticism since its inception and that has worked to "force the Other to assimilate to the values and interests of an idiosyncratic though hegemonic Western self" (265). While Carafiol believes he can displace the "American ideal" in American literary studies through a rereading of Emerson and Thoreau that essentially leaves the New England origins of "American" literature in place, Jay proposes that "we replace the idealist paradigm with a

geographical and historical one" (268) that will allow for a reevaluation of "the legacy of nationalism" and that understands that "multicultural experience is our imperative reality" (266). Where Carafiol is critical of recent feminist, minority, and New Historicist attempts to revise the study of American literature, Jay uses their work as a point of departure for a criticism based on specific locations where "the objects of study will be acts of writing committed within and during the colonization, establishment, and ongoing production of the US as a physical, sociopolitical, and multicultural event, including those writings that resist and critique its identification with nationalism" (268).

21. For a helpful discussion of the complex meanings of "creole," see Raiskin 3–5 and 79–83.

22. The lines from Susan Stewart Owens quotes are worth repeating here: "If scholars in our discipline constantly examine the relation between dominant and minority cultural forms as one of a colonizing appropriation and borrowing by the dominant, they end up, as nineteenth-century folklorists did, turning minority forms into something like nature—that is, a reservoir of spontaneity bereft of particularity and agency" (quoted on 60).

23. It should be pointed out here that Porter is not very optimistic about our ability to handle such large and complex spaces. On the one hand, Saldívar's historical and geographical framework goes a long way toward displacing the kind of idealized, mononational ground for American literary studies Carafiol criticizes. It helpfully complicates the historical context in which we pursue the study of American literature and culture by reminding us of the inextricable social and political links between the United States and the Caribbean, Mexico, and Latin America. And its attention to the transnational production and reproduction of hybrid cultures and cultural forms around border zones is a useful antidote to the melting pot pluralism Jay critiques. On the other hand, the transcultural territory or set of overlapping border zones it proposes for study is immense in geographical size and historical scope. In a forthcoming essay I try to deal with this problem, partly through a discussion of Edouard Glissant's approach to "cultural zones" and Paul Gilroy's formulation of a "black Atlantic."

24. "The real problem," Owens writes, "is that we do not have the luxury of simply opting out because . . . we already function within the dominant discourse . . . The very act of appropriating the colonizer's discourse and making it one's own is collaborative and conjunctural. We have long since entered inescapably what Pratt terms a 'contact zone'" (57).

25. This is of course just the point we saw Anzaldúa make in her discussion of borderlands. There is a remarkable convergence, in this regard, between Anzaldúa's Hispanic vantage point and Krupat's Native American one (though Krupat is not himself Native American).

26. Krupat also acknowledges another element of irony, or paradox, inherent in his project: "As a critical discourse which claims to be both on and of the frontier, traversing middle ground while aspiring to a certain centrality, descriptive

and normative at once, it should come as no surprise that Ethnocriticism and the oxymoron have particular affinities" (29).

27. In this context, Krupat links "Richard Rorty's neopragmatic demotion of philosophy to the position of just another speaker in an ongoing conversation with no claim . . . to be anything more than *interesting*" to "Gerald Vizenor's explicit linkage of what he calls the 'trickster' mode to variants of . . . postmodernist positions" (7).

28. When Krupat argues "against the politics of postmodernism," he has in mind its tendency in Rorty and Lyotard to "privilege the paradigm of a liberal, bourgeois consensus society" (10). He does, however, acknowledge the force of postmodern theory's critique of master narratives, so that Krupat continually cautions that he is *not* offering ethnocriticism as a master narrative. Indeed, Krupat sometimes seems to incorporate more of the principles of postmodern theory than he is willing to acknowledge. His reliance on postmodern theoretical principles tends, I think, to get blunted by his concern with separating himself from what he sees as the conservative or at least static politics of postmodern theory.

Works Cited

Alexander, Thomas M. *John Dewey's Theory of Art, Experience, and Nature: The Horizons of Feeling*. Albany: State U of New York P, 1987.

Anzaldúa, Gloria *Boderlands/La Frontera: The New Mestiza*. San Francisco: Aunt Lute Books, 1987.

Arnold, Matthew. "The Function of Criticism at the Present Time." *The Complete Prose Works*, vol. 3, ed. R. H. Super. Ann Arbor: U of Michigan P, 1962. 258–85.

Barilli, Renato. *Rhetoric*. Trans. Biuliana Menozzi. Minneapolis: U of Minnesota P, 1989.

Baudelaire, Charles. "The Painter of Modern Life." *The Painter of Modern Life and Other Essays*. Trans. and ed. Jonathan Mayne. New York: Da Capo, 1964. 1–40.

Bauman, Zygmunt. *Modernity and the Holocaust*. Ithaca: Cornell UP, 1989.

Bender, John, and David E. Wellbery. "Rhetoricality: On the Modernist Return of Rhetoric." *The Ends of Rhetoric: History, Theory, Practice*. Stanford: Stanford UP, 1990. 3–39.

Berman, Marshall. *All That Is Solid Melts into Air: The Experience of Modernity*. New York: Penguin, 1982.

Bernstein, Richard. *John Dewey*. Atascadero: Ridgeview Press, 1966.

Bloom, Harold. "Agon: Revisionism and Critical Personality." *Raritan* 1, no. 1 (Summer 1981): 18–47.

Bloom, Harold. *The Anxiety of Influence*. Oxford: Oxford UP, 1973.

Bloom, Harold. "Emerson: The American Religion." In *Ralph Waldo Emerson*, ed. Harold Bloom. New York: Chelsea House, 1985. 97–121.

Bloom, Harold, ed. *Ralph Waldo Emerson*, New York: Chelsea House, 1985.

Bourne, Randolph. *The Radical Will: Selected Writings, 1911–1918*. Ed. Olaf Hansen. New York: Urizen Books, 1977.

Brantlinger, Patrick. *Crusoe's Footprints: Cultural Studies in Britain and America*. New York: Routledge, 1990.

Bromwhich, David. *A Choice of Inheritance: Self and Community from Edmund Burke to Robert Frost*. Cambridge: Harvard UP, 1989.

Brooks, Van Wyck. *America's Coming-of-Age*. New York: Doubleday, 1958.

Burke, Kenneth. *Attitudes toward History*. Los Altos: Hermes Publications, 1959.

Burke, Kenneth. *Counter-Statement*. Berkeley: U of California P, 1968.

Burke, Kenneth. *A Grammar of Motives*. Berkeley: U of California P, 1969.

Burke, Kenneth. *Language as Symbolic Action: Essays on Life, Literature, and Method*. Berkeley: U of California P, 1966.

Burke, Kenneth. *Permanence and Change: An Anatomy of Purpose*. 3d ed. Berkeley: U of California P, 1984.

Burke, Kenneth. *The Philosophy of Literary Form: Studies in Symbolic Action*. Berkeley: U of California P, 1973.

Burke, Kenneth. *A Rhetoric of Motives*. Berkeley: U of California P, 1969.

Burke, Kenneth. *The Rhetoric of Religion: Studies in Logology*. Berkeley: U of California P, 1970.

Burke, Kenneth. *Towards a Better Life*. Berkeley: U of California P, 1966.

Burke, Kenneth, and Malcolm Cowley. *The Selected Correspondence: 1915–1981*. Ed. Paul Jay. New York: Viking P, 1988.

Bygrave, Stephen. *Kenneth Burke: Rhetoric and Ideology*. New York: Routledge, 1993.

Carafiol, Peter. *The American Ideal: Literary History as a Worldly Activity*. New York: Oxford UP, 1991.

Carton, Evan. *The Rhetoric of American Romance: Dialectic and Identity in Emerson, Dickinson, Poe, and Hawthorne*. Baltimore: Johns Hopkins UP, 1985.

Chai, Leon. *The Romantic Foundations of the American Renaissance*. Ithaca: Cornell UP, 1987.

Chevigny, Bell Gale, and Carl Laguardia, eds. *Reinventing the Americas: Comparative Studies of Literature of the United States and Spanish America*. Cambridge: Cambridge UP, 1986.

Clifton, James A., ed. *Being and Becoming Indian*. Chicago: Dorsey P, 1989.

Connor, Steven. *Postmodernist Culture: An Introduction to Theories of the Contemporary*. Oxford: Basil Blackwell, 1989.

Coward, Rosalind, and John Ellis. *Language and Materialism: Developments in Semiology and the Theory of the Subject*. London: Routledge, 1977.

Cowley, Malcolm. *Exile's Return*. New York: Viking, 1951.

Crane, Hart. *The Complete Poems and Selected Letters and Prose of Hart Crane*. Ed. Brom Weber. New York: Anchor, 1966.

De Man, Paul. "Literary History and Literary Modernity." *Blindness and Insight: Essays in the Rhetoric of Contemporary Criticism*. 2d ed. Minneapolis: U of Minnesota P, 1983. 142–65.

Derrida, Jacques. "The Principle of Reason: The University in The Eyes of Its Pupils." *Diacritics* 13, no. 3 (Fall 1983): 3–20.

Derrida, Jacques. *Spurs: Nietzsche's Styles*. Trans. Barbara Johnson. Chicago: U of Chicago P, 1979.

Dewey, John. *Art as Experience*. New York: Perigee, 1980.

Dewey, John. *Experience and Nature*. New York: Dover, 1958.

Dewey, John. *Philosophy and Civilization*. New York: Minton, 1931.

Dewey, John. "Philosophy and Democracy." *Characters and Events: Popular Essays in Social and Political Philosophy*, vol. 2, ed. Joseph Ratner. New York: Octagon, 1970. 841–55.

Diggins, John Patrick. *The Promise of Pragmatism: Modernism and the Crisis of Knowledge and Authority*. Chicago: U of Chicago P, 1994.

Easthope, Anthony. *Literary into Cultural Studies*. New York: Routledge, 1991.

Eichenbaum, Boris. "The Theory of the 'Formal Method.'" *Critical Theory since Plato*. Ed. Hazard Adams. New York: Harcourt Brace, 1977. 829–46.

Eliot, T. S. *The Waste Land. The Complete Poems and Plays: 1909–1950*. New York: Harcourt, Brace & World, 1952. 37–55.

Emerson, Ralph Waldo. *Ralph Waldo Emerson: Essays and Lectures*. Ed. Joel Porte. New York: Library of America, 1983.

Erkkila, Betsy. *Whitman the Political Poet*. Oxford: Oxford UP, 1989.

Farrell, Thomas B. *Norms of Rhetorical Culture*. New Haven: Yale UP, 1993.

Firmat, Gustavo Perez, ed. *Do the Americas Have a Common Literature?* Durham: Duke UP, 1990.

Fish, Stanley. "Rhetoric." In *Critical Terms for Literary Study*, ed. Frank Lentricchia and Thomas McLaughlin. Chicago: U of Chicago P, 1983.

Fisher, Philip, ed. *The New American Studies: Essays from Representations*. Berkeley: U of California P, 1991.

Foster, Hal. *Recodings: Art, Spectacle, Cultural Politics*. Port Townsend: Bay P, 1985.

Foucault, Michel. "What Is Enlightenment." *The Foucault Reader*, ed. Paul Rabinow. New York: Pantheon, 1984. 32–50.

Freud, Sigmund. *Civilization and Its Discontents*. New York: W. W. Norton, 1961.

Frothingham, O. B. *Transcendentalism in New England: A History*. Philadelphia: U of Pennsylvania P, 1959.

Fuller, Steve. *Philosophy, Rhetoric, and the End of Knowledge: The Coming of Science and Technology Studies*. Madison: U of Wisconsin P, 1993.

Gilmore, Michael T. *American Romanticism and the Marketplace*. Chicago: U of Chicago P, 1985.

Gilroy, Paul. *The Black Atlantic: Modernity and Double Consciousness*. Cambridge: Harvard UP, 1993.

Glissant, Edouard. *Caribbean Discourses: Selected Essays*. Trans. J. Michael Dash. Charlottesville: U of Virginia P, 1989.

Goddard, H. C. *Studies in New England Transcendentalism*. New York: Columbia UP, 1908.

Gouinlock, James. *John Dewey's Philosophy of Value*. New York: Humanities P, 1972.

Graff, Gerald. *Professing Literature: An Institutional History*. Chicago: U of Chicago P, 1987.

Gramsci, Antonio. *Selections from the Prison Notebooks*. Ed. and trans. Quintin Hoare and Geoffrey Nowell Smith. New York: International Publishers, 1971.

Gunn, Giles. *The Culture of Criticism and the Criticism of Culture*. Oxford: Oxford UP, 1987.

Gunn, Giles. *Thinking across the American Grain: Ideology, Intellect, and the New Pragmatism*. Chicago: U of Chicago P, 1992.

Habermas, Jürgen. "Modernity—An Incomplete Project." *The Anti-Aesthetic: Essays on Postmodern Culture,* ed. Hal Foster. Port Townsend: Bay P, 1983. 3–15.

Habermas, Jürgen. *The Philosophical Discourse of Modernity: Twelve Lectures.* Trans. Frederick Lawrence. Cambridge: MIT P, 1987.

Hansen, Olaf. *Aesthetic Individualism and Practical Intellect: American Allegory in Emerson, Thoreau, Adams, and James.* Princeton: Princeton UP, 1990.

Held, David. *Introduction to Critical Theory: Horkheimer to Habermas.* Berkeley: U of California P, 1980.

Henderson, Greig. *Kenneth Burke: Literature and Language as Symbolic Action.* Athens: U of Georgia P, 1988.

Herrnstein Smith, Barbara. *Contingencies of Value.* Cambridge: Harvard UP, 1988.

Hicks, Emily. *Border Writing.* Minneapolis: U of Minnesota P, 1991.

Horkheimer, Max, and Theodor Adorno. *Dialectic of Enlightenment.* Trans. John Cumming. New York: Continuum, 1982.

Huyssen, Andreas. *After the Great Divide: Modernism, Mass Culture, Postmodernism.* Bloomington: Indiana UP, 1986.

Jacobson, David. *Emerson's Pragmatic Vision: The Dance of The Eye.* University Park: Penn State UP, 1993.

James, Henry. *Nathaniel Hawthorne.* Ed. Tony Tanner. New York: Macmillan, 1967.

James, William. *Pragmatism, and Four Essays from The Meaning of Truth.* New York: New American Library, 1955.

Jay, Gregory. *America the Scrivener: Deconstruction and the Subject of Literary History.* Ithaca: Cornell UP, 1990.

Jay, Gregory. "The End of 'American' Literature: Toward a Multicultural Practice." *College English* 53 (1991): 264–81.

Jay, Paul. "Bridging the Gap: The Position of Politics in Deconstruction." *Cultural Critique,* no. 22 (Fall 1992); 47–74.

Jay, Paul. "Kenneth Burke and the Motives of Rhetoric." *American Literary History* (Fall 1989): 535–53.

Jay, Paul. "Modernism, Postmodernism, and Critical Style: The Cases of Burke and Derrida." *Genre* (Fall 1988): 339–58.

Kant, Immanuel. *The Critique of Judgement.* Trans. James Creed Meredith. Oxford: Oxford UP, 1957.

Karl, Frederick. *Modern and Modernism: The Sovereignty of the Artist: 1885–1925.* New York: Atheneum, 1988.

Karp, Ivan, and Steven D. Lavine. *Exhibiting Cultures: The Poetics and Politics of Museum Display.* Washington: Smithsonian P, 1991.

Kirwin, James. *Literature, Rhetoric, Metaphysics.* New York: Routledge, 1990.

Krupat, Arnold. *Ethnocriticism: Ethnography, History, Literature.* Berkeley: U of California P, 1992.

Lears, T. Jackson. *No Place of Grace.* New York: Pantheon, 1981.

Leitch, Vincent. *American Literary Criticism from the Thirties to the Eighties.*

Lentricchia, Frank. *Criticism and Social Change.* Chicago: U of Chicago P, 1983.

Levin, Jonathan. "The Esthetics of Pragmatism." *American Literary History* 6, no. 4 (Winter 1994): 658–83.

Levine, Lawrence. *Highbrow/Lowbrow: The Emergence of Cultural Hierarchy in America*. Cambridge: Harvard UP, 1988.

Lowith, Karl. *Meaning in History*. Chicago: U of Chicago P, 1970.

Mailloux, Steven, ed. *Rhetoric, Sophistry, Pragmatism*. Cambridge: Cambridge UP, 1995.

Marcell, David. *Progress and Pragmatism: James, Dewey, Beard, and the American Idea of Progress*. Westport: Greenwood P, 1974.

Marx, Karl, and Frederick Engels. *The German Ideology*. Ed. R. Pascal. New York: International Publishers, 1947.

Matthiessen, F. O. *American Renaissance: Arts and Expression in the Age of Emerson and Whitman*. New York: Oxford UP, 1941.

McDermott, John J. *Streams of Experience: Reflections on the History and Philosophy of American Culture*. Amherst: U of Massachussets P, 1986.

McGowan, John. *Postmodernism and Its Critics*. Ithaca: Cornell UP, 1991.

Nealon, Jeffrey. "The Discipline of Deconstruction." *PMLA* 107, no. 2 (1992): 1266–79.

Nelson, Cary, et al., eds. *Cultural Studies*. New York: Routledge, 1992.

Nelson, Raymond. *Van Wyck Brooks: A Writer's Life*. New York: E. P. Dutton.

Nietzsche, Friedrich. *The Use and Abuse of History*. Trans. Adrian Collins. Indianapolis: Bobbs-Merrill, 1949.

Nietzsche, Friedrich. *The Will to Power*. Trans. Walter Kaufman and R. J. Hollingdate. Ed. Walter Kaufman. New York: Vintage, 1967.

Owens, Louis. "'The Song Is Very Short': Native American Literature and Literary Theory." *Weber Studies* 12, no. 3 (1995): 51–62.

Packer, Barbara L. "'The Curse of Kehama.'" In *Ralph Waldo Emerson*, ed. Harold Bloom. New York: Chelsea House, 1985. 123–46.

Parrington, Vernon L. *Main Currents in American Thought*. 3 vols. New York: Harcourt Brace, 1927–30.

Patterson, Mark R. *Authority, Autonomy, and Representation in American Literature, 1776–1865*. Princeton: Princeton UP, 1988.

Pease, Donald. *Visionary Compacts: American Renaissance Writings in Cultural Context*. Wisconsin: U of Wisconsin P, 1987.

Pepper, Stephen C. "Some Questions on Dewey's Esthetics." In *The Philosophy of John Dewey*, ed. Paul Arthur Schilpp. La Salle, Ill.: Open Court, 1951. 369–89.

Pippin, Robert. *Modernism as a Philosophical Problem: On the Dissatisfactions of European High Culture*. Oxford: Basil Blackwell, 1991.

Poirier, Richard. *Poetry and Pragmatism*. Cambridge: Harvard UP, 1992.

Poirier, Richard. *The Renewal of Literature*. New York: Random House, 1987.

Porter, Carolyn. "What We Know That We Don't Know: Remapping American Literary Studies." *American Literary History* 6 (1994): 467–526.

Posnock, Ross. *The Trial of Curiosity: Henry James, William James, and the Challenge of Modernity*. Oxford: Oxford UP, 1991.

Pratt, Mary Louise. *Imperial Eyes: Travel Writing and Transculturation*. London: Routledge, 1992.

Raiskin, Judith. *Snow on the Canefields: Women's Writing and Creole Subjectivity*. Minneapolis: U of Minnesota P, 1996.

Reynolds, David. *Beneath the American Renaissance: The Subversive Imagination in the Age of Emerson and Melville*. New York: Knopf, 1988.

Rorty, Richard. *Consequences of Pragmatism*. Minneapolis: U of Minnesota P, 1982.

Rorty, Richard. *Contingency, Irony, and Solidarity*. Cambridge: Cambridge UP, 1989.

Rorty, Richard. *Philosophy and the Mirror of Nature*. Princeton: Princeton UP, 1979.

Rorty, Richard. "Solidarity or Objectivity?" In *Post-Analytic Philosophy*, ed. John Rajchman and Cornel West. New York: Columbia UP, 1985. 3–19.

Rosaldo, Renato. Foreword to *Hybrid Cultures: Strategies for Entering and Leaving Modernity*, by Nestor Garcia Canclini. Minneapolis: U of Minnesota P, 1995. xi–xxi.

Russell, Charles. *Poets, Prophets, and Revolutionaries: The Literary Avant-garde from Rimbaud through Postmodernism*. Oxford: Oxford UP, 1985.

Saldívar, José David. *The Dialectics of Our America: Genealogy Cultural Critique, and Literary History*. Durham, NC: Duke UP, 1991.

Santayana, George. *Santayana on America: Essays, Notes, and Letters on American Life, Literature, and Philosophy*. Ed. Richard Colton Lyon. New York: Harcourt Brace, 1968.

Schiller, Friedrich von. *Letters on the Aesthetic Education of Man*. In *Critical Theory since Plato*, ed. Hazard Adams. New York: Harcourt Brace, 1971. 418–31.

Schwartz, Sanford. *The Matrix of Modernism: Pound, Eliot, and Early Twentieth-Century Thought*. Princeton: Princeton UP, 1985.

Shusterman, Richard. *Pragmatist Aesthetics: Living Beauty, Rethinking Art*. Oxford: Basil Blackwell, 1992.

Silverman, Kaja. *The Subject of Semiotics*. Oxford: Oxford UP, 1983.

Simons, Herbert W., and Trevor Melia, eds. *The Legacy of Kenneth Burke*. Madison: U of Wisconsin P, 1989.

Southwell, Samuel. *Kenneth Burke and Martin Heidegger: With a Note against Deconstructionism*. Gainesville: U of Florida P, 1987.

Spillers, Hortense, ed. *Comparative American Identities: Race, Sex, and Nationality in the Modern Text*. New York: Routledge, 1991.

Stein, Gertrude. "Composition as Explanation." *Selected Writings of Gertrude Stein*, ed. Carl Van Vechten. New York: Vintage, 1962. 511–23.

Stewart, Susan. "The State of Cultural Theory and the Future of Literary Form." *Profession 93*. New York: Modern Language Association, 1993. 12–15.

Van Leer, David. *Emerson's Epistemology: The Argument of the Essays*. Cambridge: Cambridge UP, 1986.

Waugh, Patricia. *Practising Postmodernism/Reading Modernism*. London: Edward Arnold, 1992.

West, Cornel. *The American Evasion of Philosophy: A Genealogy of Pragmatism.* Madison: U of Wisconsin P, 1989.

Westbrook, Robert B. *John Dewey and American Democracy.* Ithaca: Cornell UP, 1991.

Wheeler, Kathleen M. *Romanticism, Pragmatism, and Deconstruction.* Oxford: Blackwell, 1993.

Whitman, Walt. *Democratic Vistas. The Works of Walt Whitman: The Collected Prose*, vol. 2. New York: Funk and Wagnalls, 1968.

Wihl, Gary. *The Contingency of Theory: Pragmatism, Expressivism, and Deconstruction.* New Haven: Yale UP, 1994.

Williams, Raymond. *Keywords: A Vocabulary of Culture and Society.* London: Fontana/Collins, 1983.

Williams, William Carlos. "The Great Figure." *The Collected Poems of William Carlos Williams: 1909–1939.* New York: New Directions, 1986. 174.

Index

The Wisconsin Project on American Writers

Frank Lentricchia, General Editor

Gaiety Transfigured: Gay Self-Representation in American Literature
David Bergman

American Puritanism and the Defense of Mourning: Religion, Grief, and Ethnology in Mary White Rowlandson's Captivity Narrative
Mitchell Robert Breitwieser

F. O. Matthiessen and the Politics of Criticism
William E. Cain

In Defense of Writers: The Poetry and Prose of Yvor Winters
Terry Comito

Get the Guests: Psychoanalysis, Modern American Drama, and the Audience
Walter A. Davis

A Poetry of Presence: The Writing of William Carlos Williams
Bernard Duffey

Selves at Risk: Patterns of Quest in Contemporary American Letters
Ihab Hassan

Contingency Blues: The Search for Foundations in American Criticism
Paul Jay

Reading Faulkner
Wesley Morris with Barbara Alverson Morris

Repression and Recovery: Modern American Poetry and the Politics of Cultural Memory, 1910–1945
Cary Nelson

Lionel Trilling: The Work of Liberation
Daniel T. O'Hara

Visionary Compacts: American Renaissance Writings in Cultural Context
Donald E. Pease

"A White Heron" and the Question of Minor Literature
Louis A. Renza

www.ingramcontent.com/pod-product-compliance
Lightning Source LLC
Chambersburg PA
CBHW052036090426
42739CB00010B/1937